Archaeological Studies of Gender in the Southeastern United States

The Ripley P. Bullen Series
Florida Museum of Natural History

Florida A&M University, Tallahassee
Florida Atlantic University, Boca Raton
Florida Gulf Coast University, Ft. Myers
Florida International University, Miami
Florida State University, Tallahassee
University of Central Florida, Orlando
University of Florida, Gainesville
University of North Florida, Jacksonville
University of South Florida, Tampa
University of West Florida, Pensacola

Archaeological Studies of Gender
in the Southeastern
United States

❧❦

Edited by

Jane M. Eastman and Christopher B. Rodning

Foreword by Jerald T. Milanich, Series Editor

University Press of Florida

Gainesville · Tallahassee · Tampa · Boca Raton

Pensacola · Orlando · Miami · Jacksonville · Ft. Myers · Sarasota

06 05 04 03 02 01   6 5 4 3 2 1

Library of Congress Cataloging-in-Publication Data
Archaeological studies of gender in the southeastern United States /
edited by Jane M. Eastman and Christopher B. Rodning; foreword by
Jerald T. Milanich.
p. cm. — (The Ripley P. Bullen series)
Includes bibliographical references and index.
ISBN 978-1-61610-113-8

1. Indians of North America—Southern States—Antiquities. 2. Indians
of North America—Southern States—Social life and customs.
3. Sex role—Southern States. 4. Southern States—Antiquities. I. Title:
Archaeological studies of gender in the southeastern United States.
II. Eastman, Jane M., 1963–. III. Rodning, Christopher Bernard. IV. Series.

E78.S65 A75 2001
975'.01—dc21   00-047667

The University Press of Florida is the scholarly publishing agency for
the State University System of Florida, comprising Florida A&M
University, Florida Atlantic University, Florida Gulf Coast University,
Florida International University, Florida State University, University of
Central Florida, University of Florida, University of North Florida,
University of South Florida, and University of West Florida.

University Press of Florida
2046 NE Waldo Road
Suite 2100
Gainesville, FL 32609
http://upress.ufl.edu

Dedication

This book is dedicated to the memory of Timothy Paul Mooney and Thomas Hargrove. Tim and Tom were both doctoral students in archaeology at the University of North Carolina in Chapel Hill. Tim died in an accident near Hillsborough, North Carolina, on an icy day in February 1995. Tom died suddenly while visiting a museum in downtown Raleigh, North Carolina, one weekend in October 1999. Both were remarkable people and talented archaeologists. Both made valuable contributions to archaeology but had many more to make.

Tim Mooney (1992, 1994, 1995, 1997) was writing his doctoral dissertation at UNC-CH about Choctaw ethnohistory and the archaeology of the Pearl River Valley in Mississippi, and he had directed archaeological field schools at Siouan sites near Martinsville, Virginia. His study of Choctaw culture change and compromise during the sixteenth and seventeenth centuries was published posthumously with an introductory essay by Vin Steponaitis. The graduate program at North Carolina was lucky to have him after his successful career as a lawyer in Washington. His enthusiasm for archaeology, his calm and humble leadership, his dependability, and his rapport with students and colleagues were remarkable. His family helped to create the Timothy Paul Mooney Fund for research by graduate students in archaeology at the Research Laboratories of Archaeology in Chapel Hill.

Tom was pursuing Ph.D. research at UNC-CH about Woodland-period archaeology along the Roanoke River in southern Virginia, and he had participated in archaeological studies of European prehistory and landscape history in Burgundy, France. His study of Piedmont ceramic traditions was only one of countless contributions that Tom made to archaeological knowledge of native peoples during every period in every part of North Carolina. It is difficult to imagine North Carolina archaeology without Tom. His abiding interest in traditional music and other folkways, his taste for barbecue and creative potluck gatherings, his vast but humble knowledge of just about everything, his creative and often comic command of language, and his quiet but palpable presence and friendship are unforgettable. Tom had run Archaeological Research Consultants for years from its legendary headquarters at the Forge in downtown Raleigh.

This book owes much to the inspiration of these men.

Contents

Figures

Tables

Acknowledgments

This book derives from our symposium about archaeological studies of gender in southeastern North America, held at the Southeastern Archaeological Conference in Birmingham, Alabama, in November 1996. Planning for this symposium must have gotten underway in the midst of Patricia Crown's plans for an archaeological symposium about sex roles and gender hierarchies in the native Southwest, held at the annual meeting of the Society for American Archaeology in Nashville, Tennessee, in April 1997. Gender is indeed a burgeoning niche within archaeology (see Nelson 1997). The publication of books about the archaeology of gender in specific cultural and geographic regions is a welcome contribution to the anthropological literature (see Kent 1998a). Ours is the first archaeological book that takes gender in the native Southeast as its main topic. We hope that it will contribute to further archaeological interests in and inquiries about gender in native Southeastern societies.

Our inspiration for the symposium and this book came from the graduate seminar about the archaeology of gender taught in 1996 by Margaret Scarry at the University of North Carolina at Chapel Hill. We appreciate her introduction to the archaeological literature about gender and her abiding interest in this and other of our projects.

Thanks very much to Meredith Morris-Babb for her encouragement ever since our symposium in 1996 and her interest in having the University Press of Florida publish this book as a contribution to its Ripley P. Bullen Series with the Florida Museum of Natural History. Judy Goffman helped us in preparing the final manuscript, and David Graham helped with the illustrations. We could not have put this book together without their guidance and the support of many others.

Of course, considerable credit is due our chapter contributors. Their patience is as commendable as their archaeology is exemplary. We thank

Vin Steponaitis, Trawick Ward, Steve Davis, Margaret Scarry, Nancy White, Jerald Milanich, and an anonymous reviewer for their comments about the book. Our thanks go to them and to Ken Sassaman, John Scarry, Stephen Williams, Tom Maher, David Hally, Lynne Sullivan, David Moore, Holly Matthews, Patrick Livingood, Tony Boudreaux, Hunter Johnson, Rob Beck, Hope Spencer, Bram Tucker, Greg Wilson, Marianne Reeves, Tiffiny Tung, Celeste Gagnon, Randy Daniel, Mark Rees, Joe Herbert, David Morgan, Mintcy Maxham, Clark Larsen, Patty Jo Watson, Kandi Detwiler, Theda Perdue, Patricia Samford, Judy Knight, Sara Bon-Harper, Kathy McDonnell, Amber VanDerwarker, and several fellow graduate students for their interests in and recommendations about this publication. Unfortunately, neither Ken Sassaman nor Marianne Reeves were able to contribute their conference papers to the book. Our thanks go to Lynne Sullivan for coming aboard after our symposium and to Janet Levy for ably authoring the epilogue. We are grateful to professors Elizabeth Brumfiel and Margaret Conkey for their inspiration and encouragement. We thank our friends and fellow archaeologists Patricia Samford and Annie Holm for their moral support and helpful brainstorming. This book owes much to all of these people.

We are also grateful for the patience of our dissertation advisors.

Foreword

To understand the past, archaeologists must uncover and interpret the material remains left by past human cultures. Because human behavior is patterned, archaeologists search for corresponding patterns in the archaeological record. When we can discern such evidence, we can better understand past human societies and events.

In this volume, Jane M. Eastman and Christopher B. Rodning—both young scholars trained at the University of North Carolina, Chapel Hill—focus on gender and how behavior associated with gender appears in the archaeological record. Women, as well as men, performed activities that are patterned and that left evidence in archaeological sites. If we are truly to understand the cultures of people who lived hundreds and even thousands of years ago, we must be cognizant of material evidence that is tied to female social statuses and roles as well as to those of males. We need to engender archaeological interpretation. Otherwise, our knowledge of the past is incomplete.

Archaeological Studies of Gender in the Southeastern United States presents cutting-edge case studies, actual archaeological and bioarchaeological projects, that demonstrate how we can engender archaeology. Using data excavated from sites, the editors and authors make clear the importance of such an approach, and they show how it enhances the archaeological record and our ability to use material remains to learn about past cultures.

This is an important book, one that breaks new ground. I am pleased to add it to the Ripley P. Bullen series.

Jerald T. Milanich
Series Editor

⚔ Introduction ⚓

Gender and the Archaeology of the Southeast

Christopher B. Rodning and Jane M. Eastman

Written accounts by European men who traveled, traded, and lived among native groups in the southeastern United States from the sixteenth through the eighteenth centuries documented a world in which there were marked differences between the lives of native men and women (Braund 1993:3–25; Galloway 1995:1–2; Hudson 1976:260–69; Perdue 1998:17–40). These accounts indicate that boys and girls in native societies learned different sets of skills and that adult women and men often conducted their daily lives apart from each other. They also suggest that men and women tended to hold different leadership roles within their communities. Given the gender distinctions apparent in native Southeastern societies during the historic period, the careful consideration of gender dynamics should benefit the archaeological study of native Southeastern cultures. The essays in this book explore the archaeology of gender in the native Southeast (see fig. I.1).

Studying Gender through Archaeology

Gender is related to but not determined by biological sex and age. It defines social categories such as men, women, boys, girls, and others like the *berdache* (a native North American who adopts an identity normally associated with the other sex). Cultural traditions about gender include significant expectations for the social roles and relationships that men,

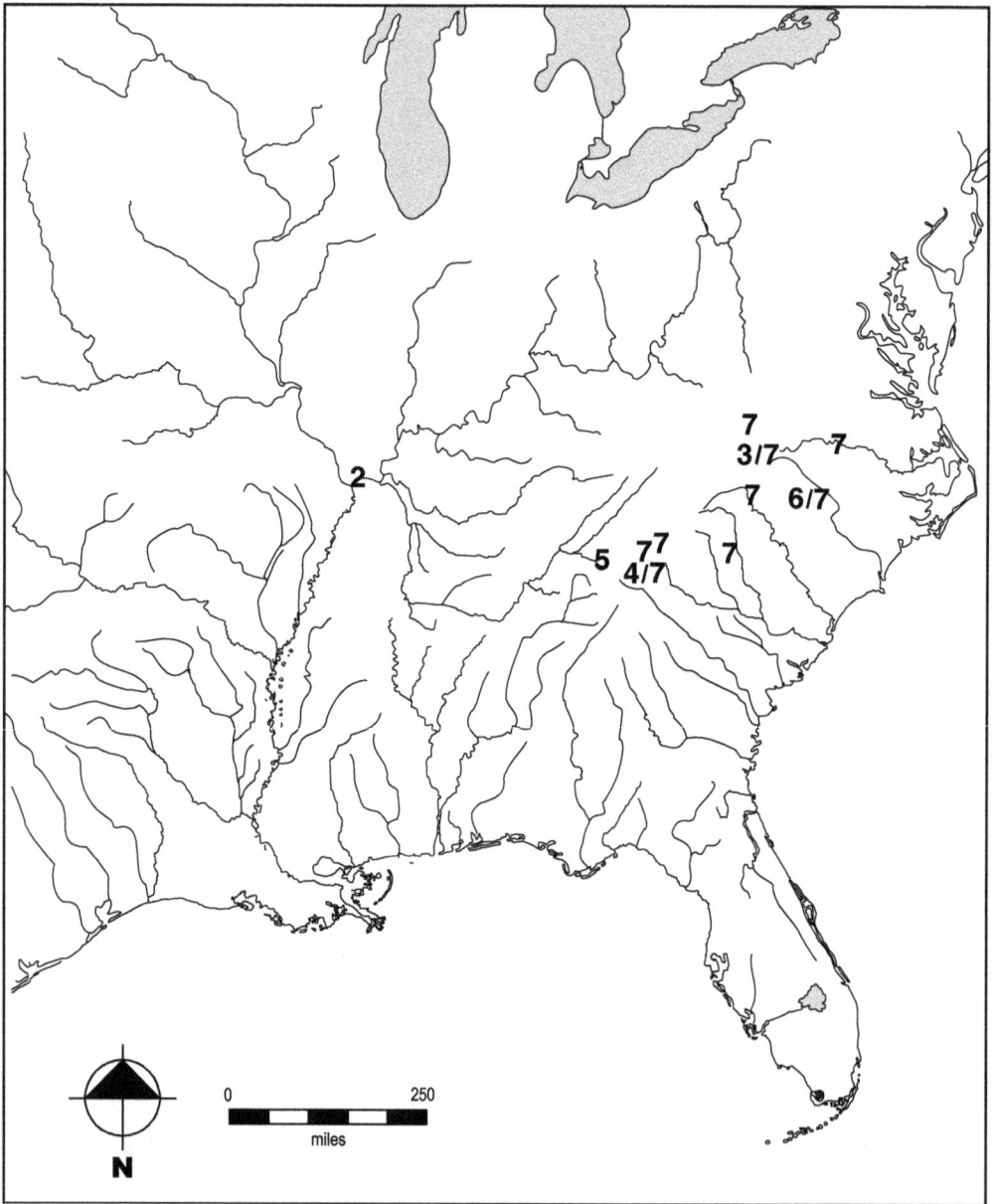

Fig. I.1. Chapter numbers placed at the locations of study areas in the Southeast.

women, and children should adopt at different stages of their lives. In their daily lives, people may choose to follow these traditions, or they may bend the rules. In either case, their gender roles and identities are formulated with reference to society's expectations. Our viewpoint is that a person's gender identity can change during the course of his or her lifetime. Gender identity is cross-cut by other factors such as a person's physical growth, development, and aging and also by progression through socially defined age classes. Gender and aging are interrelated, culturally defined processes, and the precise relationship between these processes varies from one culture and community to another.

Gender has become a prominent theme in archaeology during the past several years (Brumfiel 1992; Claassen 1997; Conkey and Gero 1991; Crown and Fish 1996; Joyce and Claassen 1997; Kent 1998a; Nelson 1997; Spector 1993; Spielmann 1995; Whelan 1995; N. M. White 1999; R. P. Wright 1996a). Archaeologists interested in gender commonly study gender roles, gender identities, and gender ideologies and how these aspects of gender are reflected in material culture. Gender *roles* refer to the differential participation of men, women, and children in activities within their communities. Gender *identities* refer to the social personalities and relationships adopted by men, women, and children at different stages of their lives. Gender *ideologies* refer to the status relationships between members of different gender categories, including all genders relevant in different cultural settings. These different components of gender have been outlined by Margaret Conkey and Janet Spector (1984:15) in their landmark essay about gender studies in archaeology. One major contribution of their essay and other archaeological literature about gender is simply the point that gender is constructed differently in different cultures and communities. Biological sex, while relevant, is not the sole determinant of gender.

The study of any of these aspects of gender through archaeology does not necessarily demand new methodologies, but it does demand new approaches. Archaeologists already are well attuned to identifying and evaluating patterns in material culture. Gender can affect these kinds of patterns significantly. By becoming informed about how gender influences the lives of people as they form households and community groups, archaeologists can prepare themselves to recognize clues in the material record that are indeed related to gender in the past.

Although we are advocating an approach to archaeology that is sensitive to the impact of gender differences on patterns in the archaeological record, we do not suggest that every shred of archaeological evidence is laden with gendered meaning and insight about gender in the past. But if archaeologists discount the archaeological record as relevant to this anthropological topic at all, they never will notice the patterns in archaeological evidence that indeed are pertinent. Archaeologists are accustomed to designing research projects to generate meaningful data sets to answer a variety of questions. Explicitly considering what roles and relationships men and women and young and old might have held within their communities, rather than making untested assumptions about their gender roles and identities, can enrich archaeological reconstructions of the past.

Gender as an archaeological topic is embedded within topics that archaeologists traditionally have studied and will continue to investigate in the future. As Conkey and Gero (1991:15) have noted, "An engendered past addresses many long-standing concerns of archaeology: the formation of states, trade and exchange, site settlement systems and activity areas, the processes of agriculture, lithic production, food production, pottery, architecture, ancient art—but throws them into new relief. *An engendered past replaces the focus on the remains of prehistory with a focus on the people of prehistory;* it rejects a reified concept of society or culture as an object of study, does away with the earliest, the biggest, the best examples of prehistoric forms, and concentrates instead on the continuities and dialectics of life, the interpersonal and intimate aspects of social settings that bind prehistoric lives into social patterns" (our italics). The consideration of gender enriches archaeological approaches to topics that are and have been major topics of interest in the field.

Another contribution of gender studies to archaeology relates to the way in which archaeologists write about the past. People are active agents in their own lives and therefore actively affect the ways their lives enter into the archaeological record. Archaeologists need heuristic devices like "phases" and "cultures" to sort archaeological evidence in analytically meaningful ways and to communicate with one another about them. Archaeologists nevertheless are interested in the experiences of people and not solely the history of different kinds of material culture. It is not uncommon to read archaeological essays about adaptive systems or settlement patterns. It is worth remembering that people constituted those systems and created those patterns.

Gender studies thus encourage archaeologists to concentrate their efforts toward reconstructing the activities of *people* in the past. They encourage archaeologists to carefully consider aspects of social roles and identities that *people* adopt during their lifetimes. They demonstrate that gender is not immutable but rather is a dynamic dimension of communities and cultures which shapes the lives of *people* and is shaped by them.

The archaeological study of gender is not about women exclusively, even though many early archaeological studies of gender did concentrate on women. As Sarah Milledge Nelson (1997:15) has written, "Given this definition of gender, it follows that a gendered archaeology considers both women and men, and any other culturally constructed genders (for example, *berdache*). Gender is not a code word for women, and gendered archaeology is *not* another way of finding women in prehistory disguised with a more neutral and inclusive term. Both women and men—people as individuals as well as in groups—become more visible in studying gender. Other constructed roles, activities, and behaviors, such as ethnicity, age, and class, may also become visible in the course of researching gender in archaeology" (italics in original). Gendered perspectives in archaeology enrich knowledge about the lives of people in the past and their interactions with people in other gender groups in their communities.

The early gender studies in archaeology have served to outline gender bias in archaeological interpretation and to remedy its traditional emphasis on patterns attributed to the lives and activities of men (Wylie 1991a:38–41). The recognition of gender as a significant topic for archaeological investigation certainly owes much to feminist scholarship and its critique of archaeological thought and practice (Gilchrist 1994:1–8). Nevertheless, archaeologists need not espouse feminist theory to find valuable insights offered in archaeological writing about gender.

Our reading of feminist anthropology and archaeology in the 1980s and 1990s has led to our recognition that a consideration of gender is a vital part of reconstructing the past. The consideration of gender has enhanced our efforts to understand social structure, social dynamics, and belief systems in the past. The studies presented here are all indebted to the ground-breaking scholarship of feminist writers and theorists, even though the authors in this volume do not write from an overtly feminist perspective. None of the case analyses focus more intently on the lives of women than on those of men or children. These chapters simply present archaeological case studies, focused on Native American cultures of the southeastern United States, that are based on the perspective that gender differences held significant meaning for these native peoples. The authors pursue many different questions about the past with reference to different kinds of archaeological evidence, but all are bound by this shared premise.

The interpretations presented in the chapters that follow are all enriched by a careful consideration of the impact that gender differences may have had on the lives of people in the past. Their reconstructions are peopled with men, women, and children who developed patterns of work, play, and ritual that reflected their gender statuses, and whose lives followed particular courses due in part to gender. The authors in this volume have all successfully embedded an explicit consideration of gender into their studies of the past, enhancing their perspectives on a variety of topics.

The chapter by Cheryl Claassen identifies several problem areas for gender studies through archaeology in the Southeast. Claassen (1992, 1997) has long championed gendered perspectives on the past. Her knowledge about gender in the past and present spans the scholarly literature about native peoples of the Americas and many other continents. In this chapter she applies that global familiarity to the tasks of learning about the past lifeways of native southeastern peoples. Her contribution to this book challenges archaeologists to revamp their perspectives about the place of men, women, and children in native southeastern societies.

The essay by Larissa Thomas compares and contrasts the gender division of labor in late prehistoric communities of southern Illinois. Thomas describes archaeological evidence of household organization at Dillow's Ridge near Mill Creek and compares it to intrasite patterning at the Great Salt Spring along the Saline River. She reconstructs patterns of hoe production as one part of Mississippian household economies at Dillow's Ridge. She contrasts this pattern at Dillow's Ridge with evidence for different forms of task specialization at the Great Salt Spring locality. Thomas thus adds a significant voice to the debate among scholars about the structure and diversity of Mississippian economies in the North American midcontinent (Cobb 1989, 1996; Muller 1984, 1986, 1997; Pauketat 1987, 1989, 1997; Prentice 1983, 1985). Archaeologists may find evidence of very different gender divisions of labor in Mississippian communities elsewhere in the Southeast, and here Thomas makes a case that archaeologists need to explore actively this aspect of Mississippian economies.

Jane Eastman explores evidence for gender differences during the life cycle of Siouan-speaking peoples who occupied northwestern North Carolina and southern Virginia during the late prehistoric period. She examines the distribution of mortuary items in burials from seven village sites in the region, and her study reconstructs the dynamic relationship between gender and age in these communities. First, gender distinctions appear to have been recognized among children from a very early age. Second, gender identities changed in different ways for men and women as they aged. The gender representation of older women in mortuary contexts differed from the treatment of adult women who died at a younger age. In contrast, gender representation of men remained consistent throughout their lifetimes. The evidence examined here indicates that Siouan women may have experienced more dramatic changes in gender roles and identities throughout their lives than did men in their communities.

Chris Rodning reviews archaeological and ethnohistoric evidence about gender ideology in Cherokee communities of southern Appalachia. Historic and ethnographic evidence about the Cherokee of the eighteenth century indicates that towns and clans in Cherokee communities gave men and women alternative tracks towards prestige among their peers. This evidence guides Rodning's interpretations of mortuary patterns at a council house and village in the upper Little Tennessee River Valley of southwestern North Carolina that likely date to the late seventeenth or very early eighteenth centuries.

Lynne Sullivan considers power relations communicated through mortuary ritual at the late prehistoric town of Toqua in eastern Tennessee. She concludes that reconstructions of hierarchical social relations within the Mississippian chiefdoms of the upper Tennessee Valley may have overstated the rigidity of these hierarchies. She argues that mortuary patterns in the upper Tennessee Valley reveal a duality in gender roles and identities that is not at all compatible with European traditions about public and private spheres of social life. More appropriate models to test archaeologically in the Southeast can be derived from a careful reading of ethnohistoric literature about Creek and Cherokee communities.

Elizabeth Monahan Driscoll, Steve Davis, and Trawick Ward review spatial patterns of graves at the site of Occaneechi Town, a native village in north-central North Carolina dating to the late 1600s and very early 1700s. Occaneechi Town was a multiethnic community deeply enmeshed in the geopolitics of the deerskin trade and English colonial expansion across the Piedmont region. Mortuary goods and demographic profiles of spatial clusters of graves reveal the structure of kinship and community at this native village on the Eno River. This study of mortuary patterns at the site of Occaneechi Town has implications for understanding changes in the social composition of eastern Siouan groups and the changing Piedmont landscape (Davis and Ward 1991:50–53;

Ward and Davis 1999:233–60). The patterns reconstructed in this chapter provide interesting opportunities for comparison with those at earlier native settlements in northern and central North Carolina.

Pat Lambert reviews bioarchaeological evidence of ceremonial practices among late prehistoric and protohistoric native communities in North Carolina. She interprets bony growths in the auditory canals of several individuals as clues about the participation of different people in sweat lodge ceremonies. Ethnohistoric evidence about these rituals indicates that after sweat baths native people would thrust themselves into nearby rivers or streams. The dramatic and rapid changes in temperature and pressure experienced during these activities could cause the kinds of growths visible on some skulls. Lambert notes that these growths are found more commonly on adult males than females. She compares this pattern to ethnohistoric evidence about the greater participation of men than women in these kinds of rituals. Her paper is one of the few published pieces that links gender-related patterns in bioarchaeological evidence to the ritual lives of people in the past. Many scholars who have explored gender-related patterns in the bioarchaeological record have concentrated on health and activity patterns rather than ceremonialism (Bridges 1989, 1991; Larsen 1994, 1995a, 1995b, 1997). This essay adds a valuable voice about the ritual lives of native peoples in southeastern North America.

The epilogue by Janet Levy draws the book to a close by relating these chapters to broader issues in archaeological thought and practice, and it notes the rich corpus of archaeological and ethnohistoric material from the native Southeast relevant to the study of gender in the past. It complements well the chapter by Cheryl Claassen about regendering our understanding of prehistory, for they both chart a challenging course for further study of gender in native southeastern societies.

Our opinion is that a gendered archaeology of the Southeast is compatible with the topics that archaeologists have studied for many years. The essays here concentrate on mortuary patterns, divisions of labor, craft production and specialization, and ceremonialism. Other topics whose archaeological correlates are related to gender are settlement patterns at local and regional scales, the architecture and composition of household groups, iconography, foodways, health, demography, and patterns of interactions with close and distant neighbors. We hope this book will alert southeastern archaeologists to archaeological patterns that may reflect the ways in which gender was constructed in native societies of the past.

Editors' Note

We thank Margaret Scarry, Vin Steponaitis, Nancy White, Janet Levy, Ken Sassaman, and our fellow graduate students for their encouragement and guidance. We are grateful to them and to Jerald Milanich, Mintcy Maxham, Bram Tucker, and an anonymous reviewer for comments about drafts of this introduction. We also thank John Scarry for providing the base map for figure I.1.

1

Challenges for Regendering
Southeastern Prehistory

Cheryl Claassen

Many contemporary archaeologists place social relations at the forefront of their investigations of the past. Some of them identify the relationships between women and men and among women as the ones most likely to reveal both new insights into technological and social change and a more people-centered reconstruction of the past. Building on a century of consensus about what activities and artifacts were women's, U.S. archaeologists since 1980 have found evidence for changes in women's and men's labor and gender organization as well as evidence for gendered sites and settlement patterns. I surveyed this literature in 1995, including that for the southeastern United States (Claassen 1997), to see what themes were emerging and what methods and theoretical positions were favored. That survey and the articles in this collection show how engendering research can revive old problems and direct attention toward new problems in reconstructing social organization and technology.

The pre-1980 literature has been criticized for its unexamined assumptions about women's roles in past societies of the Southeast, particularly the absence of women from considerations of chiefdom formation, activity areas, commodity and luxury goods production, innovations—in short, social life (see, for example, Galloway 1997; Trocolli 1992; Watson and Kennedy 1991). While the "gender" literature written largely since 1990 has examined many of these assumptions and placed gender in the foreground, revisionist authors must move carefully, for pitfalls await the unwary writer. There are five areas in which theoretical and methodological challenges exist for the archaeologist pursuing gender in the past. These challenges, which structure this paper, relate to (1) assumptions about gender held by many southeastern archaeologists: (2) the uses of skeletal data, (3) the development of suitable techniques, (4) the uses of analogy, and (5) the selection of research questions. Throughout this discussion I cite southeastern authors who have offered relevant discussion. The potential theoretical benefits of incorporating gender into archaeological studies are new hypotheses and consequently new research programs, new explanations, more satisfying depictions of the complexities of social life, and an invigorated science.

Assumptions about Gender

Assumptions about gender systems in the past abound in our literature; they are too numerous to detail here and too subtle for me to be exhaustive. My students tell me that the prehistoric landscape would have been too dangerous for women to be out in alone, that always there have been sex roles, and, of course, gender. Most professional archaeologists do not differ significantly in their opinions on these topics, even those who have taken an explicitly feminist approach.

In papers on gender written in the past by some nonsoutheastern archaeologists, I have encountered the problematic notion that gender might not have been present in some societies at some times. In both old and new papers on southeastern prehistory, the assumptions have been made that (1) the social function of gender is to organize labor; (2) sex equals gender (and therefore there always have been only two genders); and (3) the writing of southeastern prehistory is immune to gendered influences. These assumptions are problematic because neither new nor old authors within archaeology have problematized them, yet each is represented by a voluminous literature outside of archaeology.

Gender May or May Not Be Present

Southeastern archaeologists seem to assume that there always has been gender in the societies occupying the southeastern area. Certainly none of the gender papers I am familiar with for North American archaeology has attempted to argue that gender was not an important social axis, nor has any of them posited any circumstances under which gender could be expected to disappear. All North American archaeologists, past and present, appear to believe that gender always has been at play in Indian societies.

Many feminist scholars have questioned the omnipotence of gender as a social category (e.g., Rosaldo 1980), speculating that gender could disappear or appear in a society with differing social and historical circumstances. Among archaeologists, for instance, this point has been pressed by Conkey and Gero (1991:8–9), Hollimon (1991), Kornfeld and Francis (1991), and Whelan (1991b). It certainly is possible to imagine societies where gender did or does not exist, and many contemporary science fiction authors have done just that.

Feminist scholars are not the only ones to argue that gender could disappear. Some linguists have asserted that, among Native American groups, gender as we Westerners define it did not exist (i.e., it has nothing directly to do with cultural gender or biological sex). Alice Kehoe, archaeologist and ethnologist, recently asserted that gender "is a linguistic term and has no connection with biological sex or social personae" (Kehoe 1998:23). As understood by some linguists, "formal attributes of a linguistic gender system ha[ve] nothing to do with the valuation or categorization of people," or "the linguistic gender system has nothing to do with the 'gender system' in a more general sense" (Borker and Maltz 1989:412). As evidence of the discontinuity between language and culture, Kehoe offers the seemingly arbitrary sexing of objects in Indo-European languages.

Kehoe and the linguists with whom she shares company are not without their critics for the amazingly unanthropological claim that language and culture are only loosely related to each other. In fact, one of the greatest anthropological contributions to language study has been to argue for an intimate relationship between language and culture. Using linguistic gender to "refer to categorization systems tied at least in part to actual or perceived biological or reproductive roles," many anthropological linguists "have shown the nonindependence of grammatical gender from other gender systems, at least when dealing with actual linguistic usage" (Borker and Maltz 1989:412).

What linguists can offer to archaeologists wishing to pursue the gender systems of the Native American past is the insight into cultural categorization of men and women and others which can explain the association of artifacts, features, burial groupings, symbolism, and the like. Instead of telling us nothing about social gender, linguistic "gender" often signifies mental constructs of cosmic complementarity. In some native languages (e.g., Algonkian languages), "gender" demarcates animate and inanimate objects (Kehoe 1998:23), in other languages (e.g., Maya) gender demarcates high things and low things, things hot or cold

(Stone 1997). Women and men then are categorized as high or low, animate or inanimate, hot or cold, and they perform acts that are high or low, animate or inanimate, hot or cold. Birthing or growing plants is animate, as are women; killing animals is inanimate, as are men. Birds are high, as are men; shellfish are low, as are women (H. Moore 1988). Women are shellfishers, then, not because they are the weaker sex, always pregnant or nursing, but because they are associated with all things low. Archaeologists can identify other potential "low" activities and their tool kits and potentially reconstruct sex roles.

Contrary to many of my feminist contemporaries, I do think gender is always present in every human society, and consequently I think that southeastern archaeologists are right to assume that gender always has been an important means of organizing and stratifying the societies that have lived in this region. In the next section, I will argue that gender has always already been present.

The Social Function of Gender

Sex roles and gender are often conflated in our literature, such that the social function of gender is usually assumed to be to organize labor. I have previously expressed my dissatisfaction with this interpretation, for societies employ many other ways to organize labor, such as age, craft specialization, class, and caste (Claassen 1992:4; MacKinnon, in Hermann and Stewart 1994). If the purpose of gender were to organize labor, it would seem that once age, craft specialties, and class (let alone caste) take hold in a society, there no longer would be a need for gender and it would disappear. But gender doesn't disappear.

Elsewhere, Rosemary Joyce (1994) and I (1992) have put forth the idea that gender serves primarily to organize sexuality. There are no means by which societies mark and group sexuality, other than by gender. More specifically, the social function of gender is to organize and facilitate reproduction.

Speciation is the creation of sexually reproducing isolates. The basis of our being *Homo sapiens* is reproduction. Something so fundamental must have a cultural manifestation. That manifestation is the gender subsystem. As a sexually reproducing species, we experience copying and imprinting as ways of identifying sexual partners, and we must have ways of signaling sexual receptivity and fecundity. Many of those signals are culturally configured. There is no way other than with gender that our societies have organized this information. As Shulamith Firestone realized in the 1960s, gender will disappear only when a significant amount of reproduction occurs independent of the human body (Firestone 1972:197).

What differs over time and among societies, are the definitions of reproduction and the way gender is organized. Sometimes reproduction may include crop-growing, or men mimicking birth labor, or the ascension to leadership. At other times and in other places, it may simply be the birth of a human being. Sometimes the gender system is arranged hierarchically, sometimes laterally; sometimes it has two genders, sometimes more. Did gender complementarity turn into gender hierarchy at some point in political evolution in southeastern tribes?

At any rate, given this function for gender, Western notions of gender should have some utility for researchers working with other cultures. But the student must be clear whether a subsystem of gender is being compared (like hierarchy with hierarchy or two-gender system with two-gender system) or if the fundamental definition of reproduction is under examination.

Sex Equals Gender

Another assumption prevalent in archaeological writing is that skeletal sex is synonymous with gender. Feminists have separated the two terms. Typically "sex" refers to the physiology ("female"), or bluntly, soft tissue, and "gender" the social role ("woman"), with the parallel statements that sex is biological and gender is cultural in origin.

Having repeated this often-iterated understanding (sex is biological, gender is cultural), I want to take exception to it. It is erroneous for archaeologists and physical anthropologists who assign sex to skeletons to think that that act is purely the application of a biological label and not a cultural act. In fact, what we do in sexing skeletons is highly charged with our cultural notions of which characteristics are male, which female, and our need to force skeletons into those two categories. Both sex and gender labels fall within the realm of hypotheses.

The assumption that sex equals gender denies people of other cultures the prerogative to recognize more than two genders. It also denies the individuals their prerogative to choose a gender. Gender was and is recognized among many Native American groups on the basis of both dress and behavioral display, not soft tissue (Kehoe 1998; Whitehead 1981). The adult relatives are instructed as to which gender the child will assume through accounts of the child's visions and the child's favorite activities and objects. Dress and artifacts then hold the key to gender while skeletal data tell only about sex (Blackwood, in Hermann and Stewart

1994). Few archaeologists seriously contemplate whether it is sex or gender they are interested in investigating and how or whether sex data can be converted into gender data (Damm 1991).

Gender-free Writing

In addition to the assumptions about life in the past just discussed, there are troubling assumptions about gender in the way we conduct science. An extremely significant assumption made by the readers of published archaeological articles and books is that all the relevant data have been considered. There are now dozens of articles that demonstrate gender bias and class bias in citation practices, in reviewing, in conference presentations, and publications (Beaudry and White 1994; Chester, Rothschild, and Wall 1994; Claassen et al. 1999; Joyce 1994; Victor and Beaudry 1992). It is simply not true that data in articles penned by women are always recognized as relevant, are available in equally accessible formats, are read, are cited. The author who consistently settles for secondary literature sources is more likely to fall victim to this assumption than is the author who seeks out primary sources, particularly unpublished manuscripts.

Dozens of assumptions about gender are buried in our literature. Blades are made by men. Masses of shell mean women, and women mean children, and children mean a village. The presence of women's tools means the site is an overnight camp or village. Women did not travel the landscape alone, so they are never traders or the exclusive makers and users of sites. Everyone within the same social class eats the same menu. Camps move because of men's hunting needs. The landscape is not gendered, and so on.

As formidable or mundane as these assumptions are, all are surmountable, leaving positivist science intact. Doing science better by being more diligent in hypothesis testing, in particular, seems to be the solution to all of these challenges. Time will tell how successful we have been.

Use of Skeletal Data

Burials can provide extremely important information on sexed roles and sexed status. With sex as baseline data, bioarchaeologists have drawn conclusions about the type of labor habitually performed by men and women in several southeastern societies, about traumas and health, disease loads, and weaning stress (e.g., Bridges 1989, 1990, 1991, 1994; Miller-Shaivitz and Iscan 1991; Powell 1991; M. O. Smith 1996; D. Wilson 1994, 1997). Archaeologists have relied on sexed skeletons to uncover social patterns in grave preparation, grave goods, and status (e.g., Morse 1967; Rothschild 1979; Thomas 1996; Winters 1968).

Separation of sex from gender (discussed in the previous section) is not the only challenge in using skeletal data. How trustworthy are those sex assignments? The answer varies according to the decade in which the assignments were made, with greater distance from the present increasing the likelihood of sexing errors.

Many skeletons from the Southeast initially were sexed by Charles Snow at the WPA Archaeology Laboratory in Birmingham. When the analysis of sex was first accomplished in the 1930s and 1940s, the most heavily weighted criteria were found on the skull and in the grave goods. At that point in time, the act of sexing a skeleton was quite culturally charged, with strong opinions about what were male and female attributes and artifacts, and produced culturally biased sex designations. This cultural baggage has been lightened somewhat in the intervening years.

In the 1990s, the preferred criteria for sexing are characteristics of the pelvis, and four postcranial measurements involving the humerus and femur (Powell 1988:87–88). This change in criteria, centered on sexual dimorphism, has resulted in changes in sex-labeling for skeletons from all reexamined assemblages. In subsequent cases of resexing Moundville skeletons, a pattern of male bias, or overrepresentation in the sexing, has emerged (Weiss 1972). Snow's female to male ratio was one to two with Moundville skeletons. When Mary Powell resexed 424 adults in the Moundville sample, she found a female to male ratio of fifty-five to forty-four. In 11 percent of the skeletons examined by both Snow and Powell, there was a disparity in the sex assignment (Powell 1988:89–90). Powell noted that while there were discrepancies between the sex assignments made by the four physical anthropologists who have examined the Moundville skeletons over the past sixty years, there was far better agreement between them than there was with the assessments of sex made on the field forms by excavators. Excavators had attributed sex based on grave goods.

The Shell Mound Archaic skeletons from sites on Kentucky's Green River are probably the most often resexed skeletal set in the hemisphere. When I recalculated the percentages of males and females at Indian Knoll computed first by Snow (Webb 1974) and later by Marc Kelley (1980), I found that while twenty-four males were reclassified as females and twenty-four females were reclassified as males (table 1.1), the changes were significant when examining grave goods.

Table 1.1. Results of resexing skeletons from the Indian Knoll site in Kentucky

Change[a]	Count	Change[a]	Count	Change[a]	Count
I > M	44	I > F	33	I > I	43
F > F	157	F > M	24	F > I	31
M > M	168	M > F	24	M > I	32

Source: Kelley 1980 vs. Snow [Webb 1974]
a. I = indeterminate, F = female, M = male.

Of the skeletons with a sex change of male to female, seventeen had grave goods, while sixteen of the females resexed as male had grave goods. Based on Kelley's sexing of Indian Knoll skeletons, seven males, four females, and three indeterminates had carapace rattles, where the earlier sexing had the distribution of five males, seven females, and three unknowns. Pestles are now found with five males and two females, but Snow had one male, two females, and four indeterminates with pestles. This latter item is now more likely associated with one sex, while before there were not such clear patterns of association. Red ochre was originally attributed to seven males, thirteen females, and six indeterminates, whereas now the distribution is ten males, eleven females, and four indeterminates, for a more uniform distribution between genders.

The lesson to be learned from these changes in identifications of biological sex from skeletal evidence is that any assessment of status, habitual activity, diet, or the like based on skeletal data must evaluate the source of sex attributions and, if performed before 1975 (approximately), solicit an updated evaluation. These wrong sex determinations often involved wrong assumptions about the gender affiliation of tools; thus, many statements made about gendered activities, such as "this site was used for male activities," are now suspect. The biases in the old criteria and in the past use of grave goods to determine sex reaffirm the androcentric history of archaeology.

Developing Suitable Techniques

The twin challenges of assigning sex and deducing gender are hindered by a paucity of techniques suitable for identifying sex and gender. There are a small number of techniques routinely used by archaeologists or readily available to us that have proven useful: bone chemistry, DNA, site catchments, task differentiation, and handedness (not discussed here—see Sassaman 1996).

Bone Chemistry

Bone chemistry is typically used to quantify elements and proportions of foodstuffs in habitual diets. There are (at least) two ways in which prior dietary reconstructions have run aground with respect to gender: the assumptions that (1) men and women have the same diet and (2) chemical uptake is uniform in the bones of men and women.

Among the Fish Creek Aborigines in Arnhem Land, Australia, male hunters ate a greater proportion of animal foods than did nonhunters, and each individual man ate all the fish he caught. Women consumed the fish they caught while out or took it back to camp for other family members, while men brought back large game to be shared with other men (Bowdler 1976:251–52). In Kuna (Panama) dietary practices of old, women alone consumed lady fish, needlefish, and barracuda (Hale, Diaz, and Mendez 1996). In Tlingit communities in northwestern North America occupied before and after European contact, proportionately more women than men consumed shellfish, and more women and men of lower rank consumed shellfish (Moss 1993:643) and a greater variety of species (Wessen 1982). Ethnohistoric accounts suggest that Mississippian women in southeastern North America consumed diets that were nutritionally inferior to those of men (Powell 1988:78).

Isotopic assays support this challenge to uniform consumption in several cases, as do other visible aspects of skeletons, such as dental health and growth-stress indicators. Schoeninger and Peebles (1981) first recognized isotopic difference between genders. Van der Merwe and Vogel (1978) suggested that maize-farming women of the midwestern United States consumed more wild plants than did men. Diane Wilson (1997: 129–33) uncovered evidence of different female and male diets at the Powers Phase Turner site. Clark Larsen and colleagues (1992) found that while marine foods were a dietary staple for most individuals on Georgia's coast, a few individuals in the early Deptford period had diets dominated by terrestrial products. The one child in a sample of skeletons from Little Cypress Bayou (Rose, Marks, and Tieszen 1991) had a significantly different $\Delta^{13}C$ from the adults. Children between the ages of two and five years ate more plant foods and less meat than their elders in the Arikara village of Sully (Tuross and Fogel 1994:287).

It is highly likely that in most societies, the habitual gatherer of plants, gatherer of intertidal resources, fisher, or hunter will consume greater amounts of the prey over a lifetime than will those not involved in that food-procurement activity. It is highly likely that there were gender-specific diets among most hunter-gatherers (references in Bowdler 1976:251) and, to a lesser degree, among horticulturists. The methodological implication is that the bones of males, females, and children should be sampled for any dietary study and evaluated as potentially distinctive social groups, not averaged.

But are all chemical differences between men and women, children and adults, based on their diets? Buikstra cautioned investigators in 1991 that isotopic differences across age and sex groups could be independent of diet (Buikstra 1991). Carter, Dunnell, and Newell-Morris (1995) found that most archaeologists are unaware of the potential impact on strontium or calcium from reproduction and that those who are aware of this problem still favor the dietary explanation of differences in the ratio in a human population. Measurements of Sr/Ca ratio throughout the life cycle of macaques have revealed that reproduction might indeed affect the Sr/Ca ratio in human bone, a situation that compromises the use of this ratio to reconstruct diet (Carter, Dunnell, and Newell-Morris 1995). In nonprimates "the explanation for the higher ratios lies in the increased metabolic demands of pregnancy and lactation for additional Ca, combined with the discrimination by placental and mammary tissues for Ca over Sr" (Carter, Dunnell, and Newell-Morris 1995:4).

Confounding this chemical problem is the fact that while many archaeological human populations show sex differences in the ratio, modern human populations do not. The contradiction may lie in comparative demographics. Many demographers assume that modern populations have a greater proportion of postmenopausal women than did most premodern populations. This contradiction may also lie in the inappropriateness of nonprimate animal models.

DNA

Kristin Sobolik has explored the potential of DNA in coprolites to provide human sex information (Sobolik 1996; Sobolik, Gremillion, and Watson 1996). Steroid analysis of feces had proven useful for sexing some bird species prior to this application. Analysis of testosterone and estradiol in modern fecal specimens was performed and led to the creation of a hormone ratio that could distinguish between male and female. The ratio of testosterone to estradiol in males of this study ranged from 3 to 118 and in females from 0.2 to 7 (samples of four men and four women in two different menstrual-cycle phases). The same ratio was calculated by Worthman for Kalahari hunter-gatherers using serum concentrations with resulting ranges of 0.6 to 7 in females and 47 to 376 in males (Sobolik, Gremillion, and Watson 1996:288). The testosterone-to-estradiol ratio thus seems to distinguish these two sex categories.

Twelve coprolites from Early Woodland activities in Mammoth and Salts caves in Kentucky were subjected to the same type of assay and yielded ratios of twenty-four or greater. All twelve of these coprolites have been ascribed to adult males. This type of analysis holds much promise for identifying not only the sex of the depositor but also dietary and health differences among individuals.

Site Catchment

Site catchment analysis has been employed by archaeologists since the 1970s to investigate the economic foundation of past communities. Typically, one draws circles of one, two, five, or ten kilometers' radius around a camp or village and then inventories the natural resources within that area to determine what resources were locally available and which ones were foreign, as well as the economic basis for the community.

Brumbach and Jarvenpa (1997a, 1997b) have conducted ethnological work among the hunting-gathering Chipewyan of Canada for several decades. In observing the frequent participation of women in hunting they noted that women often hunted closer to the village or base camp than did men. A day's hunting typically involved travel by foot or canoe for several hours. "One archaeological implication of this is that catchment analysis of food resources located within 3 to 5 kilometers of a settlement site, or 5 to 10 kilometers if [using a canoe] will encompass the food-animal resources of primary interest to women" (Brumbach and Jarvenpa 1997b:29). The authors also concluded that women's participation in hunting is more easily recognized in the archaeological record than that of men and is "more directly mirrored in the use of tools" (Brumbach and Jarvenpa 1997b:30). The village locus and the tools recovered therein are the archaeologist's staple data and the primary inroad to women's activities. Just such a realization constitutes the artifact/activity description in Janet Spector's monograph *What This Awl Means* (1993).

Hunter-gatherer cultures are not the only ones that maintain separate spatial spheres for gendered members (even a gendered landscape?). Douglas Parrelli (1994) found that the ethnohistoric documents for the Iroquois indicated that the spatial domain for women, elderly men, and captives of either gender was village and adjacent fields, while the spatial domain for men was the forest. While Parrelli did not equate this finding with the archaeological technique of site catchment analysis, it is clear that, for this farming culture, site catchments of one, two, and five kilometers would encompass the domain of women primarily, and not the domain of men.

These writers have observed that site catchments of sizes typically used in this kind of analysis encompass primarily women's activities and contributions rather than men's. Here, then, is a classic archaeological technique suitable for gender studies. Inventorying resources within a five-kilometer radius versus those beyond that range may serve as the basis for comments about men's and women's relative dietary and economic contributions.

Task Differentiation

Janet Spector's (1983) task-differentiation approach is a common methodological tool employed by (particularly Plains) archaeologists looking for gender in the past. It is essentially the same as the behavioral chain analysis detailed by Michael Schiffer in 1975 (reprinted Schiffer 1995:55–66, or Schiffer 1976:49–55). Historically documented activities are subdivided into those activities relating to acquiring and processing food; making and repairing tools, clothing, and buildings; and maintaining social relations. For each step in an activity, one records who performed the task; where, when, and how often it was performed; what artifacts, structures, and facilities were associated. Schiffer's approach would have the researcher list the debitage associated as well. With the activities, artifacts, spatial locations, and debris specified, the researcher turns to site data to interpret the actions of men, women, and children. While numerous authors have utilized this technique, Spector (1993) now finds the approach too sterile for her own use, although the behavioral chain exercise is still useful for making assumptions apparent and for organizing arguments.

Devising more ways of focusing on sex and gender is the challenge of the immediate future. Maintaining access to skeletal material is even more important for the study of social organization.

These examples of useful techniques for exploring gender in the past fall into three categories: old techniques used with new perception (site catchment, task differentiation), old techniques incompletely understood (bone chemistry), and new techniques (DNA analysis of coprolites). The unrealized potential of site catchment analysis raises questions about the gender ramifications of other familiar techniques. The evolving understanding of bone chemistry may mean that past interpretations may not be valid. Maintaining access to skeletal material is clearly important for the study of social organization. The accessibility of DNA in curated coprolites not only holds great promise for understanding who used rock shelters and caves in the past but also offers a new way to investigate gendered differences in diet and health when skeletons are lacking. Devising more ways of focusing on sex and gender is the challenge of the immediate future.

The Use of Analogy

The direct historical approach is the favorite means by which archaeologists have raised and argued gender questions (Claassen 1997). Yet many of these authors appear to be unaware of the problems with this type of analogy or with the problems of some particular cross-cultural analogies.

Feminist critiques of the direct historical approach are many (e.g., Brumfiel 1991; Fratt 1991; Latta 1991) and center on the androcizing impact that European societies had on the natives with whom they established relations. There is no way to minimize the impact that these relations had on southeastern societies, and no ethnographies or ethnohistories have escaped the changes either in gender structures or many other cultural arenas (e.g., Ramenofsky 1987).

Ethnographic analogies from distant cultures are also popular. Often referencing the modern !Kung, authors appear to be unaware that there is both theoretical and factual trouble in the gathering image given us by the !Kung, and particularly unaware of Susan Kent's many articles on the !Kung and gender (e.g., Kent 1992, 1995, 1998b, 1999). Many anthropologists now view the !Kung as living in an environment denuded of game and therefore unusually reliant on floral foods and unusually sustained by women's gathering. If there were a depletion of game over the millennia in the Americas (a controversial issue), then gathering and plant foods generally as well as the importance of women's foraging activities would have increased as time approached the present. The large contribution of women and plants to the !Kung diet would thus not seem to be an appropriate analog for Paleoindian and Archaic cultures.

While the !Kung are problematic as analogs for North American hunter-gatherers, the writings of Robert Hall and George Hamell make it clear to me that there was and is a sea of pan-American symbolism and beliefs that is an untapped resource for analogies and hypotheses (R. L. Hall 1997; Hamell 1983, 1987). As an example of the usefulness of turning to Mesoamerican symbolism, for instance, I offer the gendered use of caves (as well as shell symbolism, as described in Claassen 1991). In central Mexico and in the Mayan area, the rituals and glyphs inside caves are the expressions of men. Perhaps caves in the southeastern United States as early as the Early Woodland period were similarly gendered, since two desiccated male bodies have been recovered from the Salts-Mammoth system, as have male coprolites. Perhaps caves were male loci throughout prehistory in this region and in the Americas. Perhaps American symbol systems, regardless of corresponding political development, need to be tapped for understanding gender in southeastern prehistory.

Archaeologists always will need cultural analogies to advance interpretation of prehistoric sites and cultures. They must be used with a full understanding of how they both constrain and enhance our interpretations. We have relied on the presumed historic or contemporary descendants of prehistoric cultures for analogies in the realm of material culture and village organization. The pitfalls of this type of analogy have been described adequately while scholars simultaneously acknowledge that the direct historical approach is the strongest type of cultural analogy we can employ. The !Kung of Africa, however, do not appear, upon extended study, to be pure hunter-gatherers, but rather are heavily influenced by their herding neighbors and an overgrazed environment—circumstances that do not pertain to prehistory in North America.

What we have been most remiss in recognizing in our use of the direct historical approach is the value of language and symbol systems. Once these cultural arenas are recognized, their analogical value can be extracted from dozens of culture groups throughout North and Central America. It is my belief that archaeologists interested in past gender systems will benefit greatly from even a cursory knowledge of native languages and American symbolism.

Research Questions

An investigation of gender is appropriate to any study concerned with social organization. It is also appropriate for any study concerned with technology or trade or demographics or animals or plants. Agency, and its concomitant issues of labor and time management, are immediately obvious inquiries: How were new technologies structured socially? How were new items absorbed culturally? How were new activities partitioned socially? We need concentrated efforts at understanding several technologies and their social ramifications: the adoption of the atlatl, fish hook, fish spear, bow and arrow, pottery and its stylistic changes, soapstone, beads, weaving, salt, canoes, and so forth.

Gender impacted how the landscape was used and perceived in the southeastern United States. I have already mentioned the possible exclusive use of caves by men. There were nutting camps and women's seclusion sites (Galloway 1997). There were locales probably sacred to matriclans and to patriclans, to warrior societies, to dance societies, and other locales for male and female initiations. There were often distinctive burial areas for women and men, particularly in Mississippian times.

While it is often assumed that men dominated public space (the village) and women private space (the home interior and yard), it may have been quite different for southeastern Indian groups. The hearth, rather than dominating private space, was, in the setting of long houses and villages, a public space. Ceremonial preparation for hunting, war, or ball games occurred in private spaces. Both men's houses and menstrual huts probably were viewed as private space. While we may not be able to investigate notions of public and private, we certainly can avoid simplistic categorization of space.

We know that, at least in historic times, there were women's languages among some southeastern societies. Surely there were other gendered symbol systems—in language, in rock art, in portable art, in decorative motifs—perhaps intelligible to the other genders but rarely made by them. Even colors are gendered among the Maya (Stone 1997) and the Dakota (Whelan 1991b). Gendered rock art in Texas has been discussed by Patricia Bass (1991), and concentrations of rock art also may have been gendered places. Gender motifs and figures have also been the focus of explication (C. Brown 1982; Koehler 1997). Statuary found in the Southeast has been given explicitly gendered interpretations on a few occasions (e.g., Galloway 1997; Kehoe 1996; Koehler 1997), as have other items of portable art such as gorgets (e.g., Hatch 1975; M. T. Smith and Smith 1989).

Many tribal peoples of North America were strongly status conscious, with high- and low-ranking families, bands, and villages; and status was hereditary. It is evident from skeletal information that women's life experiences differed according to social status, such as the experiences of women in the Middle Woodland lower Illinois Valley, at the Mississippian Turner site in Missouri (D. Wilson 1997), at Moundville in Alabama, at Dallas phase sites in eastern Tennessee, and at Chucalissa in western Tennessee (Powell 1986). Archaeologists interested in gender systems need to avoid assuming that all women were social equals and look for status differences in skeletal indications, in artifacts, and in spatial relationships.

These research questions have been offered for future research in the Southeast. The gendered use of landscape raises issues of public versus private spaces; how the landscape, particularly its physical features, was gendered; and how and why gendered social groups moved about. Gendered symbol-systems research would approach cave art, rock art, and portable art as gendered domains for communicating gender information and gender-specific concerns to the Upperworld and the Underworld. Research into social relations between women will facilitate greatly the larger research enterprise of investigating social organization while simultaneously telling us much about the interaction among women. Research into these domains in tandem will greatly enrich the anthropology of our archaeology and, no doubt, will surprise us in many ways.

Conclusion

An investigation of gender is appropriate to any study concerned with social organization. It is also appropriate for any study concerned with technology, trade, demographics, animals, or plants. We need concentrated efforts at understanding the social incorporation of various technologies, much like the recent research into the bow and arrow (Bettinger and Eerkens 1999; Nassaney and Pyle 1999) and the initial adoption of pottery (Sassaman 1993).

In our explorations of these topics, we must take care to do good science. I have discussed topics in five areas of concern. Every paper written passes into one or more of these areas: our assumptions about gender, uses of skeletal data, the development of suitable techniques, the use of analogies, and research questions. Mesoamerican ethnohistory and ethnography are to be pursued for sources of understanding past gender systems, as are language studies. We need to explore the landscape as a gendered phenomenon. New techniques for identifying sex and gender should be developed, and we need to consider the gendered ramifications of established techniques. Studies based on skeletal material or grave goods must use recent evaluations of sex.

The rewards to archaeologists who pursue information about past gender systems are many. They will contribute to a growing knowledge base about the structure of gender systems worldwide and to the generation of gender theory in anthropology. They will add to our understanding of the social organization of hunter-gatherer-fishers and agriculturalists, giving us new insights into ideological, technological and social change and a more people-centered reconstruction of the past. As we strive to regender the past, diligence and creative thinking are required to meet these challenges. The chapters to follow indicate that the results are rewarding.

Author's Note

Some fifteen months after first writing this paper, I read Sarah Nelson's *Gender and Archaeology* (1997) and discovered that we had a nearly identical set of concerns.

2

The Gender Division of Labor in Mississippian Households

Its Role in Shaping Production for Exchange

Larissa Thomas

Households were the basic economic unit of Mississippian communities in the Southeast and Midwest between A.D. 900 and 1450 (Muller 1997: 286). Households engaged in subsistence production, and in some instances they also engaged in the production of goods for exchange. Production for exchange in household contexts is evident at sites throughout the Mississippian Southeast. Households in the American Bottom, for example, produced shell beads (Prentice 1983; Yerkes 1983, 1989, 1991). Households in the Black Bottom produced fluorite ornaments (Muller 1986:239), and in the nearby Mill Creek area of southern Illinois, households produced stone hoes (Cobb 1988, 1989, 1996). In each of these cases, goods for exchange were being produced in or around domestic structures by members of the household who scheduled that activity into the rest of their domestic responsibilities.

Because the household was the locus of production for exchange, the organization of domestic production directly affected production for exchange, just as production for exchange influenced domestic production. These aspects of Mississippian economy were intertwined and interactive, and both were fundamentally structured by the gender division of labor. The gender division of labor lay at the heart of daily routines and

seasonal schedules in which different members of households were responsible for different tasks. The specific allocation of labor to various
household tasks had implications for the organization of production for
exchange. It influenced decisions about who would participate in production for exchange, how much labor they would contribute, and how
production for exchange would be scheduled among domestic productive activities.

To observe the ways in which the gender division of labor influenced
domestic economy and production for exchange in Mississippian communities, we can consider the example of two Mississippian communities in southern Illinois, represented by the Dillow's Ridge and Great Salt
Spring sites (fig. 2.1). People at these sites produced different goods for
exchange—hoes and salt—which involved different production processes
and different configurations of labor. In this chapter, I discuss the character of domestic economy and production for exchange to explore how the

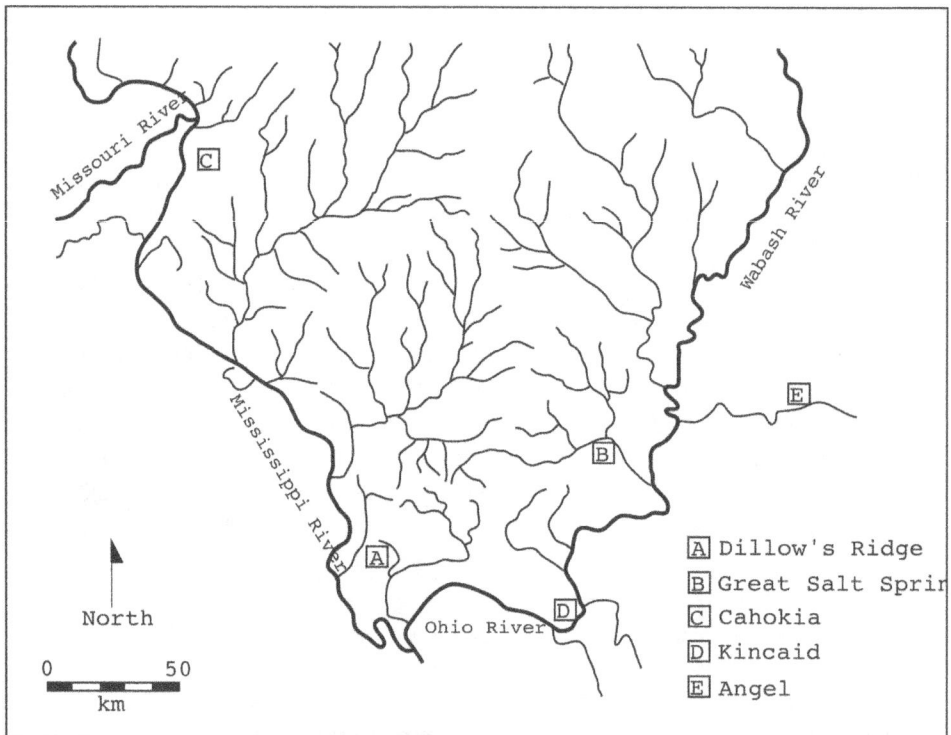

Fig. 2.1. Location of Dillow's Ridge, the Great Salt Spring, and other sites mentioned in
the text.

gender division of labor may have affected economic life in these communities.

Domestic Economy and Production for Exchange

Domestic economy or "production for use" is defined as those activities concerned with the day-to-day necessities of living related to child care, subsistence, and other forms of household maintenance (Bender 1967: 499; Sahlins 1972:82–86). Production for exchange, on the other hand, is oriented toward the accumulation of wealth in various forms (Sahlins 1972:84).

Production for exchange is often referred to as "craft specialization," a term that has been subject to extensive debate (e.g., Brumfiel and Earle 1987; Clark and Parry 1990; Costin 1991; Earle 1987; Tosi 1984). Diversity exists among definitions of specialization, in part because it has taken many forms in the diverse political economies of societies past and present. Some Mississippian archaeologists during the 1980s debated the definition of specialization and its character in Mississippian societies. On one side of the debate is Jon Muller (1984, 1986, 1987, 1997), who has argued that the term "specialist" should be reserved for individuals who derive their livelihood from the activity in question. On the other side of the specialization debate is Richard Yerkes (1983, 1986, 1989, 1991). He does not share Muller's contention that only full-time craftspeople are specialists. Rather, he has defined craft specialization as the part-time production of items—usually prestige goods for elites—at the expense of some subsistence activities, thus requiring the producer to obtain some subsistence goods through exchange (Yerkes 1983, 1989, 1991).

Debates among Mississippian archaeologists on specialization have been valuable in drawing attention to the diverse arrangements of productive labor in various Mississippian contexts. However, I prefer not to use the term "specialization." I agree with Pauketat (1997:4) that we should move beyond static, typological conceptions of specialization and begin to explore the unique political economy framing each historical case of production for exchange. As part of this project, it is necessary to consider the relationship of production for exchange and domestic production—a relationship that is mediated by the gender division of labor.

Gender Division of Labor

Only a handful of archaeological studies have focused on the gender division of labor as a critical force in the operation of prehistoric economies (e.g., Brumfiel 1991; Claassen 1991; Costin 1996; Hastorf 1991; Hingley 1990; Jackson 1991; Sassaman 1992; R. P. Wright 1996b). Such studies view gender as a fundamental social category that structures or mediates the roles and relationships involved in production. The gender division of labor establishes the range of economic activities permissible to different members of society, thus situating individuals in specific socioeconomic contexts (Costin 1996:114–15). For example, the gender division of labor associated with production for exchange can lead to gendered differences in social participation, power, and wealth, since production for exchange is usually connected, materially and ideologically, to power hierarchies (Costin 1996:115).

A focus on the gender division of labor, therefore, can enrich significantly our analyses of production for exchange and other aspects of Mississippian economy. From a methodological standpoint, addressing the gender division of labor in a prehistoric context is not a straightforward matter. The way in which tasks were distributed among various members of a society is not always evidenced in the archaeological record. In fact, methodological concerns about how to see gender in the archaeological record have been at the heart of resistance to gender studies in archaeology (Conkey and Gero 1991:11–14; Wylie 1991a). However, this methodological challenge is no greater than that of other "intangible" aspects of social reality that archaeologists have found ways of approaching, such as status (Wylie 1991a:33). One way archaeologists have sought to address issues of gender in late prehistoric contexts is through the use of relevant ethnohistoric sources (e.g., Brumfiel 1991; Dommasnes 1987; Hastorf 1991; Jackson 1991).

Although there are no ethnographic descriptions of fourteenth-century Mississippian communities, some basic elements of the gender division of labor in these societies can be reconstructed from various sources including archaeological evidence and written documents from the subsequent historic period. Archaeologists of the Mississippian period have access to descriptions of native southeasterners recorded by European observers in the sixteenth century, scattered documents from the seventeenth century, as well as later accounts from the eighteenth century. Sixteenth-century accounts from the expeditions of De Soto, De Luna, Cabeza de Vaca, and Pardo are valuable in that they describe groups that had not yet been affected by prolonged relationships with foreign cultural systems. Documents from the eighteenth century, written by men who lived and/or traveled extensively among the groups they are describing—Adair, Bartram, Lawson, and Le Page du Pratz—often provide greater detail than the early accounts by explorers. However, they describe south-eastern people who, to varying degrees, had been ravaged by European diseases, involved in economic relationships with Europeans, affected by missionary activity, and who had begun using many forms of European material culture. Southeastern societies were not static in the centuries that preceded and succeeded the Spanish entrada. But neither were the basic cultural patterns of these societies obliterated by the arrival of Europeans.

Using ethnohistoric information requires an assumption of continuity over the period of time separating the people described in the documents and the people who created the archaeological context at issue. It also requires an assumption of shared cultural content between the two. Although there is no way to prove that the gender division of labor was the same in all Mississippian communities, it seems a reasonable supposition given what appears to have been a shared worldview across the Mississippian Southeast (Knight 1986). Continuity through time in the gender division of labor is suggested in the cases where archaeological evidence exists to corroborate documentary accounts. Although I have discussed more extensively elsewhere my use of ethnohistoric information in this study (Thomas 1997:32–39), I can summarize my rationale as follows:

1. Archaeological evidence makes clear that there was some amount of continuity between the prehistoric and historic periods and that the accounts are not wildly inaccurate.
2. The information I have sought required only straightforward empirical observations rather than interpretive input from the observer.
3. The existence of multiple sources allows one to evaluate consistency synchronically and diachronically.

Information from the sixteenth-century accounts, the major eighteenth-century accounts, as well as more obscure accounts from throughout the historic period have been assembled and supplemented by ethnographic information collected in the nineteenth and early twentieth centuries by the ethnographer and ethnohistorian John Swanton (e.g., 1928, 1946). Swanton's compilation *The Indians of the Southeastern United States* (1946) is particularly useful because it places information from different sources side by side and allows one to evaluate consistency and divergence among different accounts, among different societies, and through time.

Multiple lines of evidence, including ethnohistoric information (e.g., Swanton 1946), iconographic representations (e.g., Emerson 1989), and bioarchaeological remains (Bridges 1989) all indicate that women were responsible for most of the agricultural work during the Mississippian period. Southeastern men in the historic period cleared agricultural fields and occasionally might have helped with planting and harvesting (Swanton 1946:286, 710, 713, 717). Women were responsible for the remainder of the agricultural tasks: from preparing the fields, to planting, weeding, and harvesting (Swanton 1946:710, 713, 717). Not only were women the main producers of agricultural foods, they probably were also responsible for collecting wild food plants such as nuts and fruit. In this activity, women probably received help from children and older people, as was the case among some southeastern people in the eighteenth and nineteenth centuries (Campbell 1959:11). Women also likely collected some animal foods like shellfish (Claassen 1991:277, 286; Waselkov 1987:99).

Women were the ones who processed and cooked food (Swanton 1946:710–11, 715, 717). The Keller figurine from the BBB Motor site in the American Bottom and the "Figure at Mortar" from Spiro both depict women grinding corn (Emerson 1989:52–56). In fact, implements used for food production are universally associated with females in Mississippian iconography (K. E. Smith 1991:131). Adult women probably shared with young girls a considerable amount of the work involved in preparing food (e.g., Swanton 1946:718). As girls matured and learned the necessary skills for food preparation, they likely made greater and greater contributions. The same was probably true of all of the other domestic tasks in which girls took part as they learned the skills expected of southeastern women.

Historic accounts from the sixteenth century onward consistently report that men's main contributions to subsistence were hunting and fishing (Campbell 1959:11; Swanton 1946:710, 715, 717). Just as young girls learned gender-appropriate skills from their mothers and other female relatives, young boys learned skills expected of men from their male relatives, including older brothers, fathers, and uncles (Swanton 1946:714, 717). Learning to hunt—practicing with a bow and arrow and accompanying older men on hunts—was foremost in boys' education (Swanton 1946:714, 716–17).

Child care responsibilities among historic southeastern groups depended on the age and sex of individual children. Women took care of young children, but somewhere around the age of four or five, boys came under the supervision and tutelage of their fathers, elder brothers, or the oldest uncle of the clan (Swanton 1946:714–15). Girls remained in the care of their female relatives, learning from and helping their older sisters, their mothers, and their mothers' clan sisters (Swanton 1946:715).

Beyond involvement in subsistence production and child-rearing, women contributed to Mississippian economies through the production of utilitarian goods. Women likely made the clothing that protected people from the elements. Every early account that describes the production of textiles and basketry in the Southeast ascribes this activity to women (Drooker 1992:11–12; Swanton 1946:710–11, 715, 717). Furthermore, most of the work involved in preparing skins and making leather clothing also was done by women (Swanton 1946:715, 717). Thus, women made clothing as well as many other items of textile, basketry, and leather—from bags to mats to fishing nets.

Women also made ceramics, a fact evidenced in ethnohistoric accounts and in the ceramics themselves. Ethnohistoric information from the southeastern United States describes pottery making as women's work (e.g., Swanton 1946:549–55, 710). At least one Mississippian ceramic vessel actually shows a woman engaged in this activity (Holmes 1903: plate 28). It is reasonable that women, who did most of the cooking, would make the tools necessary to prepare food.

Men also produced many economically important types of material culture. For example, throughout the historic period, men built houses and other household facilities like corncribs (Swanton 1946:715, 717). In fact, men did most woodworking, making many useful objects such as bows, arrows, mortars, and canoes (Swanton 1946:710, 715, 717). The importance of men's woodworking skills in supplying Mississippian families with a wide array of household equipment is underestimated by the rarity of wood in archaeological contexts.

Ethnohistoric sources are largely silent on the issue of flint knapping in the Southeast (Swanton 1946:544). However, the manufacture of arrows is generally attributed to men, and men are said to have performed the majority of activities that in prehistoric times would have required the use of stone tools (Swanton 1946:717). Therefore, men may have been the primary producers of stone tools in southeastern communities, and they probably were the ones who exchanged lithic raw materials and finished tools in contexts like the Mill Creek area where stone hoes were produced and exchanged. Although most flint knapping was probably done by men, lithic technology was not foreign to Mississippian women, who undoubtedly made and used a variety of expedient and formal tools for their daily tasks. Recent discussions of lithic technology in relation to gender division of labor have argued that lithic debris in most household contexts is likely the result of women and men alike making and using stone tools (Gero 1991; Sassaman 1992). Gero (1991:169) argues that, since a great deal of women's work typically centers around the household, women's activities are most visible in household refuse, which often includes evidence of tool manufacture and use. At sites in the Southeast, women, like men, would have needed stone tools in many of their daily tasks, and "it is inconceivable that they sat and waited for a flake to be produced, or that they set out each time to borrow one" (Gero 1991:170). Many tools probably were used by both men and women since they lived together in households, where they likely shared certain tools that would have been useful to more than one member of the group (Bruhns 1991: 421–22).

Overall, historic sources from the Southeast describe the gender division of labor as very rigid and reinforced by a spatial segregation of activities (Hudson 1976:260). Let us now consider how that gender division of labor affected production for exchange in two Mississippian contexts.

Domestic Economy and Hoe Production at Dillow's Ridge

Dillow's Ridge was a village in southwestern Illinois occupied between A.D. 1250 and 1450. The village was located in the Mill Creek area, a locality encompassing small mound sites, villages, quarries, and workshops— each involved in the production of hoes (fig. 2.2). Mill Creek hoes were one of the most commonly exchanged items during the Mississippian period (Cobb 1989:79), when people from the Mill Creek quarries and workshops produced thousands of hoes for export to sites throughout the Mississippi Valley and beyond (Winters 1981:28). They also produced Ramey knives, finely crafted knives that seemed to serve both utilitarian and ritual or status-marking functions; the knives appear in both domestic and mortuary contexts, and are depicted in Mississippian iconography (Cobb 1996:282). Rare ceremonial objects such as maces and swords also were made of Mill Creek chert (Cobb 1989:84).

The Mill Creek area is the source of Mill Creek chert, a lithic material well suited for use in agricultural hoes because of a number of unique qualities. Mill Creek chert occurs in nodules of sufficient size for the manufacture of large bifaces such as hoes. The lenticular shape of Mill Creek nodules makes them natural preforms for hoes and knives, requiring minimal reduction and shaping in manufacture (Dunnell et al. 1994:81; Phillips 1900:42). Scanning electron microscopy has revealed that Mill Creek chert has a grainy texture with large crystalline structures, making

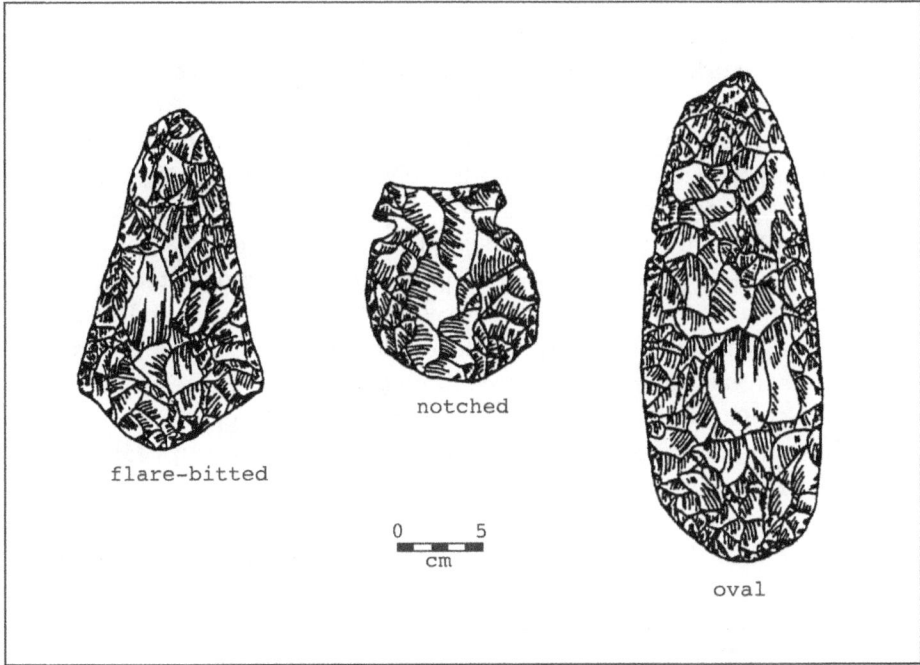

Fig. 2.2. Mill Creek hoes (after Cobb 1996:270).

it more durable than finer-textured cherts (Cobb 1988:87). The microstructure of Mill Creek chert is riddled with voids created by minerals leaching out since the chert's formation. These voids arrest crack propagation and partly account for Mill Creek chert's durability and resistance to fracture and wear (Dunnell et al. 1994:81). The chert was extracted from at least four quarries, where the nodules are suspended in clay subsoil. At the quarries today, the ground surface is pockmarked with hundreds of slumped-in quarry shafts (Phillips 1900:43) and littered with lithic debris from the testing of nodules and the manufacture of hoes.

Dillow's Ridge is located on a ridgetop overlooking the small You-Be Hollow Valley, across from the largest Mill Creek quarry (fig. 2.3). Shallow depressions representing the remains of house basins appear across the surface of the site. Three seasons of excavations led by Charles Cobb have shown that structures were rebuilt as many as three or four times.[1] Extensive midden deposits contain ordinary domestic refuse, such as ceramics, daub, animal bone, botanical remains, and an assortment of lithic tools. Present also is refuse related to the production of hoes for exchange, including flint knapping tools like abraders, hammerstones, and antler mallets as well as tool-production failures and massive amounts of debitage. Thus, in addition to being an ordinary village, Dillow's Ridge was also a workshop where large bifaces were produced for exchange. Judging from the number of production failures recovered, it appears that both Ramey knives and hoes were the principal products at Dillow's Ridge. Charles Cobb and Brian Butler (1996) have estimated the annual output of producers at Dillow's Ridge based on debitage volume and biface replication data. They argue that production intensity was quite low, with the average annual output only in the hundreds of tools.

Hoe production at Dillow's Ridge seems to have been pursued autonomously by residents of the site. Hoes were produced at four quarries and numerous workshops scattered throughout the Mill Creek area. The dispersed nature of quarrying and hoe production suggests that local leaders did not control access to the chert resource. It also appears that local leaders neither controlled nor profited from the labor of hoe producers. The mound burials at the nearby Hale site contain very few prestige goods (Cobb 1989:85). Despite the Hale site's strategic location and

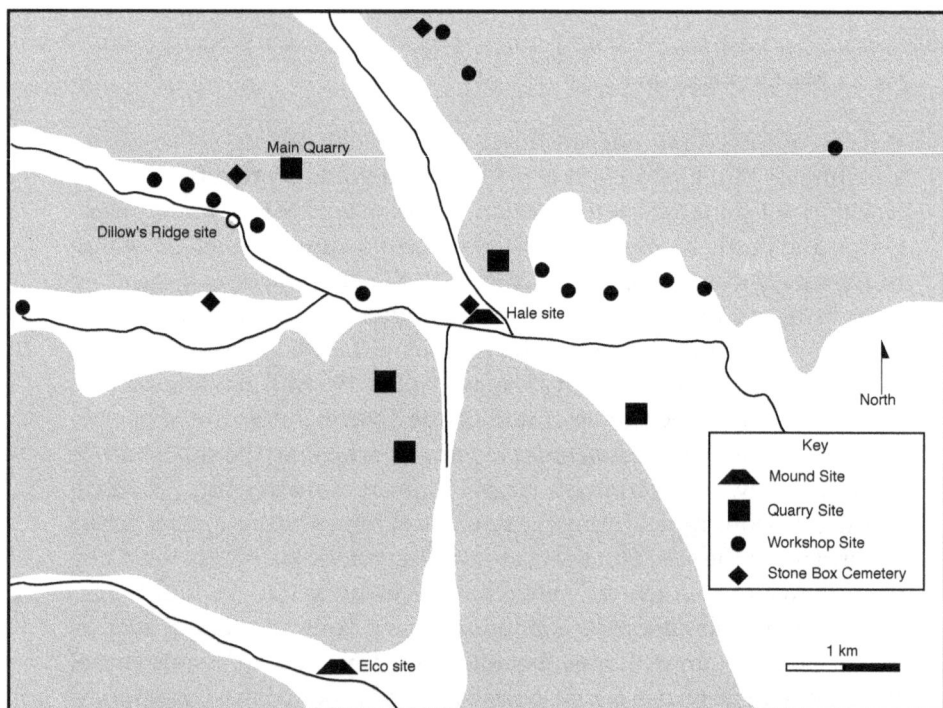

Fig. 2.3. Mississippian occupation in the Mill Creek area (after Cobb 1996:276).

the availability of a chert resource over which elites potentially could have extended monopoly control, leaders in the Mill Creek area do not appear to have controlled production. Nor is there any evidence that powerful elites from distant polities at Cahokia or Kincaid controlled hoe production.

Despite their involvement in the production and exchange of hoes, people at Dillow's Ridge carried on a rather normal Mississippian existence (Thomas 1997). It has been argued in the past that chert exploitation in the Mill Creek area was carried out by small groups of nonspecialists who visited the area periodically for short periods of time before returning to their homes elsewhere (Muller 1986:233–34, 1987:15). This argument has been controverted by data gathered in four seasons of survey and excavation in the Mill Creek area and at Dillow's Ridge. People at Dillow's Ridge lived at the site year-round and were able to support themselves without the hoe trade.

A diverse assortment of Mississippian cultigens has been found at the Dillow's Ridge site (table 2.1). With the recovery of a large number of hoe-resharpening flakes (n = 70), we know that these cultigens were grown at Dillow's Ridge rather than being obtained through trade or brought from elsewhere by the site's residents. People at Dillow's Ridge also collected a variety of wild food plants, especially nuts and fruits. They hunted, trapped, fished, and collected many different animals, but relied heavily on deer (table 2.2). It is clear that people at Dillow's Ridge were largely self-sufficient in their subsistence production, given the presence at the site of the many artifacts needed to procure and process the foods recovered there (tables 2.3 and 2.4).

Aside from possible hunting and fishing trips outside of the Mill Creek area and trips related to the exchange of hoes, it appears that people occupied Dillow's Ridge year-round. The archaeobotanical assemblage from the site offers some evidence regarding seasonality. Seasonally ripening plants suggest occupation in the fall, summer, and possibly the spring. Plants that become ripe in different seasons (such as maygrass and nuts) are found in the same contexts at the site, suggesting continuous occupation rather than discrete occupational episodes in different seasons. Although winter and spring occupation is difficult to demonstrate, the presence of storable foods, like nuts and corn, could suggest occupation during these seasons. The faunal assemblage also provides information about seasonality. Data on dental wear, epiphyseal fusion, and the hibernation schedules of certain animal species together suggest occupation sometime between spring and fall. Furthermore, the

Table 2.1. Summary of identified floral remains from Dillow's Ridge

Taxa	Common name	Frequency
Amaranthus sp.	Pigweed	1
Carya spp.	Hickory	5,313
Carya illinoensis	Pecan	2
Chenopodium spp.	Goosefoot	24
Crataegus spp. cf. *C. rotundifolia*	Hawthorn	2
Curcurbitaceae	Squash/gourd	7
Diospyros virginiana	Persimmon	3
Iva annua	Sumpweed	11
Juglans spp.	Black walnut	12
Liquidambar styraciflua	Sweetgum	1
Panicoid grass	Panic grass	1
Phalaris caroliniana	Maygrass	6
Phaseolus sp.	Domestic bean	1
Phytolacca sp.	Pokeweed	1
Polygonum erectum	Knotweed	217
Polygonum spp.	Knotweed	2
Portulaca sp.	Purslane	1
Quercus spp.	Oak acorn	19
Rhus sp.	Sumac	2
Rubus spp.	Blackberry	4
Sambucus canadensis	Elderberry	1
Solanum sp.	Nightshade	2
Strophostyles helvola	Wild bean	4
Vitis spp.	Wild grape	37
Vitis rotundifolia	Muscadine grape	1
Zea mays	Maize	1,196
Kernels		107
Cupules		81
Small fragments		1,008
Total		6,871

Note: The data in this table reflect the contents of five 6-liter flotation samples plus four larger samples totaling 43 liters, for a volume total of 73 liters. Analysis was carried out by Lee Newsom and Linda Parry at the Center for Archaeological Investigations, Southern Illinois University, Carbondale.

Table 2.2. Summary of identified faunal remains from Dillow's Ridge

Taxa	Common name	NISP[a]
Total mammals		3,520
Odocoileus virginianus	White-tailed deer	361
Procyon lotor	Raccoon	16
Urocyon cinereoargenteus	Gray fox	2
Canis familiaris	Domestic dog	59
Marmota monax	Woodchuck	8
Sciurus carolinensis	Gray squirrel	5
Sciurus niger	Fox squirrel	1
Sciurus spp.	Unidentified squirrel	90
Tamias spp.	Chipmunk	2
Oryomys palustris	Rice rat	1
Peromyscus sp.	Deer mouse	1
Unidentified rodents		75
Didelphis marsupialis	Opossum	7
Sylvilagus floridanus	Cottontail rabbit	6
Sylvilagus spp.	Unidentified rabbit	9
Unidentified mammals		2,877
Total birds		137
Meleagris gallopavo	Turkey	17
Anas spp.	Duck	2
Podilymbus podiceps	Pied-billed grebe	2
Unidentified birds		116
Total reptiles		340
Unidentified snake		1
Pseudemys sp.	Terrapin	1
Trionyx/Chelydra sp.	Softshell/snapping turtle	5
Chrysemys/Graptemys spp.	Map/painted turtle	11
Terrapene carolina	Box turtle	37
Unidentified turtle		286
Total amphibians		1
Unidentified salamander		1
Total fish		322
Aplodinotus grunniens	Freshwater drumfish	4
Micropterus salmoides	Largemouth bass	1
Micropterus sp.	Unidentified bass	1
Ictalurus natalis	Yellow bullhead	4

(continued)

Table 2.2 *(continued)*

Taxa	Common name	NISP[a]
Ictalurus spp.	Unidentified catfish	4
Catostomus sp.	Sucker	1
Moxostoma cf. *carinatum*	River redhorse	3
Moxostoma cf. *erythrurum*	Golden redhorse	1
Ictiobus cf. *bubalus*	Smallmouth buffalo	1
Dorosoma sp.	Unidentified shad	1
Amia calva	Bowfin	15
Unidentified fish		286
Total molluscs		216
Amblema plicata	Three-ridge	3
Lasmigona costata	Fluted-shell	1
Ligumia recta	Black sandshell	1
Campeloma sp.	Aquatic snail	1
Terrestrial snail		28
Unidentified shell		182
Total identified specimens		4,537

Note: The data in this table are compiled from the analyses of the 1993, 1994, and 1995 assemblages made by Peter Stahl and Emanuel Breitburg.

a. The number of identified specimens.

built environment at the site sheds light on seasonality in that the presence of substantial, well-built houses could indicate year-round occupation.

The evidence for domestic production at Dillow's Ridge mirrors what one would expect from a site *not* involved in production for exchange. Dillow's Ridge was not a temporary camp. It was not supported by food traded into the site. People did not seem to focus narrowly on particular resources and productive activities to avoid conflicts with hoe production. In short, it appears that involvement in hoe production did not significantly affect domestic production at Dillow's Ridge. Hoe production was one activity scheduled into a primary preoccupation with domestic production. The reason why hoe production did not affect domestic production became most clear to me as I reconstructed a seasonal schedule of production for the site.

Seasonal Schedule of Production

Drawing together the evidence for resource use, productive activities, seasonality of site occupation, as well as ethnohistoric information on the gender division of labor and task scheduling in southeastern societies, I

Table 2.3. Lithic tool assemblage from Dillow's Ridge

Domestic tools		Tools produced for exchange	
Tool type	Frequency	Tool type	Frequency
Projectile points	50	Ramey knives	20
Drills/perforators	12	Hoes	14
Scrapers	21	Tested nodule	1
Knives	4		
Celts	2		
Adzes	1		
Chisels	1		
Gravers/notches	36		
Denticulates	26		
Eccentric lithic	1		
Bifaces	32		
Unifaces	1		
Retouched flakes	2		
Utilized flakes[a]	178		
Cores	3		
Totals	370		35

Note: The data in this table are from the lithic assemblage recovered in the 1993 excavations.

a. The number of utilized flakes identified in the sample is low. Because of the massive quantities of debitage recovered from the site, each flake was not carefully inspected.

have assembled a seasonal schedule of production at Dillow's Ridge. Given that men and women were responsible for certain essential tasks, they had varying amounts of time from season to season that they could use with more flexibility and discretion.

Spring

In terms of subsistence, early spring posed the greatest challenge to the residents of Dillow's Ridge. Men had hunted intensively through the late fall and winter. In the spring, they continued to hunt, since meat was one of the few foods available at this time of the year. But over time, deer must have become increasingly difficult to find. Similarly, people had relied on stored foods to sustain them through the winter. But at some point in the spring, stored foods like maize, nuts, and dried meat were probably exhausted. In the historic period, stored food from the fall har-

Table 2.4. Ceramic vessels from Dillow's Ridge

Vessel type	Frequency[a]	Percentage[b]
Jars		
Short-neck jars	6	2.3
Everted-rim jars	79	30.5
Bowls		
Straight-rim bowls	25	9.6
Outslanting bowls	38	14.7
Rounded bowls	21	8.1
Restricted-rim bowls	26	10.0
Pans	23	8.9
Terraced bowl	1	0.4
Rectangular bowl	1	0.4
Tippets bean-pot handle	1	0.4
Effigy-rim bowl	1	0.4
Plates	4	1.5
Miniature bowls	12	4.6
Other	1	0.4
Bottles		
Straight-rim bottles	10	3.9
Everted-rim bottles	5	1.9
Human-effigy bottle	1	0.4
Complete bottle missing neck	1	0.4
Stumpware	3	0.2
Total	259	100

a. Frequencies are based on diagnostic sherds large enough to display vessel morphology. Sherds that join were counted as one sherd. The sherds were recovered in the 1992 shovel tests and the 1993 and 1994 excavations.

b. Percentages may not total due to rounding.

vest was not expected to last until the next crop came in, and it rarely did (Swanton 1946:256–57).

Few plant foods were available in the early spring to supplement dwindling supplies of stored food. One exception was sap, which could be collected and processed into sugar and syrup. Later in the spring, other plant foods became available. Greens, blossoms, buds, cambium, fruits, bulbs, and tubers might have been important foods, but as is the case for sap production, archaeological evidence of the use of these foods would be difficult to identify (Lopinot 1984:96). As more plant foods became available for women to collect, men continued to hunt, but this activity probably shifted gradually to a more supplemental role (Lopinot 1984:101).

Beyond immediate subsistence concerns in the spring, women at Dillow's Ridge also likely planted the crops that their families would rely on later in the year—principally maize. Among the other crops planted at Dillow's Ridge, maygrass was unique in that by the end of spring it was mature enough to be harvested (Lopinot 1984:101), providing an important food source in the late spring and early summer, when relatively few other plant foods were available (Yarnell 1976:269).

In the late spring, aquatic resources probably became important parts of the diet, along with maygrass. Men probably began fishing and collecting turtles at this time, as was done elsewhere in the Southeast as late as the nineteenth century (Campbell 1959:10–11). All of the fish recovered at Dillow's Ridge spawn in the spring and/or summer and therefore are more accessible during this period (P. W. Smith 1979). Freshwater mussels are also available primarily during the warmer months of the year (Parmalee, Paloumpis, and Wilson 1972:58); therefore, this was likely the time when women and children began collecting them.

At some point in the spring, men likely transported hoes to destinations where they were exchanged. Some hoes were transported by an overland trek west into the Mississippi floodplain. Some hoes were transported to the lower Ohio Valley, which could be reached by canoe. Canoe travel out of the Mill Creek area was likely restricted to times when You-Be Hollow Creek and Mill Creek were swollen, since the water level in these creeks can be quite low at other times. Rainfall in southern Illinois is highest in the spring. Spring also would have been a time when men had few conflicting responsibilities. Furthermore, toward the end of spring, stored foods may have been running low and wild resources scarce. When necessary, men could have exchanged hoes for subsistence goods to supplement their household's dwindling supplies. Indeed, it is possible that the large fish recovered from Dillow's Ridge, which cannot be found locally, were among the goods obtained through exchange by men who produced Mill Creek hoes.

Summer

In the summer, people at Dillow's Ridge continued many of the subsistence pursuits that were begun in the spring, particularly the use of aquatic resources. Agricultural work also continued in the summer. From the time the crops were planted in the spring until harvest time, the fields were minimally tended—occasionally women would weed the fields, and boys probably spent some of their time protecting the fields from birds and other animals through expedient hunting. Soon field maintenance gave way to harvesting as the focus of agricultural work, for in the late summer a number of cultigens besides maygrass also became available. These include the first maize crop, squash, beans, and knotweed. Many wild plant foods also were collected. Blackberries, elderberries, and purslane were only available in the summer. Other foods, like wild beans, panic grass, and the fruit of certain nightshades, became available late in the summer and into the fall.

While collecting wild plant foods, women also may have spent time in the summer gathering plant fibers for textile production. Processing the fibers, spinning yarn, and weaving fabric could then be worked into the women's schedules at their discretion. Unlike the time-sensitive nature of hide working, a great deal of flexibility existed in the scheduling of textile production, which required a significant amount of time but not constant attention and work (Drooker 1992:165–68). Textile production is most likely to have been pursued in the summer, because fibers were abundantly available at this time of year, and in the fall women would have been busy with more pressing tasks.

In addition to making textiles, women probably made ceramics in the summer. In the Mississippian Southeast, women potters probably made a large number of pots all at once, to last throughout the year. There are economies of scale involved in producing many ceramic vessels at once rather than making one at a time. Unlike lithic tools, which can be made quickly any time they are needed (as long as raw materials are available), ceramic vessels involve a long production sequence: gathering and preparing the clay; burning and crushing shell; mixing the paste; forming, decorating, drying, and firing the vessels. The early summer is the most likely time for most ceramic production because of the relatively warm, dry weather and the amount of discretionary time women would have had. The summer was also a likely time for the production of Mississippian ceramics, since shell (for temper) would have been available from harvesting mussels in the spring and summer.

Beyond fishing, men probably were involved in few subsistence-related tasks. Because they had more discretionary time in the summer than in any other season, it is likely that this was when most quarrying and flint knapping of hoes and Ramey knives were carried out. Flint knapping is an activity that can be easily interrupted and resumed, and therefore pursued in small parcels of time between other activities. However, quarrying requires sustained, cooperative effort for significant lengths of time. Men probably went to the quarry in pairs, or more likely groups, and spent several hours at a time digging the deep shafts that exposed the chert nodules suspended in the clay subsoil. While at the quarry they also spent time testing the suitability of the nodules for knapping. Those not actively digging and lifting chert out of the shafts did some flint knapping while at the quarry. After working at the quarry, the men brought nodules as well as partially worked bifaces back to the village to be finished later at their discretion. The flint knapping involved in producing hoes and Ramey knives may have continued intermittently in the fall, winter, and spring. However, because men would have been busier with subsistence activities in these seasons, it is reasonable to suppose that most hoe production took place in the summer.

Fall

The fall would have been the busiest time of year for women and men at Dillow's Ridge. Most of the staple foods that sustained people through the winter and into the spring had to be harvested within a short period during the fall. Some of the foods whose harvest began in the late summer continued to be gathered in the fall: maize, beans, squash, and knotweed, for instance. A number of other important food sources could only be harvested in the fall. These include cultigens such as goosefoot, pigweed, and sumpweed, as well as nuts and fruits such as hickories, walnuts, acorns, hawthorn, persimmon, and grapes.

Because so many foods had to be harvested at once, women carried out this work with some help from men and children. But the actual work involved in gathering these foods was only the beginning. Women spent a significant amount of time processing the food so that it could be stored. Like the actual harvesting, preparing foods for storage had to be done within a short span of time.

While the harvest and the work involved in storing foods were the major preoccupations of women at Dillow's Ridge in the fall, men focused their energies on hunting. The greatest quantity of venison would have been available during the fall and early winter from acorn-fattened deer (B. D. Smith 1975:33). Deer also had thicker fur and hides as well as fully hardened antlers at this time of year (B. D. Smith 1975:38). Furthermore, the animals would have been easier to capture because of rutting and because the barren landscape facilitated locating and tracking them (Lopinot 1984:94; B. D. Smith 1975:37). In addition to deer, other animals that feed on acorns, such as turkey and squirrels, would have been hunted intensively in the fall.

The animals obtained in the hunt had to be processed immediately after they were brought home. First they had to be skinned and butchered. In the case of turkeys or other birds, the feathers were plucked and kept to be used in textiles. When the animals were butchered, some meat was cooked and eaten. Deer supply a large amount of meat, and many deer were killed in this season. As a result, people would have been able to obtain much more meat than they could consume, and much of this meat likely was dried and stored so that it could be used through the winter and into the spring.

Preparing meat for consumption or storage was only part of the work necessary after the hunt. Other useful materials, such as sinew and bone, also were collected from the carcass. Other than meat, perhaps the most important material taken from deer was the hide. It had to be processed immediately, by means of a fairly time-consuming process; otherwise, the material would harden and become unusable.

Winter

Other than living off stored foods, the only major subsistence task pursued in the winter was hunting. Men hunted, and women turned deerskins into clothing. In addition to working with leather, women also may have done some weaving in the winter. As mentioned previously, most textile production probably took place in the summer, and certainly yarn was made in the summer. But skeins of yarn may have been saved for weaving projects in the winter. Early in the winter, women must have given high priority to stocking their households with warm clothing and bedding, made from furs, hides, or textiles.

In conjunction with hunting, the other major activity that men pursued in the winter was land management: intentional burning and clearing to induce secondary succession, and burning farm fields to prepare them for cultivation (Campbell 1959:10; Speck 1946:29). When this was done, animals driven out by the flames were hunted (Swanton 1946:319).

Between hunting excursions and field clearing, men had discretionary time in the winter. It is possible that they spent some of this time flint knapping, producing hoes and Ramey knives that would be exchanged in the spring. As mentioned previously, most quarrying and flint knapping probably took place in the summer. However, through their quarrying efforts, men probably were able to stockpile a number of nodules to be worked later in the idle hours of the winter.

Summary

From this discussion of the seasonal schedule of production at Dillow's Ridge, three facts are most important to convey:

1. Women were responsible for the vast majority of work in the domestic economy throughout the year, while men had fewer domestic responsibilities and mainly were occupied with hunting and fishing, clearing land, building and maintaining houses, woodworking, and working with stone.

2. Men probably were the ones quarrying chert and producing hoes.

3. Much of the work involved in hoe production could be easily interrupted and resumed among men's domestic responsibilities, which were relatively few.

Given these conditions, hoe production would not have interfered with domestic production, which was carried out largely by women.

The Economy of Salt Production at the Great Salt Spring

The relationship of production for exchange to domestic production at Dillow's Ridge is very different from that evident at the Great Salt Spring. The Great Salt Spring site is located on the banks and the bluff overlooking the Saline River in Gallatin County, Illinois. The site has been the focus of six seasons of archaeological fieldwork under the direction of Jon Muller (Muller 1984, 1990, 1991, 1997:308–29). The saline spring at the site was exploited primarily during the Mississippian period from ca. A.D. 1000 to 1450 (Muller 1990:303; Muller and Renken 1989) but also was used for commercial salt production in the nineteenth century. Today, only one saline spring and one freshwater spring flow at the site; however, there may have been additional springs in the past (Muller 1990:41).

There is no evidence that the Great Salt Spring was controlled directly by elites at a large mound center like Kincaid or Angel (Muller 1990:59). Differences in decorative techniques between domestic ceramics from the Great Salt Spring and Kincaid suggest that people using the Great Salt Spring may not have lived within the sphere of that chiefdom (Muller 1991:79). In fact, Muller (1991:79) argues that the Great Salt Spring's ceramic styles reflect geographic diversity in the origins of the salt makers. Just as the Great Salt Spring was not controlled by a distant mound center, neither does it appear to have been controlled locally. There are no mound sites near the Great Salt Spring and very little Mississippian occupation in the area at all, except at the Half Moon Lick—another salt spring near Equality, Illinois, approximately five kilometers away (Muller and Avery 1990:80). Because there are no nearby mound centers and no permanent occupation at the Great Salt Spring, it is unlikely that anyone maintained exclusive access to the resource.

The prehistoric production of salt differed from hoe production in two important ways: First, it took place at a location distant from people's homes; second, women were the primary producers. People traveled to the Great Salt Spring to make salt and stayed for short periods of time. Across the entire site, there is only one substantial structure and one light shelter, and there is very little domestic refuse characteristic of Mississippian settlements. For example, debitage from the manufacture of household tools is rare at the site, and utilized flakes (n = 10) are nearly absent (Muller 1991:61–68). The small number of bifaces recovered (n = 64) include a small range of tool forms (projectile points, scrapers, and bifacial knives) necessary for tasks carried out during short visits to the site, such as hunting and butchering (Muller 1991:68). Relatively few ceramics were for domestic use. Of the 926 identifiable rim sherds recovered in the 1981–90 seasons, 63 percent were salt pans (n = 583), 27 percent were jars (n = 247), and 9 percent were bowls (n = 87) (Muller 1991:69). It is not surprising that some domestic ceramics would be found at a site that people visited for short periods of time. During those visits, people still had to prepare and consume food. Overall, the archaeological assemblage from the site is dominated by equipment used in the manufacture of salt.

Early historic accounts of salt production describe people traveling to distant locations where they would stay for limited periods to make salt before returning home (Foreman 1936:134; Tregle 1975:153). Such a pattern also is exhibited in the archaeological evidence from the Great Salt Spring. Although there are spring-, summer-, and fall-ripening species in the ethnobotanical assemblage, the context of these materials suggests that occupation in any particular season was discrete and discontinuous. For example, Lopinot observes that maygrass, which ripens in the late spring to early summer, appears in contexts separate from fall-harvested foods like nuts, suggesting that they were deposited in separate occupational episodes (Lopinot 1990:398). Seasonally discrete deposits are not typical at residential sites (Lopinot 1990:398). By way of comparison, the six seeds of maygrass recovered from Dillow's Ridge all came from a flotation sample containing many fall-ripening plants such as hickories, walnuts, acorns, amaranth, chenopodium, sumpweed, hawthorn, persimmon, and grapes.

Not only did the Great Salt Spring differ from Dillow's Ridge in the seasonal use of the site, it also differed in that women performed most of the work in the production of the exchange good. Women made the main pieces of equipment needed in salt production: ceramic vessels called "salt pans," used to boil the brine. Such vessels probably had relatively short use lives due to the effects of thermal stress and fatigue, and they probably had to be replaced often. Southeastern women in the historic period also were reported to have carried out the lion's share of work involved in reducing brine to salt, while the men of their households hunted or relaxed (Bartram 1928:45; Foreman 1936:134; Tregle 1975:153). Some of the main tasks in salt making included constructing hearths, bringing brine from the spring to the hearth, adding more brine as the liquid boiled down, and maintaining a fire in the hearth. Although most of the work was done by women, children probably participated as well, by gathering and carrying firewood.

Evidence from the Great Salt Spring reveals that salt production was carried out at rather low intensity (Muller 1991:299–300, 391). The most telling evidence comes from the ethnobotanical assemblage. The wood used for fuel in the salt-reduction hearths consisted of a narrow range of hardwood species out of proportion to their representation in the upland forests of southern Illinois (Lopinot 1990:391–94). It appears that people had the ability to be selective in their choice of fuel woods. Moreover, there are substantial amounts of fungus in the assemblage, suggesting that people used fallen limbs and dead or rotting wood rather than chopping down healthy trees for fuel (Lopinot 1990:391). During the nineteenth-century commercial venture at the Great Salt Spring, the nearby vicinity was quickly deforested. Ultimately, they began piping the brine to locations where wood was still available as fuel (Muller 1991:31). In the prehistoric period, it does not appear that fuel supplies were strained at any time during the site's use.

In the aggregate, salt production was pursued at low intensity; nonetheless, when individual groups visited the Great Salt Spring, women's time would have been dominated by activities related to the production of salt. As a result, evidence of domestic activities at the site reflects women managing their time differently from their practice in contexts without an added set of tasks. Women organized domestic production to minimize the amount of work they had to do while visiting the Great Salt Spring. For example, the preponderance of maize kernels rather than cob fragments suggests that this food was brought to the site in a preprocessed form, and not grown there (Lopinot 1990:396). To save space and to reduce the time and equipment needed to process the corn, it is likely that people traveling to the Great Salt Spring most often would have brought parched maize kernels and/or meal, less frequently bringing maize dried on the ear.

Taken as a whole, the floral assemblage from the Great Salt Spring (table 2.5) displays a very limited range of species compared to the assemblage from Dillow's Ridge. Since women were the likely salt producers, they would have had less time for subsistence activities while visiting the Great Salt Spring. It has already been posited that women brought maize with them to the site. As table 2.5 indicates, maize is the most common food plant recovered. It is unlikely that women would have spent inordinate amounts of time collecting many other food plants during the short time they would spend at the site. It is more likely that they used the resources that would be the quickest and easiest to collect and prepare. Women probably enlisted the help of children, enjoining them to collect whatever nuts and other fruits and seeds could be obtained easily near the site. Children's help, both in subsistence production and in the salt-making process, was undoubtedly vital for women doubly charged with the bulk of subsistence and salt-making duties. It is also possible that plant foods were less important at the Great Salt Spring than they were at permanent Mississippian settlements. Salt-producing women probably relied more heavily on the productive labor of men for subsistence while they were at the Great Salt Spring, eating meat and fish that men obtained by hunting, trapping, and fishing (table 2.6). The limited range of plant-food refuse at the Great Salt Spring may reflect the concentration of female labor in the activities related to salt production.

The organization of salt production, including its gender division of labor, raises some interesting issues about production intensity, about who made economic decisions in Mississippian households, and about the character of exchange. For instance, it is possible that women's primary involvement in salt production may have acted to constrain the intensity of the activity. Based on ethnohistoric information, we can surmise that Mississippian women had far less discretionary time than their male counterparts. Because of more pressing responsibilities related to the support of their families, women may not have had time to do more than produce small amounts of salt in excess of what they needed themselves. Producing larger quantities of salt would have required longer or more-frequent stays at the Great Salt Spring. Meanwhile, domestic production would have languished. Perhaps the preeminence of women's domestic responsibilities explains why no one lived at the Great Salt

Table 2.5. Summary of identified floral remains from the Great Salt Spring site

Taxa	Common name	Frequency
Carya spp.	Hickory	143
Chenopodium berlandieri	Goosefoot	39
Diospyros virginiana	Persimmon	3
Fagus sp.	Beech	Present
Gleditsia triacanthos	Honey-shuck	1
Juglans spp.	Walnut	142
Phalaris caroliniana	Maygrass	15
Polygonum lapathifolium	Knotweed	1
Portulaca oleracea	Purslane	1
Quercus spp.	Oak	704
Rubus spp.	Blackberry	2
Viburnum sp.		1(?)
Vitis spp.	Wild grape	1
Zea mays (total)	Maize	846
Cob		7
Kernel		839
Total		1,899

Source: After Lopinot 1990: 388–90, 392–94, 396–97.

Note: The data in this table present the floral remains excluding charcoal from fourteen 12-liter flotation samples and one analytical sample containing maize.

Spring full-time as they did at Dillow's Ridge. It would seem, then, that the gender division of labor may have conditioned the volume of trade in salt and perhaps other goods.

The gender division of labor also may have affected the means by which different goods were traded. Since women made salt, were they also responsible for exchanging salt? Ian Brown (1980:10) has argued, based on historic-period information, that men traded salt. But it is possible that this arrangement may have resulted from European gender constructs, influencing expectations about appropriate trading partners. If women in prehistoric times traded salt, it is interesting to speculate whether they participated in the same exchange networks as men, or if there existed dual trade networks in which different goods were exchanged—some goods traded by women among women, and others

Table 2.6. Summary of identified faunal remains from the Great Salt Spring site

Taxa	Common name	NISP[a]
Total mammals	2,925	
Odocoileus virginianus	White-tailed deer	335
Cervus canadensis	Wapiti	2
Procyon lotor	Raccoon	14
Mephitis mephitis	Striped skunk	1
Ursus americanus	Black bear	2
Urocyon cinereoargenteus	Gray fox	2
Canis familiaris	Domestic dog	2
Castor canadensis	Beaver	1
Marmota monax	Woodchuck	3
Sciurus carolinensis	Gray squirrel	12
Sciurus niger	Fox squirrel	20
Sciurus spp.	Unidentified squirrel	3
Tamias striatus	Chipmunk	1
Unidentified rodent		1
Didelphis marsupialis	Opossum	7
Sylvilagus floridanus	Cottontail rabbit	9
Sylvilagus aquaticus	Swamp rabbit	1
Unidentified mammals	2,509	
Total birds		162
Meleagris gallopavo	Turkey	12
Anas spp.	Duck	2
Tympanuchus cupido	Prairie chicken	1
Unidentified birds		147
Total reptiles		615
Colubrid spp.	Nonpoisonous snake	2
Crotalid spp.	Poisonous snake	5
Trionyx spiniferus	Spiny softshell turtle	3
Chelydra serpentina	Eastern snapping turtle	1
Chrysemys/Graptemys spp.	Map/painted turtle	9
Terrapene carolina	Box turtle	173
Sternothaerus odoratus	Stinkpot	2
Unidentified turtle		420
Total fish		49
Aplodinotus grunniens	Freshwater drumfish	10
Ictalurus punctatus	Channel catfish	2
Ictalurus spp.	Unidentified catfish	2
Amia calva	Bowfin	12
Lepisosteus spp.	Garfish	23

Total molluscs		4,681
Polygyra spp.		6
Lithasia spp.		2
Pleurocera spp.	Periwinkle	1
Amblema plicata	Three-ridge	66
Cyclonaias tuberculata	Purple warty-back	1
Elliptio crassidens	Elephant's ear	3
Elliptio dilatus	Spike	38
Fusconaia ebenus	Ebony-shell	35
Fusconaia flava	Wabash pig-toe	14
Fusconaia sp.		1
Lampsilis ovata	Pocketbook	2
Lampsilis radiata	Fat mucket	12
Lampsilis teres	Sandshell	4
Lampsilis ventricosa	Pocketbook	1
Lampsilis spp.		2
Lasmigona complanata	White heel-splitter	3
Ligumia recta	Black sandshell	4
Ligumia subrostrata		1
Obovaria olivaria	Hickory-nut	1
Obovaria retusa	Pink	1
Obovaria subrotunda		2
Plagiola lineolata	Butterfly	3
Plethobasus cyphyus	White warty-back	1
Pleurobema cordatum		19
Pleurobema spp.		4
Proptera alatus	Pink heel-splitter	9
Quadrula metanerva	Monkey-face	3
Quadrula pustulosa	Pimple-back	7
Quadrula quadrula	Maple-leaf	5
Quadrula sp.		1
Tritogonia verrucosa	Pistol-grip	6
Villosa cf. *iris*	Rainbow-shell	1
Terrestrial snail		8
Unidentified shell		4,414
Total identified specimens		8,432

Source: After Breitburg 1990:352–53.

Note: This table presents those fauna identified in the excavated samples from the 1982 and 1989 field seasons.

a. The number of identified specimens.

traded by and among men. What else might women have produced for exchange? Subsistence goods? Beads?

The possibility that women participated in trade networks brings us to the question of women's power in the economic realm. The anthropological view of households has tended to stress cooperation and collective interest over conflict and self-interest (Wilk 1989:26). Is it possible that there were power struggles between men and women at the Great Salt Spring over the exchange of salt, over what would be sought in trade, and over who would receive the goods? Did women's salt production provide them greater influence and access to wealth than women at Dillow's Ridge, for instance? Did women's production of this exchange good allow them to accumulate wealth of their own, or perhaps to contribute to their household or kin group's communal wealth in a such a way that they achieved status uncommon for most Mississippian women? In view of their unusual economic contribution, did salt-producing women have greater input on economic matters than women in other Mississippian households? For example, did women decide when they would schedule a trip to the Great Salt Spring, even if the entire household went together? It is possible that gender relations in salt-producing households had a different flavor than in most Mississippian households.

Exchange, in the vulgar economic sense, was not necessarily the only means through which salt was distributed. Gift-giving in the context of social interaction may have accounted for the circulation of substantial amounts of prestige goods as well as subsistence goods, particularly in the context of feasting (Blitz 1993a, 1993b). In at least one of the towns visited by the De Soto expedition (Cofitachequi), salt was among the goods presented to the Spaniards as gifts for honored guests (Clayton, Knight, and Moore 1993:278). There is no way of knowing if salt was regularly offered as a gift during the Mississippian period, but such a practice is well within the realm of possibility. Like direct exchange, the reciprocal circulation of goods through gift exchange may have been an indirect means for salt producers to obtain wealth items as well as status. Again, in the context of gender relations, it is interesting to wonder who was earning this social capital through the distribution of salt.

Discussion

Examining the organization of production for exchange at Dillow's Ridge and the Great Salt Spring makes clear the importance of gender division of labor in our analyses. In order to understand how production for exchange was carried out in Mississippian societies, it is necessary to consider how labor was organized within households. The gender division of labor is more than just an interesting piece of trivia about Mississippian society. It was an integral component of economy that affected other aspects of Mississippian production and society.

As we have seen, hoe production did not have a noticeable effect on the domestic economy of hoe producers at Dillow's Ridge. This may be partly due to the low intensity of hoe production: People at Dillow's Ridge did not devote enough time to hoe production to significantly interfere with domestic productive activities. Another partial explanation may be the gender division of labor in which men produced hoes and women carried out the greater share of domestic production. If men were contributing all the labor toward hoe production, labor was only being drawn away from male activities, like hunting, which were intermittent and few, leaving most domestic activities unaffected. Although the scheduling of male productive activities may have been impacted by hoe production, women's attention to farming, collecting, and food processing was not interrupted.

Like hoe production, salt production was carried out at low intensity. While they were away from the Great Salt Spring, the lives of salt producers were not affected by salt production, except insofar as it provided some small amount of goods obtained through exchange. However, while they were at the Great Salt Spring, the women who produced salt modified their routines to minimize the amount of time they had to devote to food procurement and processing as a means to accommodate the large amounts of time they were devoting to the whole process of salt production. At the same time, it appears that men at the Great Salt Spring were making greater contributions to subsistence through hunting to help lighten women's work load.

The contrasts between the household economies of Dillow's Ridge and the Great Salt Spring illustrate the economic variability that existed during the Mississippian period. Whereas Dillow's Ridge was a permanent village, the Great Salt Spring was a limited activity site. At the former, hoes were produced for exchange by a group of resident producers; at the latter, salt was produced by visitors during brief stays. At Dillow's Ridge, production for exchange was carried out by men, while at the Great Salt Spring, production and perhaps exchange of salt was carried out by women. Archaeologists have long known that diverse economic arrangements existed in Mississippian communities. It is now worthwhile to consider how the social organization of labor within households related to economic diversity in the Mississippian period. Considering gender encourages archaeologists to think about the past in terms of real human actors, their motivations, and constraints on their action. Envisioning ordinary people and their concerns is necessary to the pursuit of "emic" interpretations of prehistoric economy and social life (e.g., Drooker 1992:1–3; T. M. N. Lewis and Kneberg 1946; Spector 1991, 1993; Tringham 1991). Because gender was part of social reality in the past, it should inform our interpretations of that past.

Note

1. Excavations at Dillow's Ridge were initiated in 1993 by Charles Cobb as part of a major research program funded by the National Science Foundation. In 1994, Cobb continued his work at Dillow's Ridge and elsewhere in the Mill Creek area through a National Geographic Society grant and in collaboration with Southern Illinois University at Carbondale's field school in archaeology, which was led by Charles R. McGimsey. Cobb returned to Dillow's Ridge in 1995 as director of Southern Illinois University's field school.

Editors' Note

Dillard's Ridge is managed by the U.S. Forest Service. We are grateful for the service's efforts in preserving this important resource and contributing to our further understanding of prehistory in southern Illinois.

❧ 3 ❧

Life Courses and Gender among Late Prehistoric Siouan Communities

Jane M. Eastman

Gender as a cultural process rather than a biologically determined status has the potential to change throughout one's life course and may take on different levels of significance during different stages of life. The goal of this chapter is to explore these aspects of gender. Specifically, I analyze mortuary data from seven village sites in the western Piedmont of Virginia and North Carolina. These sites were occupied during the fifteenth and sixteenth centuries by Siouan peoples who were probably ancestors of the Sara, Tutelo, and Saponi. I have attempted to characterize the nature of gender differences in these tribal communities by comparing the distribution of grave goods associated with children, adolescents, and adult males and females of different ages.

The use of the terms "gender role" and "gender identity" in this study are consistent with Spector and Whelan's (1989:69) definitions. "Gender role" refers to "what men and women actually do," including their activity patterns, social relations, and behaviors. "Gender identity" concerns an individual's own sense of his or her gender. "Gender representation" includes the material clues that are used to mark gender identities. "Life cycle" refers to culturally recognized stages in the process of physiological growth, development, and aging, with special reference to changes in productive and reproductive capacity.

Many ethnographic, ethnohistoric, and archaeological studies indicate that gender roles and identities change during an individual's life cycle (J. K. Brown 1985; Brumbach and Jarvenpa 1997a, 1997b; Crown and Fish 1996; Derevenski 1994, 1997a, 1997b; Gilchrist 1997; Ginn and Arber 1995; Hudson 1976; Joyce and Claassen 1997; Lesick 1997; Rubinstein 1990; Sullivan, this volume). These studies also reveal that gender changes are often experienced differently by men and women. The present study indicates that this may well have been the case in late prehistoric Siouan communities of the western Piedmont, and I suggest that women in these communities experienced more profound changes in their gender roles and identities as they aged than did men.

This study is organized into several sections, beginning with a discussion of the relationship between gender and the life cycle; an outline of the sex and age categories used to parse the mortuary data; and a review of the geographical, chronological, and archaeological background for the study. Following these preliminary sections, I present mortuary data from seven archaeological sites in the study area. I am especially interested in gender-based differences in the distribution of mortuary items.

Gender as Life Cycle Process

As mentioned above, many researchers have made the point that gender, as a culturally defined status, is malleable throughout an individual's lifetime and is intimately tied to aspects of physical development and aging. From this perspective, gender is viewed as a process that unfolds throughout one's lifetime. Gender roles, relations, and identities may be subject to reinterpretation and change as one progresses through different stages of physiological development and through different social age classes. Derevenski (1997a:876) has noted that stages within the life cycle may be demarcated as bodies grow and senesce and as reproductive capacity changes. Changes in gender roles throughout the life cycle may be represented by changes in dress, in expectations about appropriate behavior, and in the division of labor. Life cycle changes that involve relinquishing one role and assuming another are often marked by social ceremonies (rites of passage) (Hudson 1976:319–35; Silverman 1975:309). This type of cultural demarcation provides the opportunity for archaeologists to reconstruct patterns of gender difference in the past through such archaeological evidence as material remains of dress, association of tools and other objects representative of gender roles and identities, and physical traces of habitual activities left on the human remains themselves.

Sex and age at death provide a means for subdividing burial populations in the Piedmont into subgroups that may represent different gender groups within living communities. The populations considered here have been divided into five age groups, and adults have been divided further into males and females. Homes Hogue (1988) has made age and sex estimates for the skeletal population from the Shannon site (44My8), and Patricia Lambert (Davis et al. 1996) has identified the skeletal material from the other six sites referenced in this study. Subadults have been divided into two age groups: children (zero to five years) and adolescents (six to fifteen years). Adults have been classified as either males or females and further divided by age at death into young (sixteen to twenty-five years), mature (twenty-six to thirty-four years), or older (thirty-five and over) adults.

Children up to five years constitute the youngest age group, and it is anticipated that during these first years of development mothers in the study area were primarily responsible for the care of both boys and girls (Hudson 1976:323). Childhood is often considered to be a time when gender differences are absent or ambiguous (Schildkrout 1978; Lesick 1997), and gender may or may not have played a profound role in determining the activities and experiences of very young children in Siouan communities.

As children developed and began to learn subsistence skills, gender differences likely took on greater significance. Young girls probably would have remained with their mothers, to be trained by them and their female kin, while young boys most likely left their natal household and were taught important life skills by their mother's brothers. The adolescent age group (six to fifteen years) represents the stage when gender roles and subsistence skills were instilled and when young people likely began to make economic contributions to their households (Claassen 1992:5; Derevenski 1997a:887; Swanton 1946:714–15). Most individuals at the older end of this age group (fifteen years of age) would have reached sexual maturity and would have been able to take on adult roles and responsibilities.

Adulthood (sixteen years and over) has been subdivided into three age groups: young, mature, and older. These subdivisions are intended to represent both potential differences in the productive and reproductive capacities of adults and different stages in the growth and development of households and families. The young adult class (sixteen to twenty-five years) incorporates the early childbearing years for women and those in which their child-rearing responsibilities may have been greatest because they would not have been able to enlist the help of older children. Early adulthood for males in native tribal societies probably would have been marked by efforts to achieve social recognition for individual skills like hunting, trade, warfare, or diplomacy. Mature adults (twenty-six to thirty-five years of age) were likely to be at the height of their productive and reproductive lives, and by this time their older children would be contributing significantly to the household economy. The older adult category (over thirty-six years) incorporates the period within the life cycle when reproductive and productive capacities decline and some capacities may cease altogether. During the later stage of life, new avenues for exerting influence would have to be pursued as physical capacities declined. Advanced age itself may have brought older adults respect, veneration, and decision-making power within Siouan communities (Lefler 1967:43). Lesick (1997) indicates that gender differences may assume less importance in structuring the lives and activities of older adults and may become especially ambiguous for postmenopausal women.

The following section divides the burial population into these groups based on sex and age at death. I look for patterns in the distribution of mortuary items that reflect changing gender roles, relations, and representation throughout the life course of men and women in Siouan communities of the western Piedmont in North Carolina and Virginia.

The Study Area

The upper Dan drainage is located in the northern Piedmont woodlands of North Carolina and southern Virginia. The headwaters of the Dan River originate in the Blue Ridge region of western Virginia, flow south into the northwestern North Carolina Piedmont, then flow east into the Roanoke River in south central Virginia near the town of Clarksville. The Roanoke River has its headwaters in the eastern Ridge and Valley Province of Virginia and flows through a large gap in the Blue Ridge into the Piedmont, where it eventually joins the Dan in southern Virginia.

Seventeenth- and eighteenth-century documents suggest that Siouan-speaking peoples occupied this area at the time of European contact. The archaeological record indicates cultural continuity in ceramics and settlement patterns between the early-contact-period inhabitants of the study area and the late prehistoric peoples studied here. The late prehistoric sites in the upper Dan drainage probably were occupied by ancestors of the Sara tribe, while the site in the upper Roanoke Valley was probably occupied by ancestors of another Siouan tribe, the Tutelo. These tribes were present in the study area at the time of the first European explorations, and their eventual movements outside these drainages were documented later during the contact period (Davis 1999; J. Mooney 1894; Swanton 1946:110, 200–201; L. B. Wright 1966:413).

A sample of burials from seven late prehistoric and protohistoric archaeological sites in the Dan and Roanoke drainages is used to explore differences in the mortuary treatment of men, women, and children who died at different stages in their life cycle. The location of these sites is presented in figure 3.1. Archaeological evidence indicates that although the late prehistoric communities represented by these sites exhibited some diversity, many aspects of their cultures were similar. Social groups were organized into small tribes, which typically resided in nucleated villages. These communities practiced a mixed economy of horticulture, hunting, and gathering and crafted very similar pottery, tools, and ornaments. In addition, all groups considered here are thought to have spoken Siouan languages (Dickens, Ward, and Davis 1987; K. T. Egloff 1992; Hudson 1976; J. Mooney 1894; Swanton 1946:813; Ward and Davis 1993, 1999:99).

The Mortuary Data

Archaeological research on fifteenth- and sixteenth-century village sites in the study area has recovered evidence of mortuary ritual prior to any sustained contact or trade with European colonists and exposure to Old World epidemic disease. Unfortunately, there is no single site from this period in the study area with a large excavated burial population, so information from six sites in the upper Dan drainage and one large site in the upper Roanoke drainage was compiled to create a large sample of prehistoric burials. The combined sample includes fifty-four burials from sites in the Dan drainage and ninety-six burials from the Roanoke drainage. All subadult burials with an estimate for age at death and all adults for whom age at death and sex could be estimated were selected for study. Roughly half of these burials (n = 73) have associated artifacts, and the distribution of those mortuary items is of primary concern in this analysis (see table 3.1). When the number of burials with grave goods is compared to those without grave goods, no significant differences are present between different gender groups (see table 3.2). Therefore, all gender groups were given comparable recognition in mortuary ritual through offerings of grave goods. The remainder of my analysis will focus on the distribution of mortuary items in the seventy-three burials with intact grave goods.

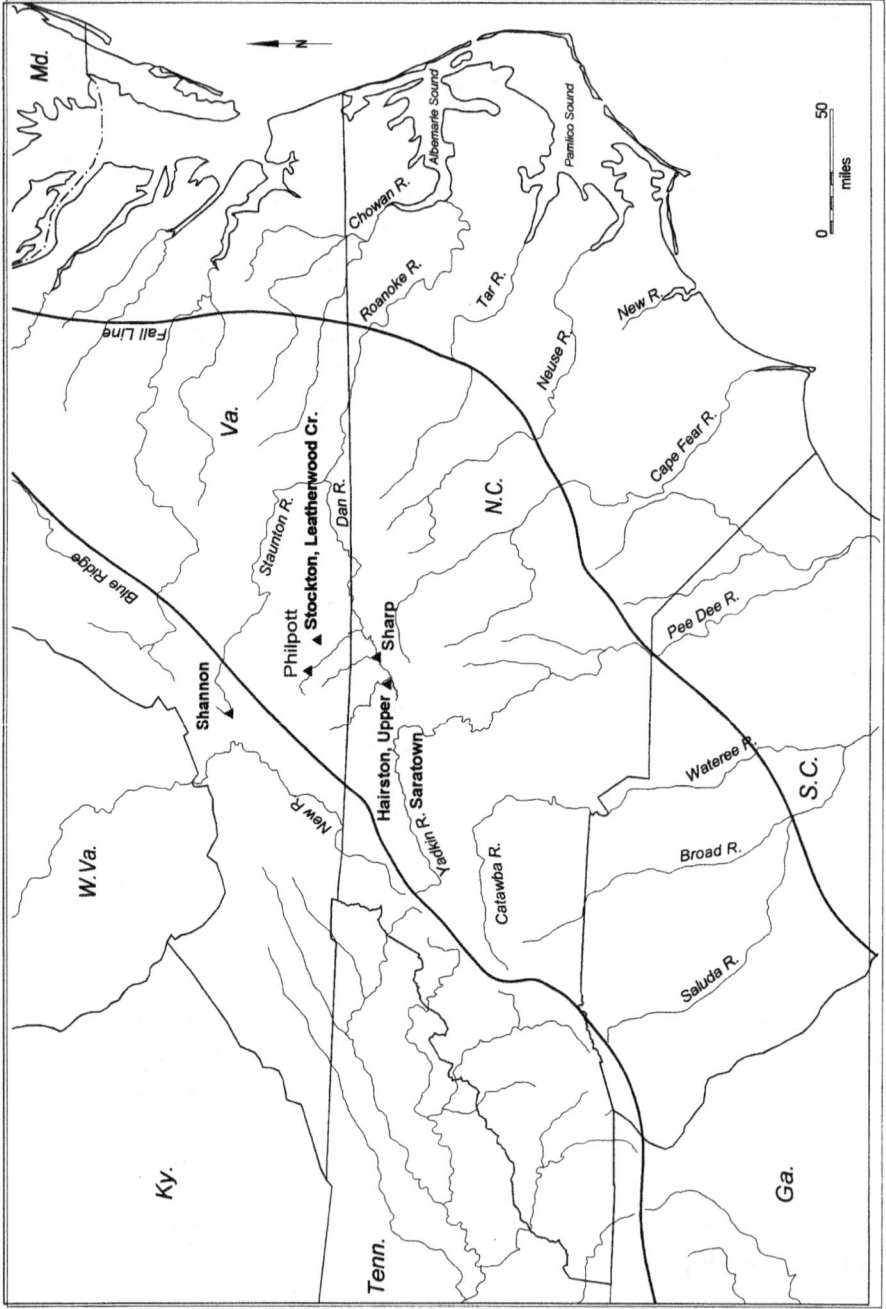

Fig. 3.1. Archaeological sites in the upper Dan and Roanoke drainages of the North Carolina and Virginia Piedmont.

Table 3.1. Distribution of mortuary items in burials from late prehistoric and protohistoric archaeological sites in the Dan and Roanoke drainages

Class[a] Site[b]	Burial	Associated artifacts

Child (n = 40; 16 without associated artifacts)

44Hr1	5	27 columella beads, 4 drilled elk incisor beads
44Hr4	5	58 marginella beads
44Hr4	8	1 conical shell gorget, 2 perforated shell disks, 2 triangular shell pendants, 7 tubular columella beads
44Hr35	2	527 shell disk beads
44Hr35	11	1 circular shell pendant
44Hr35	22	232 marginella beads, 1+ tubular columella bead, >11 columella beads
31Sk1	2	1 columella bead, 1 "rattlesnake" shell gorget, 8 copper tube beads
31Sk1	5	5 columella beads
31Sk1	6	1 ceramic vessel, 1 copper bar gorget, 1 "rattlesnake" shell gorget, 1,478 shell disk beads, 477 marginella beads, 5 columella beads, 1 serrated mussel shell, 2 pearl beads, 411 turkey wingtip beads, 47 rabbit innominate beads, 3 squirrel mandible beads, 1 turkey tarsometatarsus awl
44My8	6	6 columella beads, 4 bone beads
44My8	12	959 marginella beads
44My8	17	90 marginella beads
44My8	26	15 columella beads, 1 bone bead
44My8	48	2 tubular columella beads, 1 marine shell pendant
44My8	51	61 marginella beads, 2 columella beads
44My8	59	4 shell pendants, 26 columella beads, 423 marginella beads
44My8	86	1 shell pendant, 27 turkey wingtip beads, 255 marginella beads
44My8	74	384 marginella beads
44My8	94	103 marginella beads
44My8	73	12 columella beads
44My8	37	2 columella beads, 4 bear canine beads
44My8	99	1,669 disk beads, 3 bear canines
44My8	72	2 mountain lion claws
44My8	77	2 projectile points

continued

Table 3.1 *(continued)*

Class[a] Site[b]	Burial	Associated artifacts

Adolescent (n = 12; 3 burials without associated artifacts)

44Hr1	1	11 olive beads
31Sk1	4	12 columella beads, 779 shell disk beads
44My8	5	1 shell gorget
44My8	34	26 olive beads, 7 mountain lion claws, 6 projectile points
44My8	52	555 marginella beads, 68 columella beads, 4 wolf canines, 2 quartz crystals
44My8	41	1 bone bead
44My8	43	1 ceramic vessel
44My8	95	2 projectile points, 4 columella beads
44My8	98	1 hammerstone

Young adult females (n = 26; 16 burials without associated objects)

44Hr1	3	3 ceramic vessels, 1 miniature vessel, 6 plain shell gorgets, 4 tubular columella beads, 33 drilled columella beads, 1,948 marginella beads
44Hr1	9	6 drilled columella beads
44Hr35	6	342 marginella beads
31Rk12	3	3 ceramic vessels, 1 shell gorget blank, 900+ columella beads, 118 shell disk beads, 400+ turkey wingtip beads, 231 ground bone beads, 75 bird longbone beads, 39 rabbit innominate beads
31Sk1	3	1 "rattlesnake" shell gorget, 2 columella earpins, 1,100+ columella beads, 72 shell disk beads, 4 columella tubular beads, 1 marginella bead, 1 turkey tarsometatarsus awl, 2 bone splinter awls, 50 pebbles (part of a turtle shell rattle), 3 quartz flakes, 2 mussel shells, 11 bird longbone beads, 100+ turkey wingtip beads
44My8	11	300 marginella beads, 39 disk beads, 20 columella beads
44My8	20	330 marginella beads, 2 columella beads
44My8	75	2 columella beads, 1 bone hairpin
44My8	22	1 turtle carapace cup
44My8	29	1 bone bead

Mature adult females (n = 6; 3 burials without associated artifacts)

31Sk1a	79	chipped stone end scraper
44My8	16	245 marginella beads
44My8	68	1,296 marginella beads, 48 disk beads, 18 columella beads, 37 turkey wingtip beads

Old adult females (n = 18; 10 burials without associated artifacts)

44Hr35	12	1 turkey tarsometatarsus awl
31Rk12	1	1 chipped stone hoe
44Hr35	3	2 columella earpins, 106 columella beads, 2 columella tubular beads, 551 marginella beads
44My8	1	7,400 marginella beads, 52 columella beads
44My8	8	126 disk beads, 15 columella beads
44My8	63	7 columella beads
44My8	46	1 celt
44My8	60	1 celt, 9 bone beads

Young adult males (n = 4; 4 burials without associated artifacts)

44My8	15	30 marginella beads, 42 tubular columella beads

Mature adult males (n = 3; 2 burials without associated objects)

44My8	58	193 columella beads, 1 projectile point

Old adult males (N = 33; 16 burials without associated objects)

44Hr4	16	1 clay pipe
44Hr35	1	2 deer ulna awls, bone tool, fish hook blanks
44Hr35	8	1 clay pipe, 3 deer ulna awls
44Hr35	13	1 fish hook, 3 bone splinter awls
44Hr35	15	1 clay pipe
31Sk1a	110	ochre
44My8	61	2 fish hooks
44My8	82	1 clay pipe, 1 turkey tarsometatarsus awl
44My8	18	1 turtle shell cups, 1 turkey tarsometatarsus awl
44My8	45	2 bone chisels, 3 turkey tarsometarsus awls, 1 polished stone celt, 7 projectile points, 2 chipped stone drills, 1 stone abrader, 2 bone flakers, 3 beaver incisors, 5 columella beads, 2 copper fragments
44My8	4	2 turtle carapace cups, 2 elk teeth, 1 eagle talon, 1 amethyst crystal, 1 end scraper, 2 bone awls, 1 bone tube made from a human humerus, 1 turkey longbone bead
44My8	25	5 bear canine beads
44My8	56	2 bear canine beads, bear mandible
44My8	65	5 mountain lion claws
44My8	92	1 chipped stone knife
44My8	10	56 marginella beads
44My8	97	46 columella beads

a. Classes include children, adolescents, young adult females, mature adult females, old adult females, young adult males, mature adult males, old adult males.

b. Sites included in this analysis are Upper Saratown (31Sk1a), Hairston (31Sk1), Sharp (31Rk12), Leatherwood Creek (44Hr1), Philpott (44Hr4), Stockton (44Hr35), and Shannon (44My8).

Table 3.2. Distribution of graves with mortuary items

Gender category	Present	Absent	Total	% with mortuary items
Children	24	16	40	60
Adolescents	9	3	12	75
Total subadults	33	19	52	63
Young adult females	10	16	26	39
Mature adult females	3	3	6	50
Older adult females	8	10	18	45
Total females	21	29	50	42
Young adult males	1	4	5	20
Mature adult males	1	2	3	33
Older adult males	17	16	33	48
Total males	19	22	41	47
Total adults	40	51	91	44

Table 3.3. Distribution of sex-specific mortuary items

Gender class	Present	Absent	Total	Percent with sex-specific mortuary items
Children	13	11	24	55
Adolescents	6	3	9	66
Total subadults	19	14	33	58
Young adult females	5	5	10	50
Mature adult females	1	2	3	33
Older adult females	1	7	8	13
Total adult females	7	14	21	33
Young adult males	1	0	1	100
Mature adult males	0	1	1	0
Older adult males	13	4	17	76
Total adult males	14	5	19	74
Total adults	21	19	40	53
Grand total	40	33	73	56

Table 3.4. Distribution of certain mortuary items at late prehistoric and protohistoric components in the Dan and Roanoke drainages

Mortuary item	Children	Adolescents	Adult females			Adult males		
			Young	Mature	Old	Young	Mature	Old
Female items								
Plain gorgets/pendants	+	+	+	-	-	-	-	-
"Rattlesnake" gorgets	+	-	+	-	-	-	-	-
Hairpins or earpins	-	-	+	-	+	-	-	-
Disk beads	+	+	+	+	-	-	-	-
Turkey wingtip beads	+	-	+	+	-	-	-	-
Rabbit innominate beads	+	-	+	-	-	-	-	-
Ceramic pot	+	+	+	-	-	-	-	-
Male items								
Projectile points	+	+	-	-	-	-	+	+
Crystals	-	+	-	-	-	-	-	-
Animal teeth/claws	+	+	-	-	-	-	-	+
Clay pipe	-	-	-	-	-	-	-	+
Ochre	-	-	-	-	-	-	-	+
Age-specific items								
Large formalized tools	-	-	-	-	+	-	-	+
Nonspecific items								
Carapace cup	-	-	+	-	-	-	-	+
Small flake tools	-	+	+	+	-	-	-	+
Bone tool	+	-	+	-	+	-	-	+
Tubular beads	+	-	+	-	+	+	-	-
Columella segment beads	+	+	+	+	+	-	+	+
Marginella beads	+	+	+	+	+	+	-	+

Distribution of Mortuary Items in Burials

Just over half (56 percent) of the burials have sex-specific mortuary goods (see table 3.3). That is, more than half of burials have artifacts found exclusively in burials of either females or males but not both (see table 3.4). Mortuary items found only with females include bone beads made from rabbit innominates and turkey wingtips; hairpins and earpins made from conch columella and bone; and gorgets, pendants, and disc beads made from the outer whorl of conch shells (fig. 3.2). In addition to these ornamental items, pottery vessels are also associated with females but

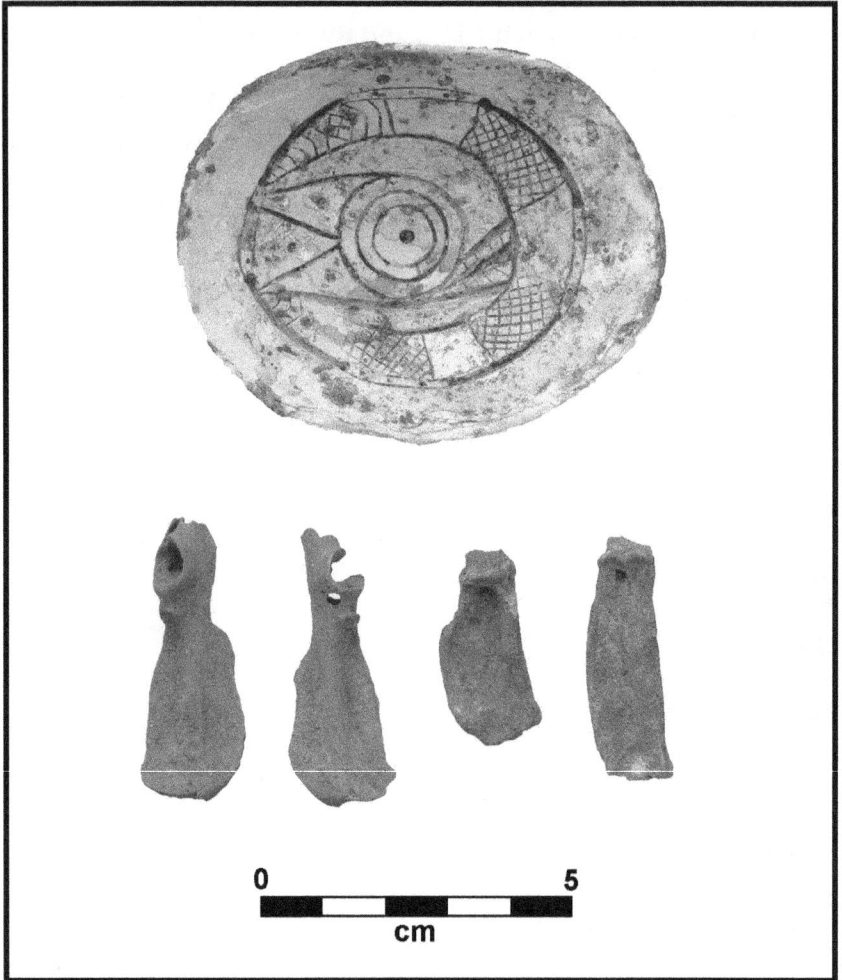

Fig. 3.2. Female-related artifacts from the Stockton site.

not males. Mortuary items found only with males include animal teeth and claws, projectile points, crystals, clay pipes, bone fishhooks, and ochre (fig. 3.3).

These grave goods may have been used to represent gender differences in Siouan communities in the study area. To explore this possibility, the strength of the association between each of these items and the sex of the individual was measured. Contingency tables were constructed, and two measures were used to evaluate the association: the phi coefficient

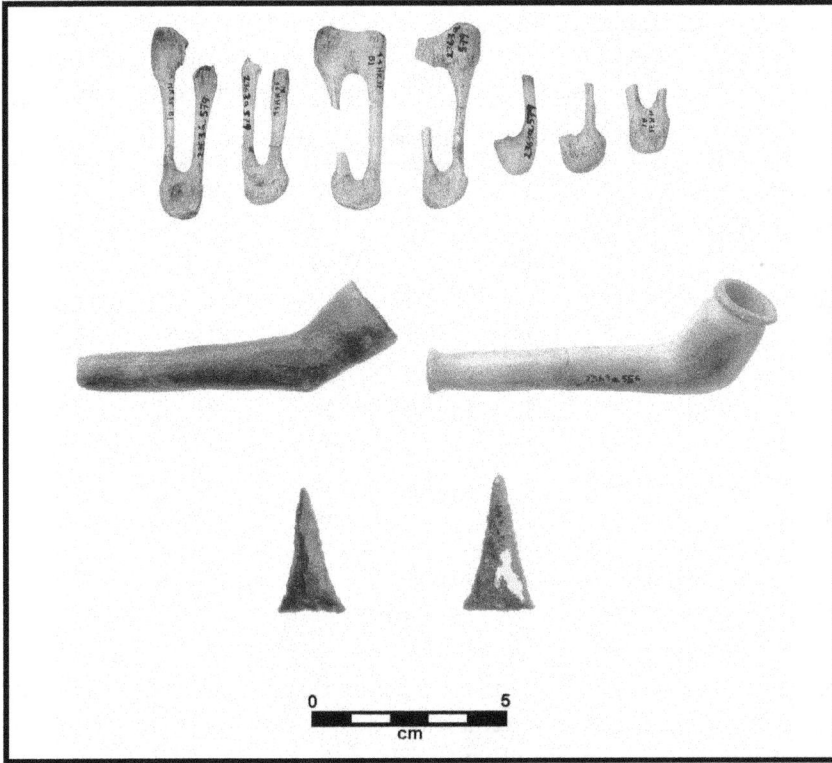

Fig. 3.3. Male-related mortuary items from the Stockton site.

(Wilkinson et al. 1992) and Cole's coefficient of association (Cole's C^7), which is equivalent to phi/phi_{max}. The value of each measure varies between +1 and -1, with 0 indicating no association. Using phi, a perfect association is achieved only when both cells b and c or cells a and d of the contingency table have a value of 0. This goal model for perfect association is theoretically unlikely. Cole's C^7 uses a less stringent goal model for perfect association. A perfect positive association is achieved with Cole's C^7 if either cells b or c of the contingency table have a value of 0, and a perfect negative association is achieved if either cells a or d equal 0. Table 3.5 indicates that Cole's coefficient measures a perfect association between sex and the sex-specific artifacts, while the phi coefficient indicates that even though these artifacts were interred exclusively with females or males but not both, the association between each of these mortuary items and sex is weak.

The lack of a strong association (as measured by the phi coefficient)

Table 3.5. Frequency of burials with certain mortuary items by sex

Mortuary item	Male		Female		Phi coefficient[a]	Cole's C[7] phi/phi$_{max}$
	Present	Absent	Present	Absent		
Shell gorget	0	19	3	18	-0.271	-1
Earpin/hairpin	0	19	3	18	-0.271	-1
Bone beads[b]	0	19	3	18	-0.271	-1
Columella beads	4	15	12	9	-0.368	-0.47
Marginella beads	2	17	9	12	-0.362	-0.62
Clay pipe	4	15	0	21	0.350	+1
Projectile point	2	17	0	21	0.219	+1
Fish hook	3	16	0	21	0.299	+1
Teeth/claws	4	15	0	21	0.350	+1
Bone awls	7	12	2	19	0.327	0.06

a. Measuring strength of association between mortuary items and males.
b. Rabbit innominate beads and turkey wingtip beads.

between these mortuary items and sex is due in part to the rarity of these artifacts. Only a few females and males in the sample were interred with these items. In other words, none of these objects was used in a general way to distinguish males from females in burial practices, and none of these items appears to have marked gender in exclusion of other statuses. Only a few females or males in the sample were interred with any of these sex-specific objects, and this distribution leads to the conclusion that these grave goods signify other social differences in addition to gender. Vertical social status or horizontal statuses like kinship or cohort affiliation may also have determined which men or women within the communities would have been buried with these mortuary items.

Though these objects were not used in a general way to mark gender differences, their distribution among children and adolescents provides support for the interpretation that two distinct sets of mortuary items are present. The two groups of sex-specific mortuary objects are mutually exclusive even when interred with children and adolescents. When any of these items was interred with a child or an adolescent, either female- or male-specific items were present, but not both. There is only one exception to this rule: An infant burial at the Shannon site (44My8, Burial

99) was interred with both disc shell beads and bear canines. No other evidence indicates that this infant held a unique status, and the significance of both male- and female-related mortuary objects in its grave cannot be evaluated at this time.

What can be concluded from the distribution of grave goods at these sites is that certain objects mark opposing statuses. Within the study area, these opposed statuses were recognized from childhood and continued to be recognized in consistent ways by mortuary practices into adulthood. That is, in burials of children and adolescents, mortuary items were used in ways similar to their use in adult burials. Given that these objects have sex-specific distributions among adults, gender appears to have been one of the statuses that was commonly marked in mortuary practices for all age groups. Though gender may not have been as important a status for children as it was for sexually mature individuals, the mourners responsible for the burial of children appear to have recognized gender as one basis for selecting appropriate mortuary items for inclusion with children.

In order for any object to signify effectively female or male in mortuary ritual, it would have to have gender-specific associations in daily life as well. In most cases, the gender-specific mortuary items at these sites are consistent with our understanding of a division of labor based on gender in many historic native cultures of eastern North America. For example, fishhooks, projectile points, ochre, and the teeth or claws of mountain lion, bear, wolf, and elk are male-related mortuary items. These items probably relate to men's habitual activities, like hunting, warfare, and fishing. Female-related mortuary items, like ceramic vessels and miniature clay vessels, may refer to women's pottery-making or cooking and possibly salt production (see I. W. Brown 1980). The bone beads interred only with females were those made from turkey and rabbit bones. This may indicate that Siouan women hunted or trapped small mammals and turkeys. The ethnographic literature provides several examples of women hunters and trappers who focus on small prey animals (Brumbach and Jarvenpa 1997a, 1997b; Estioko-Griffin and Griffin 1997; Nelson 1997:92–93). If women did not acquire these animals themselves, they likely would have processed and cooked them. These bone beads may have served as charms, trophies, or amulets in a fashion similar to that of the teeth and claws of large mammals found in male burials. Mortuary items made from marine shell, especially gorgets and pendants, probably related to women's role in reproduction. Shell had, and still has, a symbolic link to the creation of life and the continuity of life among many native groups in eastern North America (see Hamell 1983). This association between shell gorgets and pendants and reproduction is further supported by the fact that they are found only with young adult females of prime childbearing age and young children and infants (girls?).

Other ornaments made from marine shell, especially beads made from conch columella and marginella shells, are more widely distributed among late prehistoric burials. Nearly 60 percent of all burials in this sample with mortuary items had columella or marginella beads. These types of beads were buried with members of all ages and gender groups. In her analysis of marine shell beads in the North Carolina and Virginia Piedmont, Thomas (1996:36) found that "shell beads were used in the same way by women and men" in terms of the type of beads, their placement in burials, and the frequency of beads in burials. Shell was an important item in social negotiation among community members. In many southeastern cultures, shell beads were exchanged as wealth items and used for payment of social debts like bridewealth or reparation (Lefler 1967:204; A. Moore 1988:45; Thomas 1996). Their use as an important medium of exchange, combined with the symbolic importance of shell, probably accounts for the widespread use of shell beads in mortuary practices.

In addition to these types of beads, several other common mortuary items were not distributed differentially among different gender groups. These include small flake tools and bone awls. The presence of bone awls and flake tools with children and both male and female adults of all ages may indicate a lack of technological specialization in the production of these items and may reflect their widespread use by most members of the community.

Gender and the Life Cycle

Age is intricately linked to gender identities and roles, and I will now consider how age and sex together influenced the structure of mortuary practices. Older women were more likely to have stone or bone tools buried with them than were young women. These older women were also less often buried with sex-specific shell items. Of the eight older females in this sample, only two were buried with female-related shell items, while four were interred with formalized stone or bone tools. The older adult females buried with tools lacked any associated items made from shell. This suggests that the qualities selected for representation in burial may have changed throughout a woman's life. During the prime childbearing years of early adulthood, a woman's status as reproducer was commonly marked in mortuary practices, but following menopause, work-related items more often marked a woman's status and achievements as producer. The work-related tools interred with older females do not have gender-specific distributions.

Other archaeological and ethnographic work supports this interpretation of changing gender roles of postmenopausal women. In his review of the changes in the lives of older women, Rubinstein (1990:117) noted that aging women often experience a degree of inner freedom that accompanies the lessening of domestic responsibilities associated with raising young children. He suggests that the role of work becomes a more significant factor in the lives of older women and that in traditional societies older women may also assume roles as ritual leaders. Other studies also suggest that postmenopausal women are often free to assume special roles or to take up activities normally reserved for males (Brumbach and Jarvenpa 1997a, 1997b; Crown and Fish 1996; Lesick 1997:35; J. Moore 1997). This type of life change may have been experienced by older Siouan women in the study area.

This database is a poor one to use to explore status changes during the life of men because of the small number of males in the sample younger than thirty-five years at death. Eighty percent of adult males in this sample were over thirty-five years at death (see table 3.6). This pattern is present at the Stockton (44Hr35) and Shannon (44My8) sites, which have the largest number of identifiable male skeletons. This distribution could indicate several things:

1. a low mortality rate for males between the ages of sixteen and thirty-five;
2. mortuary treatment other than burial within the village for young adult males (perhaps because they were often away from the village on extended hunting trips or raids);
3. an analytical bias toward identification of older males in the analysis of the skeletal material;
4. a sampling bias based on incomplete excavation of the archaeological sites;
5. low fertility in the population, which would result in fewer younger individuals in a burial population.

Despite the small number of adult males in the sample who were younger than thirty-five at death, one observation about the distribution of mortuary items can be made: Both of the younger males in the sample with associated mortuary items were interred with marine shell beads,

Table 3.6. Frequency of males by age group

Site	Males <35 years at death	Males >35 years at death	Total
Leatherwood Creek (44Hr1)	0	1	1
Philpott (44Hr4)	0	2	2
Stockton (44Hr35)	0	7	7
Upper Saratown (31Sk1a)	0	1	1
Hairston (31Sk1)	0	1	1
Shannon (44My8)	8	21	29
Total	8	33	41
Percentage	19.5	80.5	

while only three of the seventeen older adult males were buried with marine shell beads. This distribution mirrors that of shell bead use with females in this sample and indicates that older males are less likely to be buried with shell beads than younger males. Younger males, like younger females, may have been more concerned with reproduction and/or longevity than were those over thirty-five years old.

In contrast to the pattern observed for females in this sample (that is, a decline with age in the use of sex-specific items in mortuary ritual), three-fourths of older males have sex-specific mortuary items. This may indicate that the basis for men to achieve status throughout their lifetime was more consistent than that of women. What I suggest is that as males aged, their identification with activities habitually performed by men may not have diminished, while the opposite may have been true for women. The avenues for men to achieve status may not have changed throughout their lifetimes as drastically as those of women, whose prominent role as a reproducer ended with menopause. For example, the presence of fishhooks and fishhook blanks in several burials of older males indicates that fishing may have been an important productive activity that males undertook as their skills in hunting and warfare waned. The presence of large-mammal incisors and claws with older males points to their continued identification with hunting or hunting rituals, even if they may not have been actively hunting in their later years.

As the above discussion indicates, age and sex often are woven together intricately to form the basis for status during life and for the distribution of many mortuary items after death. The distribution of some mortuary items, however, seems to be associated more directly with the age of the individual without regard to sex. I already have discussed evidence that indicates shell beads were used similarly by men and women. I now would like to examine the distribution of shell among individuals who died at different stages in the life cycle. The distribution of shell items is not even across all age groups in this study. Table 3.7 lists shell artifacts from burials in different adult age groups, allowing comparisons of the associations of beads with adults younger and older than thirty-five years at death. The table indicates that shell artifacts, as a whole, and certain common types of shell beads are distributed differently between younger and older adults. Marginella beads and columella segment beads are found more often with younger than with older adults. Perhaps shell, with its symbolic link to reproduction and continuity of life, was a more important item for young adults to possess and display. Older adults may have been less concerned about fertility than younger adults and therefore less attracted to shell items. Similarly, the death of an older adult may have had less effect on the reproduction and physical continuity of the kin group than the loss of a younger adult, and, therefore, the mourners responsible for burying older people may not have felt that shell items adequately expressed the loss of these individuals to the community.

The use of large formalized stone tools as mortuary items appears to have been related primarily to age. Tools like ground stone celts occur only with older men and women. Similarly, the only chipped stone hoe in the sample was interred with an older female. It may have been only during the later years of life that age, as a status separate from gender, was signified in mortuary ritual by non-sex-specific productive imple-

Table 3.7. Frequency of burials with certain mortuary items by age group

Mortuary item	Adults <35 years Present	Absent	Adults >35 years Present	Absent	Phi coefficient[a]	Cole's C[7] phi/phi_{max}
Columella beads	10	5	6	19	0.422	0.44
Marginella beads	10	5	3	22	0.565	0.63
All shell artifacts	12	3	7	18	0.504	0.62

a. Measuring association between mortuary items and young adults (16–34 years at death) and mature adults (>35 years old at death).

ments.

Conclusion

This study indicates that during the fifteenth and sixteenth centuries the ancestors of Siouan-speaking groups like the Sara and Tutelo marked gender identities through mortuary practices. Certain objects were associated with different gender groups. More than half of all infants and adolescents were buried with items that were interred with either males or females, but not both; this pattern likely reflects the prospective gender identities of these young people. Young adult women were buried with sex-specific objects more often than were older women. A different pattern is present for males. Although the sample of males is heavily skewed toward older individuals, it seems that sex-specific grave goods were more often interred with older males than with any other segment of the burial population. This may indicate that gender as a recognized social status and identity was more important to older men than to older women. For women, gender may have been supplanted by other statuses associated with being a community elder, while male-related objects and male roles appear to have remained important to men into older adulthood. For both males and females, the likelihood of being buried with a bone or stone tool instead of shell beads or other shell ornaments increased with age. I think this reflects two interrelated aspects of aging: First, shell may have been linked symbolically to reproduction and therefore may have been more often interred with burials of young adults and subadults; second, the frequency of stone and bone tools in burials of older people may indicate that elders spent more time making implements following the cessation of their involvement in other activities or perhaps that they spent more time using these implements in productive craft activities than did younger individuals.

This study demonstrates that gender was one of the statuses recognized in mortuary practices for individuals who died early in life. Gender representation remained relatively consistent for males throughout their adult years, but, in contrast, gender representation appears to have changed dramatically for females as they aged. This study has demonstrated the dynamic potential of gender in the lives of late prehistoric peoples of northwestern North Carolina and southern Virginia.

⋊ 4 ⋉

Mortuary Ritual and Gender Ideology in Protohistoric Southwestern North Carolina

Christopher B. Rodning

The major premise of this book is that gender traditions guide the lives of people and the social roles and identities they develop at different stages of their lives. Gender affects the daily lives of people and the ways in which they interact with others in their communities. Gender should therefore relate in some way to the landscapes in which people have lived in the past. Several archaeologists have indeed demonstrated relationships between gender and past landscapes, including the built environment of towns and villages as well as the natural environments of whole regions (Claassen 1991; Conkey 1991; Galloway 1997; Gilchrist 1994; S. Hall 1998; Handsman 1991; Hastorf 1991; Hendon 1997; Jackson 1991; Lane 1998; Parkington 1998; Schmidt 1998; Spector 1991; Tringham 1991). This study of the relationship between gender and past landscapes contributes to broader archaeological interests in the ways in which symbolic meanings become embedded in the spaces and places where men, women, children, and members of other gender groups live their lives (Barrett, Bradley, and Green 1991; Lawrence and Low 1990; R. B. Lewis, Stout, and Wesson 1998; Rapoport 1994; Spain 1992; Tilley 1994). This chapter considers the relationship between gender and the cultural landscape at and around the protohistoric town represented by the Coweeta Creek archaeological site in southwestern North Carolina. My primary interest is the arrangement of burials and buildings at this site, situated just north of the confluence of Coweeta Creek and the upper Little Tennessee River. Ethnohistoric evidence offers clues for reconstructing mortuary ritual and social dynamics within this native community.

I begin with a review of ethnohistoric evidence about gender roles and identities in Cherokee and other native communities during the eighteenth century. Ethnohistorians have noted significant distinctions between the social domains of native women and men in eastern North America (Trigger 1978:802–3). Some evidence indicates that these gendered social spheres may have corresponded to different spatial domains within past cultural landscapes of native North America (Fenton 1978:297–98). Women wielded power as household leaders, whereas men derived status from activities that often took them to the forests between towns and along the trails and waterways connecting them.

I then review archaeological evidence from southern Appalachia that reflects gender distinctions communicated through mortuary ritual. Considerable archaeological fieldwork has been done in western North Carolina and surrounding areas with an interest in town layout and regional settlement patterns (fig. 4.1). Contiguous excavations at Coweeta Creek

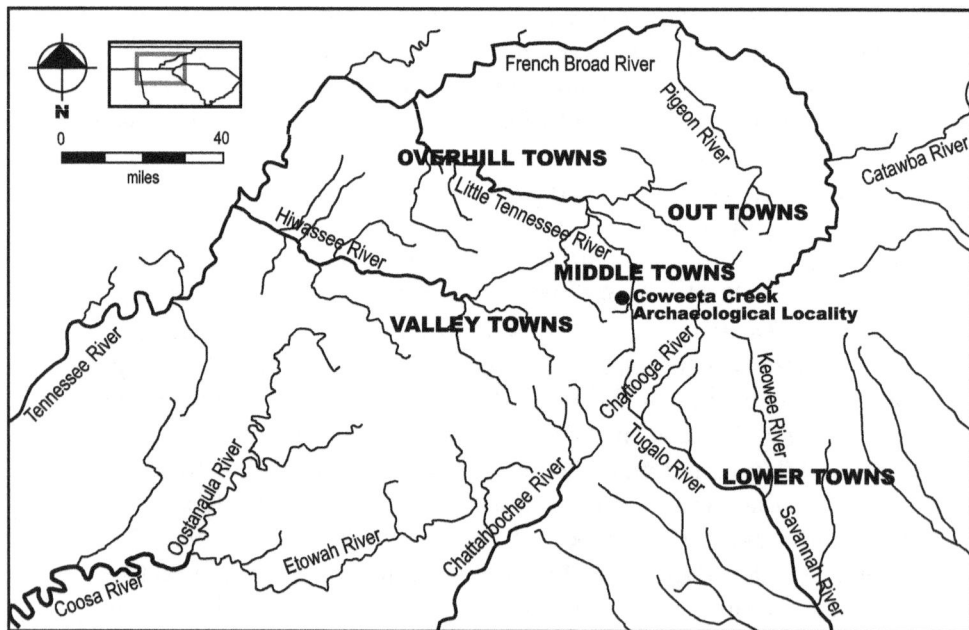

Fig. 4.1. Cherokee town groups in southern Appalachia. Courtesy of the UNC Research Laboratories of Archaeology and the *Journal of Cherokee Studies* (Rodning 1999a:10–11; see also B. J. Egloff 1967:4; Ward and Davis 1999:140).

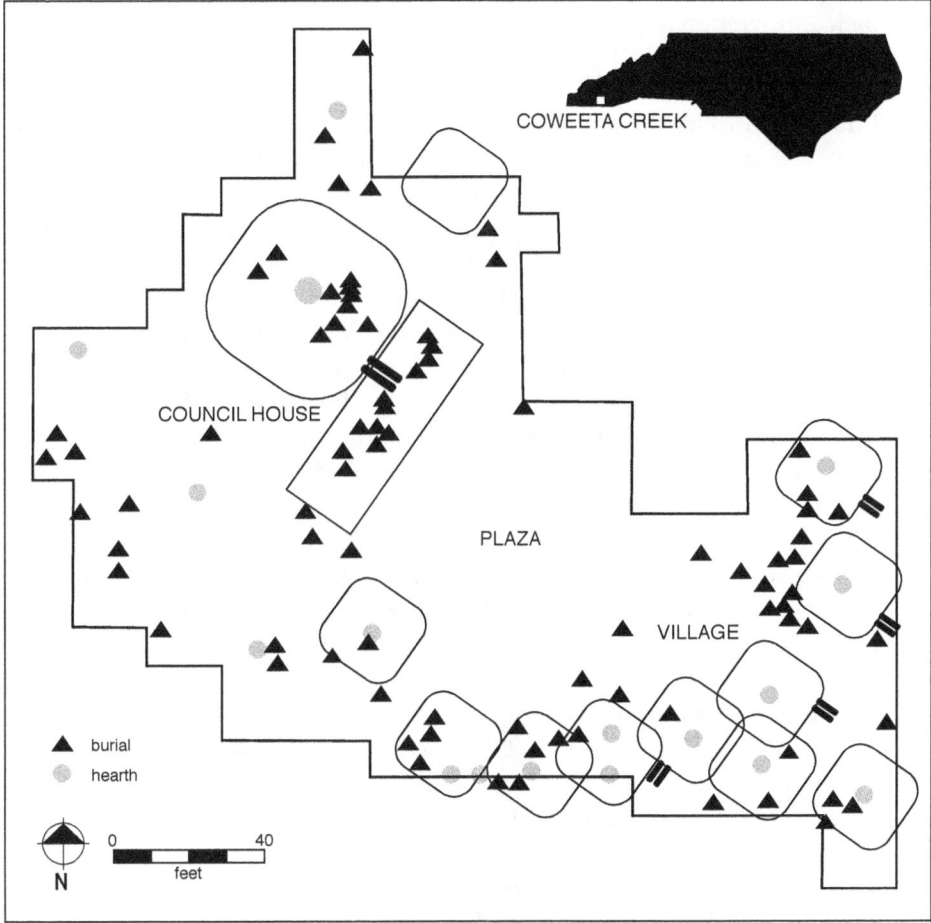

Fig. 4.2. Coweeta Creek site in southwestern North Carolina. Courtesy of the UNC Research Laboratories of Archaeology and the *Journal of Cherokee Studies* (Rodning 1999a:11–13; see also K. T. Egloff 1971:44; Ward and Davis 1999:185).

have revealed the layout of a council house and village area surrounding a town plaza and the presence of graves in these different architectural spaces (fig. 4.2). This and other sites give some clues about how gender ideology may have become manifest in the built environment, if not the regional cultural landscape in the seventeenth and early eighteenth centuries.

My conclusions reconstruct the gender distinctions made through mortuary ritual at Coweeta Creek and relate them to gender ideology within the native town centered there. This ideology seems to have recognized distinct but complementary tracks to prestige and power for men and women in the Coweeta Creek community.

Ethnohistoric Background

Ethnohistoric clues about Cherokee culture and community in southern Appalachia come from journals and maps left by explorers and traders as well as colonial soldiers (Beck 1997; J. N. Brown 1999; J. Chapman 1985; Gearing 1958, 1962; Goodwin 1977; Harmon 1986; Hatley 1989, 1991; Hudson 1977, 1986, 1990, 1997; King 1979; King and Evans 1977; King and Olinger 1972; J. Mooney 1900; Randolph 1973; Riggs 1989; Schroedl 1978; B. A. Smith 1979; M. T. Smith 1992). Primary sources were authored by men and thus reflect greater knowledge of the ritual and routine lives of native men than those of women (Galloway 1989, 1997; Hatley 1995:52–53; Perdue 1998:3–4). Of course, many written journals and maps post-date the beginning of the slave and deerskin trades and the many native cultural changes spurred by these developments in the seventeenth and eighteenth centuries (Galloway 1993, 1995; Goodwin 1977; Hatley 1995: 17–41). Here I concentrate on written materials about several different native groups to develop a model of Cherokee gender ideology during the eighteenth century. Then I interpret southern Appalachian archaeological materials that most likely date to the seventeenth century with this ethnohistoric model as a guide.

Men and women in historic Creek societies in Alabama and Georgia tended to pursue distinct lives as adult members of their communities (Braund 1993:14; see Sullivan, this volume). Women made contributions to their communities as leaders of matrilineal clans and households. They were also the main keepers of gardens and fields, from which they harvested maize, beans, and squash as well as wild berries, grasses, nuts, birds, game, and probably materials for making baskets. Town chiefs were mostly adult men, many of whom had made their mark as hunters, warriors, and traders, and these pursuits often took them far away from their hometowns. Men often gathered in square grounds in Creek towns for social reasons. Men prominent within their towns were often the first of their communities to interact with European travelers and traders during the seventeenth century.

People in historic Iroquois communities of New York state and sur-rounding areas of the eastern Great Lakes region recognized spatial do-mains primarily related to the activities of men and women in different parts of their landscape (Prezzano 1997:91; see Claassen, this volume). Longhouses were the domain of Iroquois women, and these architectural spaces housed members of several lineages within matrilineal clans. The power of Iroquois women resided within villages of longhouses that housed several lineages and in the fields that they tended just outside their village palisades. Men, though they certainly helped with farming, were better known for their roles as hunters and warriors. Meanwhile, men were traders and diplomats, conducting many expeditions to far-away villages and colonial forts. Forests between villages and the pathways winding through them were male space. Longhouses and other areas within villages formed the spatial domain of women.

These gender distinctions were comparable to those in the eighteenth-century Cherokee cultural landscape. Local members of matrilineal clans formed households within towns (Hill 1997:69; Perdue 1998:42–43). Buildings and gardens related to households would thus have become landmarks for the clans of which they were members (Champagne 1990:11; Hill 1997:27–28). Apart from these dwellings stood communal council houses, the setting for many rituals and town council meetings. Men conducted purification rituals there before leaving and upon returning to their hometowns, and some old men may have all but lived in them. All members of communities would have gathered for ritual events at and beside council houses, and they all would have been members of one household or another. This point notwithstanding, there seems to have been a symbolic relationship between women and household space, on one hand, and men and council houses, on the other.

The leaders of clans and towns wielded different kinds of power within Cherokee communities. Male town leaders were spokespersons for their clans in Cherokee town council deliberations (Champagne 1990: 16–17; Persico 1979:93–95). Meanwhile, these men were Cherokee only because of their relationship to a woman who was a member of one clan or another (Hill 1997:25–27; Perdue 1998:41–42). During the early eighteenth century, there are neither specific clans nor lineages that seem to have outranked others in any hereditary hierarchy of town leadership (Champagne 1983:89, 1990:16); egalitarianism prevailed within these towns. Nor were there paramount towns, whose leaders had coercive power over other towns (Hudson 1976:202–3, 1990:94–101). Everybody within a town was a member of one clan or another, and this membership contributed much to their place within the community. Most, if not all, people were affiliated with a town, including those living beside town centers and those in the countryside between towns.

This evidence indicates that leaders within native societies in western North Carolina and some other areas of eastern North America during the eighteenth century emerged from both matrilineal clan kin groups, on one hand, and social entities called towns, on the other. Women derived power and prestige as clan leaders and linchpins in matrilineal kin networks, and they devoted much energy toward tending gardens, gathering nuts and other resources from woods around their towns and farms, making baskets and perhaps pots, and preparing foods and beverages for ritual events and routine meals (Hill 1997; Wetmore 1983:52). Men commonly contributed to their communities as town leaders, and they were primarily involved in hunting, warfare, diplomacy, trade, woodcutting, and rituals such as the ballgame (Gearing 1962; Hill 1997: 120). Children in Cherokee towns in southern Appalachia probably would have been enculturated from an early age with this gender ideology and these gender roles.

Archaeological Background

Archaeology at several late prehistoric- and early historic-period sites in greater southern Appalachia offers opportunities to compare the layouts of towns with this model of historic Cherokee gender ideology (Anderson 1990, 1994; Anderson, Hally, and Rudolph 1986; Dickens 1978, 1986; Hally and Kelly 1998; R. B. Lewis and Stout 1998; R. B. Lewis, Stout, and Wesson 1998; T. M. N. Lewis and Kneberg 1946; T. M. N. Lewis, Kneberg Lewis, and Sullivan 1995; Polhemus 1987, 1990; Schroedl 1989, 1998; Schroedl and Riggs 1990; Setzler and Jennings 1941; Sullivan 1987, 1989, 1995; Ward and Davis 1999). Excavations at several localities have revealed the layouts of burials relative to architectural spaces at these sites. Late prehistoric and early historic towns in this region tend to have dwellings placed beside a communal council house and town commons devoted to public gatherings. The burial of someone in one architectural space or another would have communicated the relationship of that person with the activities and symbolic significance of that space. People would have attached to these architectural spaces their memories of dead ancestors laid to rest in them. Archaeologists have not identified monuments in the southern Appalachians specifically built as landmarks for the dead that date as late as the seventeenth century. Graves at late Mississippian and protohistoric towns seem to have been placed within areas where daily activities and ritual events took place. Some burials have been found in platform mounds and more recent communal council houses. Others have been found in and beside household architecture. Thus, the resting places of ancestors would have become marked by those architectural forms in southeastern North America. This overlap in the spaces of the living and the dead is visible at several sites in western North Carolina.

Archaeologists affiliated with the Research Laboratories of Archaeology (RLA) at the University of North Carolina (UNC) at Chapel Hill conducted considerable surveys and excavations in the western part of the state during the 1960s and 1970s. This fieldwork was part of the Cherokee archaeological project initiated by Joffre Coe to study the development of Cherokee culture in western North Carolina (Coe 1961; Dickens 1976, 1986; Ferguson 1971; Holden 1966; Keel 1976). Other archaeological materials significant to this topic have been recovered through fieldwork in northeastern Georgia and southeastern Tennessee (Hally 1986; Schroedl 1986a, 1986b; Sullivan 1995).

Considerable excavations have been conducted at Warren Wilson, in the French Broad River watershed in Buncombe County, North Carolina (Ward and Davis 1999:160–71). The palisaded village built here most likely dates to the fifteenth century, and there are earlier settlements represented at the site. The palisade was rebuilt several times, presumably as the village grew outward. Houses, represented archaeologically by postholes, foundations of entryways, and hearths, were placed around communal space within the village. Dickens (1976:125–28) has argued that graves in and around one house have a richer suite of grave goods than other houses at Warren Wilson, indicating that this house may have been home to an elite group within this rural farming village.

Significant excavations have been conducted at Garden Creek, in the upper Pigeon River Valley in Haywood County, North Carolina (Ward and Davis 1999:171–75). Excavated materials from Garden Creek Mound #1 have enabled archaeologists to trace the development of public architecture from communal earthlodges to a platform mound atop which elite families may have lived. Underneath and beside Garden Creek Mound #1 were the architectural remnants of a village predating the mound. Dickens (1976:128–30) notes some seventeen burials in this mound at Garden Creek, representing all age groups.

Fieldwork at Coweeta Creek (31Ma34) in Macon County, North Carolina, was directed toward studying Cherokee culture at the temporal divide between prehistory and protohistory (Keel and Egloff 1999). Brian Egloff led fieldwork from 1965 through 1967. Bennie Keel directed excavations from 1967 to 1971. Originally, the Cherokee project had planned to spend one field season at Coweeta Creek.

Plans for major excavations at other sites in the upper Little Tennessee River Valley, such as Cowee (31Ma5) and Nequassee (31Ma2), never materialized (Keel and Egloff 1999). Earlier in the Cherokee project, UNC teams had excavated a mid-eighteenth-century burned house at the Tuckasegee site—31Jk12 (Dickens 1978:123; Keel 1976:63–64)—some twenty miles northeast of Coweeta Creek. As part of the Cherokee project, UNC teams had also done fieldwork at a late-eighteenth-century dispersed settlement at the Townson site—31Ce15 (Dickens 1967:17, 1976:15, 1978:123; Keel 1976:14–16)—some thirty-five miles west of Coweeta Creek. One reason that the members of the Cherokee project never got around to extensive excavations at Cowee and Nequassee was the richness of what they found at these other sites and at Coweeta Creek.

For several seasons, excavations concentrated on the Coweeta Creek mound (K. T. Egloff 1971:43–69; Rodning 1999b). This mound actually represents a layer cake of one council house built atop the toppled and covered remnants of its predecessors. Archaeologists have found evidence of at least six manifestations of the council house in this mound. These council houses were probably comparable in some characteristics of architectural materials and visual form to those found in the Estatoe and Tugalo mounds in northeastern Georgia (Anderson 1994:205–13; Hally 1986:95–97).

As fieldwork continued, excavations were done in the plaza and village area beside the Coweeta Creek mound (K. T. Egloff 1971:69–70; Rodning 1999a). This fieldwork revealed several constellations of postholes and hearths representing dwellings that are comparable in architectural form to written descriptions of Cherokee winter lodges (Faulkner 1978:87; Waselkov and Braund 1995:84). The bewildering maze of postholes and entrance trenches in the village section of the site suggests that many houses were rebuilt one or more times, and it is difficult to know for sure if there were covered sheds comparable to historic Cherokee summer houses beside these winter lodges (Perdue 1998:43; Waselkov and Braund 1995:253). The layout of this residential sector of the town at Coweeta Creek looks rather like that of many others in late prehistoric western North Carolina and surrounding areas (Dickens 1978: 127–31; Sullivan 1995:107–9).

For several reasons, Coweeta Creek has never received the comprehensive archaeological treatment that it deserves. Its artifact collections are vast. Its traces of architecture are rich datasets about how this native town was built and rebuilt. Due to the expertise of those who conducted the fieldwork, Coweeta Creek stands to make major contributions to archaeology and the history of Cherokee peoples in southern Appalachia during the early historic period.

Coweeta Creek Town Plan

The town at Coweeta Creek most likely lasted for less than one hundred and perhaps less than fifty years. The council house and village houses were rebuilt more than once. Rebuilding nevertheless preserved a town plan that seems to have been consistent throughout the tenure of this locality as a major town center. Each stage of the council house at Coweeta Creek opened through vestibule doorways to the southeast. Doorways of dwellings in the village pointed in this same direction toward the confluence of the creek and the Little Tennessee River itself. For these reasons, it is meaningful to consider the archaeologically visible layout of Coweeta Creek as one planned town.

The council house was built and rebuilt at least six times (see Ward and Davis 1999:183–86). Its shape and dimensions, roughly forty feet square with rounded corners, were consistent from its earliest to its latest known stages (K. T. Egloff 1971:66; Dickens 1978:123–25; D. G. Moore 1990). Ceramics from the earliest stages of the council house are very much like those from its latest stages, in surface treatment and form, and they have contributed much to the characterization of the Qualla ceramic series, which is well represented at several historic Cherokee towns (Baden 1983:144–49; B. J. Egloff 1967:73; Russ and Chapman 1983:77–83). It is conceivable that the Coweeta Creek village predated the council house, or that the first council house was built only after the village had been standing for some time. It seems most likely that the formal town at Coweeta Creek did not last more than five or six generations, if that long. Further study of archaeological materials at Coweeta Creek should help to pinpoint the dates of this town and its architectural history.

Ceramics from Coweeta Creek are comparable to pottery from nearby towns dating to the sixteenth and early eighteenth centuries (Ward and Davis 1999:181–83). Many characteristics of sixteenth-century Tugalo-phase ceramics are visible in Coweeta Creek pottery—burnished interiors, curvilinear complicated stamping on the outsides of globular jars, incised motifs between the rims and shoulders of carinated bowls, and other characteristics that place pottery here within the Lamar tradition (see Hally 1986:99, 1994a:147; Hally and Langford 1988:78; Wynn 1990:54). There are similarities as well to early eighteenth-century Estatoe-phase pottery in Coweeta Creek ceramics—burnished interiors, some check stamping as surface finish, and some cases of coarser grit temper than what is common in earlier Lamar pottery (see Hally 1986:111, 1994a:174; Hally and Rudolph 1986:63; Wynn 1990:58). Ceramics from Coweeta

Creek thus seem to place it within the seventeenth or perhaps the very early eighteenth century.

European trade goods from Coweeta Creek seem generally consistent with this posited date. Glass beads and pieces of kaolin pipes have been found in the council house (Ward and Davis 1999:183). These artifacts are not found in other parts of the site (Ward and Davis 1999:187). This restricted distribution and variety of European trade goods suggests an early form of interaction with Europeans, before the intense interactions between natives and European colonists through the deerskin trade of the eighteenth century (Baden 1983:10–17; Rodning 1999a:15). At later Cherokee towns in southern Appalachia, archaeologists have found a broader range of European goods in many different burials and buildings (Guthe 1977:217–26; Schroedl 1986b:535). The effects of the colonial trade in deerskins and slaves upon the lives of men and women in the Coweeta Creek community and other communities in this region merit further archaeological study.

Coweeta Creek thus represents a protohistoric Cherokee council house built and rebuilt beside a plaza and village area close to the confluence of Coweeta Creek and the Little Tennessee River. The council house sat atop a river terrace, though not at its highest point (K. T. Egloff 1971:69–70). The first council house most likely was built when the village was still standing, although the chronological relationship between them is still grounds for further consideration (K. T. Egloff 1971:63–69). One unresolved problem is the significance of the semicircular trench and the burials and hearths in the southwestern corner of the site. Another problem is the uncertainty about what kinds of architecture might have been built just north of the council house. At this point, it seems reasonable, nonetheless, to differentiate between the council house and village areas as distinct architectural spaces at this town.

Coweeta Creek Mortuary Program

For the purposes of this paper, I have allocated each of the Coweeta Creek burials to the architectural space associated with either the council house or the village. The remnants of the council house were found in the mound at the northwestern corner of the excavations at 31Ma34. The village area was found to the south and east of the plaza at 31Ma34. Although this spatial distinction between "public" council house and "domestic" village space is apparent from just looking at the map, I would add that further archaeological study of Coweeta Creek and surrounding areas could change our understanding of the layout of the town.

Archaeologists have found eighty-three graves at the site (fig. 4.2). These graves represent the burials of some eighty-eight individuals (table 4.1). Seventeen are shaft-and-side-chamber graves, and one is a shaft-and-central-chamber burial. The rest are simple oval or oblong pits. Thirty-four people were buried within or beside the council house in some thirty-two distinct graves, including those in clusters right outside and inside its vestibule doorway. Fifty-four people were buried within the fifty-one distinct graves in the village, although excavations have not uncovered all of the space that was likely part of this town. Twenty-nine people at the site were placed in the ground facing east, southeast, or northeast. Twenty-three were buried facing west, southwest, or northwest. Ten faced north. Thirteen faced south.

All but sixteen adults were identified as male or female.[1] Anybody who died before reaching the age of sixteen was not identified as male or female but only as a subadult.

Archaeologists have found mortuary goods clearly placed in the ground with the deceased in twenty-nine of the burials.[2] Figure 4.3 shows the grave goods found in all the known Coweeta Creek burials. Figure 4.4 shows grave goods from burials in the Coweeta Creek mound. Figure 4.5 shows mortuary artifacts from graves in the Coweeta Creek village. Each rectangle in these charts represents one grave at the Coweeta Creek site (see Sherratt 1982:22). The layout of the icons representing different grave goods within individual rectangles does not follow any spatial patterns in their placement within the actual graves. These figures are merely schematic representations of the presence or absence of grave goods in different burials at the site.

The suite of grave goods at Coweeta Creek is comparable to those found at other late prehistoric and early historic sites in western North Carolina and surrounding areas (Dickens 1976:132; Keel 1976:218; M. T. Smith 1987:98–108; M. T. Smith and Smith 1989; Thomas 1996). The most elaborate sets of grave goods are those with two different male elders in the council house. Within Burial 9 was an adult male with seven arrowheads, one gaming stone, four knobbed shell ear pins, columella beads, olivella beads, drilled pearls, and impressions of what may have been some sort of woven shroud or basket; within Burial 17 was an elderly male with a carved stone pipe, an engraved rattlesnake gorget, and knobbed shell pins. Turtle-shell rattles, which were most likely used in ritual dances, were found in two graves in the village. Within Burial 43 was a young adult woman with turtle-shell rattles; within Burial 41 was a young adult woman with turtle-shell rattles and shell beads. One ground

Table 4.1. Excavated graves and grave goods at Coweeta Creek

Burial[a]	Setting[b]	Age[c]	Sex[d]	Grave[e]	Orient[f]	Artifacts[g]
1	CH	E	I	OP	SE	
2	CH	MA	I	OP	N	
3	CH	C	U	OP	SE	
4	CH	E	M	OP	S	
5	CH	A	U	SC	SW	
6	CH	E	M	SC	SE	1 ground stone celt, 2 knobbed shell ear pins
7	CH	MA	F	OP	NW	
8	CH	MA	M	OP	S	
9	CH	E	M	OP	SE	7 stone arrowheads, 1 gaming stone, 4 knobbed shell ear pins, 93 columella shell beads, 11 olivella shell beads, 14 drilled pearls, fragments of basketry
10	CH	C	U	OP	E	
11	CH	E	M	OP	N	
12	CH	MA	M	OP	N	32 shell beads
13	CH	YA	I	OP	S	
14	CH	E	M	OP	S	
15	CH	E	M	SC	N	6 shell beads
16	CH	C	U	OP	NE	1 shell mask gorget,[h] 8 columella shell beads
17	CH	E	M	SC	N	1 circular engraved gorget,[i] 1 carved stone pipe, 2 knobbed shell ear pins
18	CH	E	M	OP	SW	1 bone hair pin
19	CH	C	U	OP	S	3 shell pendants, 4 columella shell beads, 5 olivella shell beads
20	CH	MA	I	OP	NE	
21a	CH	YA	I	OP	SW	1 shell bead, 1 animal mandible fragment
21b	CH	E	I			
21c	CH	C	U			
22	V	C	U	OP	?	
23	CH	YA	M	SC	NE	1 shell mask gorget, 2 columella shell beads
24	CH	MA	F	SC	NE	
25	CH	YA	M	SC	NE	
26	V	E	F	OP	NE	

Burial[a]	Setting[b]	Age[c]	Sex[d]	Grave[e]	Orient[f]	Artifacts[g]
27	CH	C	U	SC	SE	1 shell-tempered clay jar (with restricted neck), 1 shell mask gorget, 2 knobbed shell ear pins, 14 drilled pearls
28	CH	YA	M	SC	S	
29	CH	YA	I	SC	SE	
30	CH	YA	M	SC	NE	1 shell mask gorget[j]
31	CH	C	U	OP	SW	4 shell pendants, 12 columella shell beads
32	CH	MA	M	OP	SE	2 knobbed shell ear pins
33	CH	E	M	OP	NE	2 shell beads
34	V	C	U	SC	NE	
35	V	E	M	OP	SE	
36	V	E	F	OP	SW	
37	V	MA	F	CC	SE	10 animal bone fragments
37a	V	MA	M			
38	V	C	U	OP	NE	1 grit-tempered clay bowl (with four strap handles)
39	CH	A	U	SC	NE	
40	V	YA	I	OP	SE	1 clay pipe, 2 shell bead fragments
41	V	YA	F	OP	NW	turtle shell rattle fragments, 24 shell bead fragments
42	V	E	F	SC	S	1 ground stone celt, 75 columella shell beads
43	V	YA	F	OP	S	turtle shell rattle fragments
44	V	MA	M	OP	W	24 columella shell beads
45	V	YA	F	OP	W	1 shell hair pin
46	V	YA	I	OP	NE	
47	V	YA	I	OP	SW	
48	V	MA	M	OP	NW	
49	V	C	U	OP	?	
50	V	E	M	OP	SW	
51	V	A	U	OP	N	1 shell mask gorget
52	V	MA	I	OP	NE	
53	V	MA	M	OP	SW	
54	V	YA	F	OP	NE	
55	V	MA	M	OP	N	
56	V	A	U	OP	N	
57	V	MA	F	OP	SW	
58	V	YA	M	OP	NE	

continued

Table 4.1 (continued)

Burial[a]	Setting[b]	Age[c]	Sex[d]	Grave[e]	Orient[f]	Artifacts[g]
59	V	YA	I	OP	SE	
60	V	MA	F	OP	NW	
61a	V	YA	I	OP	S	
61b	V	C	U	OP	—	
62	V	YA	M	OP	S	1 shell mask gorget
63	V	MA	F	OP	N	1 clay pipe
64	V	A	I	OP	SW	
66	V	YA	I	OP	SW	
67	V	YA	I	OP	W	1 shell bead
68	V	C	U	OP	SW	
69	V	C	U	OP	E	
70	V	C	U	OP	?	
71	V	C	U	OP	?	
72	V	MA	F	OP	S	
73	V	MA	M	OP	NW	
74	V	MA	M	OP	N	
75a	V	MA	M	OP	NE	
75b	V	YA	M	OP	—	
76	V	YA	I	OP	SW	
77	V	C	U	OP	?	
78	V	MA	M	OP	W	
79	V	C	U	OP	?	
80	V	C	U	OP	?	2 stone discs
81	V	E	F	SC	S	
82	V	C	U	SC	S	
83	V	A	U	OP	?	
84	V	C	U	SC	SW	4 glass beads

a. Burials were numbered sequentially during excavations. The excavators at 31Ma34 never designated any burial as Burial 65.

b Setting within the site: "CH" designates the council house and plaza, "V" denotes village area (see fig. 4.2).

c. Age group: "E" for elders, "MA" for mature adults, "YA" for young adults, "A" for adolescents, "C" for children (see fig. 4.3).

d Biological sex: "M" for male, "F" for female, "I" for indeterminate adults, "U" for unknown subadults (see fig. 4.3).

e. Grave type: "SC" for shaft-and-side-chamber graves, "CC" for the one shaft-and-central-chamber grave, "OP" for simple-oval-pit burials (see Ward and Davis 1999:165).

f. Orientation of the individual: cardinal direction in which the individual faced when placed in the ground.

(continued)

g. Artifacts placed in the grave with the deceased individual; see also figs. 4.3, 4.4, 4.5.

h. There is a trace of a forked-eye motif around one of the suspension holes of this shell mask. Several variations of this motif have been illustrated by Marvin Smith and Julie Barnes Smith (1989:13).

i. There is one carinated jar from Coweeta Creek that has incised scrolls and punctations between its rim and shoulder. This design looks similar to the rattlesnake motif engraved on this gorget found in the burial of an old adult man in the Coweeta Creek council house. Underneath the shoulder there are curvilinear complicated stamped scrolls on the outside. This pot has been photographed by Ward and Davis (1999:182).

j. There is a remnant of a long-nose motif between the suspension holes of this shell mask. Noses like this on shell masks have been illustrated by Marvin and Julie Barnes Smith (1989:10).

stone celt each is found with a male and female elder (Burials 6 and 42). The only pots found as grave goods are associated with children (Burials 27 and 38). One stone pipe and several clay pipes are found with adults and elders (Burials 17, 21, 63)—smoking was probably still reserved for ritual events rather than practiced as widely as it was after native people became enmeshed in trade and interaction with Europeans.[3] Shell mask gorgets (one has traces of what looks like an engraved forked-eye motif) and shell pendants (both oval and bi-lobed in shape) are found with children and young adults (Burials 16, 19, 23, 27, 30, 31, 62)—shell artifact forms may have been commonly associated with young people at protohistoric sites in the greater southern Appalachians.[4]

Nothing in the grave goods at Coweeta Creek indicates the presence of rigid social and political hierarchies like those characteristic of some earlier chiefdoms in southeastern North America in which ruling elites outranked other social groups (B. D. Smith 1986:50–63; M. T. Smith and Williams 1994; Steponaitis 1986:387–93; Trigger 1978:801–2; H. H. Wilson 1986). Certainly, some mortuary goods such as engraved shell gorgets may have communicated membership in elite echelons of South Appalachian Mississippian societies or descent relationships with ancient chiefs (Anderson 1990:196–99, 1994:311–13; M. T. Smith 1987:98–108). However, no pronounced distinctions in rank and status are evident in mortuary goods from burials in native towns in the Appalachian Summit as appear in other regions (Dickens 1979:210–14, 1986:87–90; H. H. Wilson 1986:52–68). This point likely relates to the relative egalitarianism of these communities as compared to the more rigid social hierarchies within paramount chiefdoms in other parts of the Southeast. It meanwhile suggests the potential significance of other kinds of social distinctions which may have been communicated through mortuary ritual by protohistoric and perhaps late prehistoric native groups in the southern Appalachians.

It is interesting that the adult male in Burial 9—just outside the doorway to the council house—was buried with seven arrowheads (Ward and Davis 1999:188–89). Five are made of Knox black chert from eastern Tennessee.[5] One may have been crafted from rhyolite from the Morrow

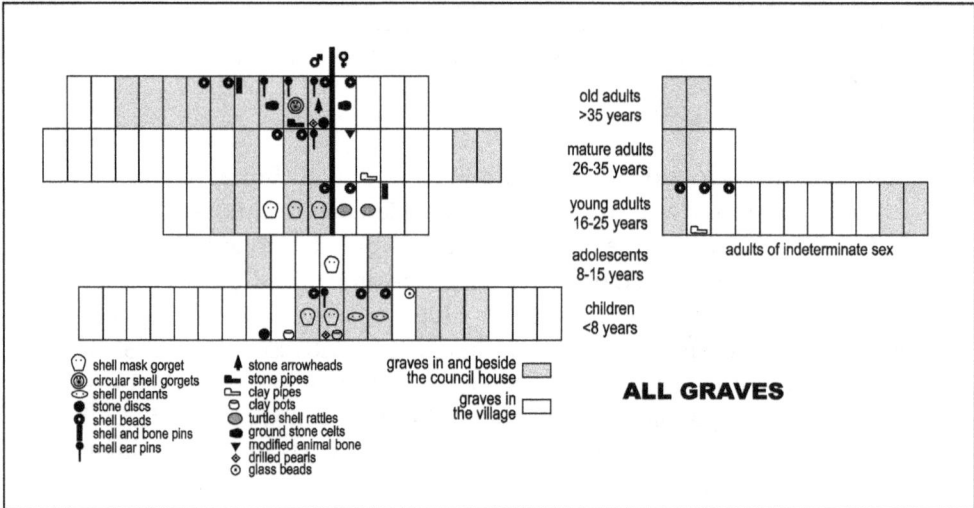

Fig. 4.3. Mortuary goods from all graves at the Coweeta Creek site.

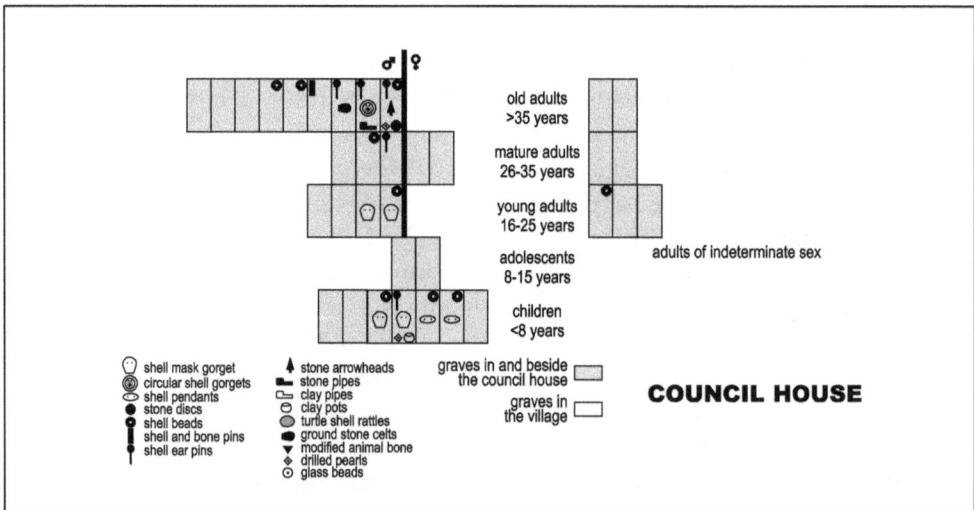

Fig. 4.4. Mortuary goods from graves in the Coweeta Creek mound.

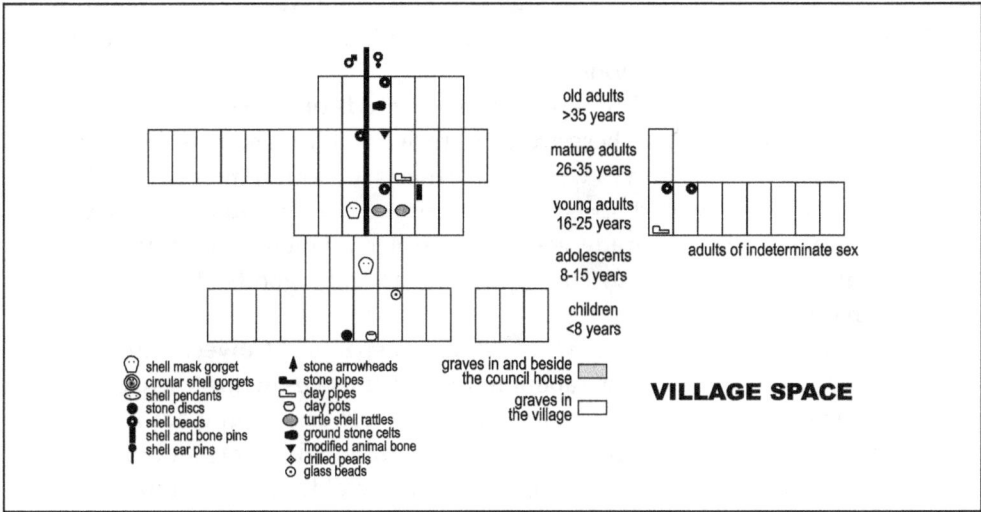

Fig. 4.5. Mortuary goods from graves in the Coweeta Creek village.

Mountain region in central North Carolina.[6] The last is made of the kind of quartzite found in most areas of western North Carolina and thus probably represents raw material found along the upper Little Tennessee. This man was most likely a prominent warrior and a leader of this protohistoric Cherokee town. It may or may not be a coincidence that there were seven traditional Cherokee clans, the same number of arrows placed in the ground with this town leader.

The only gorget with an engraved rattlesnake motif that was found in a grave is the one found with a male elder in Burial 17 (just outside the council house), whose suite of mortuary goods included a carved stone pipe and knobbed shell pins that most likely were worn as ear ornaments (Ward and Davis 1999:187–88). Such gorgets have been interpreted as markers of leadership within regional paramount chiefdoms, or alliances of chiefdoms, in southern Appalachia (M. T. Smith 1987:145–46). This prestige good almost certainly communicated his status as an eminent town leader, or descendant of an eminent chief of an earlier era, to members of his own and neighboring communities in southern Appalachia (M. T. Smith 1987:108–12).

Knobbed shell pins are found most commonly with male elders buried in the council house. For this reason, they may represent badges of status among people associated with rituals and other activities conducted in this space. An exception to this is the child in Burial 27 in the council house, buried with shell pins, one shell mask gorget, drilled pearls, and one ceramic pot. I suggest that this child is a close clan relative of one of the men buried in the council house, as perhaps were other children in the council house.

Shell artifacts probably represent trade goods or at least trade in the raw material for them. These artifacts are derived from marine shell. Fifteen of twenty-two graves with shell artifacts are found in or beside the council house. I would speculate that this set of individuals may have had greater access to trade goods than others, which is supported by the almost exclusive restriction of European trade goods at the site to the mound.

The placement of graves within different spaces at Coweeta Creek is indeed interesting evidence about mortuary practices in this town. Eight of at least eleven male elders and seven mature and young adult men were laid to rest in the council house. All four female elders and nine of eleven adult women—and several men and children—were buried in graves within the village. This gendered pattern is visible at the Overhill Cherokee towns of Chota and Tanasee in southeastern Tennessee during the eighteenth century (Schroedl 1986b:204). Its presence at Coweeta Creek indicates that the pattern may have its roots in native tradition in southern Appalachia before the Cherokee and their native neighbors became enmeshed in the deerskin trade during the eighteenth century (Rodning 1999a:18).

Several clusters of graves are present within and beside the Coweeta Creek council house (Ward and Davis 1999:187). One cluster (Burials 18, 17, 16, 9) was placed just north of the doorway to the council house; within these graves were placed many grave goods, including pipes, shell beads, knobbed shell pins, and shell gorgets. Another cluster (Burials 11, 12, 13, 14, 15, 19) was placed just south of the doorway to the council house; neither the four adult males nor the one indeterminate adult in this cluster were associated with any mortuary artifacts, but the one child in that cluster had shell beads and one shell pendant. Mortuary goods aside, the placement of these graves within the Coweeta Creek council house space would have communicated the deceaseds' prominence within the social sphere symbolically represented in that architectural form.

Other clusters of graves are visible in the Coweeta Creek village area (Ward and Davis 1999:189). One cluster (Burials 75, 76, 78, 79), beside a residential house in the northeasternmost corner of the site, includes the resting places of three adult men, one child, and one adult of indeterminate sex. Another cluster (Burials 56, 57, 58, 59, 60, 72, 73, 74, 83), beside a dwelling space just south of the aforementioned, includes the graves of three adult women, three adult men, two adolescents, and one unidentifiable adult. Two clusters are associated with dwellings in the southeastern corner of the site (Burials 80, 81, 82, 84, on one hand, and Burials 51, 52, 54, on the other). Two clusters are attributable to houses beside the southernmost corner of the town common (Burials 35, 50, 53, 62, 63, 64 in the center and edges of one house and Burials 42, 43, 44, 45 around one hearth). As with the council-house graves, the placement of these people in the ground would have communicated the acknowledgment by their peers of their significant contributions as leaders within their households and perhaps their clans.

My interpretation of these mortuary patterns at Coweeta Creek is that they reflect in part the gender roles adopted and statuses achieved by people during their lifetimes. There are many more male elders than people of other gender categories buried in the council house, indicating that burial in this space was achieved primarily by men rather than inherited by all members of one highly ranked family, which fits ethnohistoric evidence of egalitarianism and gender roles of adult men in Cherokee communities (Perdue 1998:27). Likewise, there are clues that adult women may have been honored by burial in architectural spaces associated with their households; this pattern in the placement of graves at the site is consistent with ethnohistoric evidence about the role of historic Cherokee women as publicly prominent leaders in their clans and households (Perdue 1998:46). The conscious decisions to place male elders in graves within and beside the council house and adult women in village burials most likely reflects the gender ideology prevalent within this protohistoric town.

Older adult men were commonly buried in the Coweeta Creek council house because of their contributions as town leaders. As town leaders, they would have met with one another and perhaps with leaders from other towns within their council house. As warriors and hunters, they likely conducted rituals of purification within their council house before and after journeys away from their hometown. These gender roles would have been remembered during the events at which prominent town leaders were laid to rest, in an architectural space that continued to serve as a community center after their deaths. Their burial in the council house would have confirmed their identities within the living community as significant ancestral town leaders, an identity related closely to gender. I would argue that these interpretations are consistent with written clues about Cherokee gender roles and gender identities during the eighteenth century (see Hill 1997:27; Perdue 1998:40; Sattler 1995:18).

Adult women were commonly buried in the Coweeta Creek village and probably close to the architecture of the households of which they were members during their lives. I would not argue that their exclusion from burial within the council house indicates a lack of power or a lack of public prominence of women within the Coweeta Creek community. I would argue instead that burial in these architectural spaces was consistent with the roles of women as leaders of households and perhaps clans within the Coweeta Creek community. Homes Hogue Wilson (1986:58–61) has described similar spatial patterns in the mortuary program at Warren Wilson along the Swannanoa River in western North Carolina, although there is not a council house at that palisaded village. Sullivan (1987:27–28) has noted comparable patterns in the burials at Ledford Island, along the lower Hiwassee in southeastern Tennessee, where there is a discernible communal building and town plaza beside the village area. At Warren Wilson, graves placed within and beside houses are most commonly those of adult women. At Ledford Island, the same pattern is present with most adult women in graves beside houses. I suggest that the prevalence of prominent women within household cemeteries and even in some cases under household hearths is consistent with ethno-historic evidence of the prominent roles of Cherokee women as clan and household leaders during the eighteenth century (see Hatley 1991:43; Perdue 1998:42; Sattler 1995:228).

Children are found in graves in all architectural spaces at this town. I would argue that the placement of their graves was guided by the status and decision of close clan kin relatives—hence the burials of children with many mortuary goods in the Coweeta Creek council house. I would argue further that people eventually reached an age where their social identities were shaped more by their own accomplishments than by those of their kin—hence the burial of many more male elders than young adult men in the Coweeta Creek council house, even though the numbers of each age group in the burial population are comparable. Mortuary goods are most common in graves of the oldest and youngest people buried at the site.

Of course there are exceptions to these patterns. Some adult women *were* buried in the council house. Many young adult men *were* buried in the village. However, there is a tendency for male elders to have been laid to rest in the council house. Meanwhile, even the adult women with turtle-shell rattles and one ground stone celt are found in the village. Therefore, it seems that there were not vertical distinctions in rank communicated through the placement of some graves within the council house and others in the village. Rather, gender distinctions often were communicated through the location of burials in one architectural space or another within the town. Gender identities of the deceased perhaps were one of the most significant determinants of mortuary treatment by living members of the community.

This relationship between gender and the spatial dimension of mortuary patterns must have paralleled the prevalent gender ideology within the Coweeta Creek community. Men achieved status primarily through their contributions as town leaders and through their interactions with leaders of other towns. Women achieved status primarily through their contributions as leaders of households, which perhaps comprised local members of the same clan. Gender ideology at Coweeta Creek espoused egalitarianism and alternative pathways to prestige rather than subordinate and superordinate rank. Mortuary patterns at Coweeta Creek reflect this gender ideology. Men and women of renown were laid to rest in architectural spaces at Coweeta Creek that became vested with gender symbolism themselves.

Gender Ideology and the Cultural Landscape of the Southern Appalachians

My interpretations of mortuary patterns at Coweeta Creek reflect my opinion that native mortuary ritual in this region was guided by social dynamics within communities for whom the dead became ancestors. My treatment of the mortuary evidence from Coweeta Creek recognizes gender categories related to age groupings of adult males and females. The first premise is only one of many ways in which rituals surrounding the dead may have been related to the social structure and dynamics of communities and to their religious beliefs (Braun 1981; J. A. Brown 1990, 1995; Carr 1995; R. W. Chapman 1981, 1995; Goldstein 1995; Hodder 1984; Howell 1995; Mainfort 1985; Huntington and Metcalf 1979; O'Brien 1995; O'Shea 1984; Shanks and Tilley 1982; Tainter 1978; Tilley 1984; Whelan 1991a, 1991b, 1995). The second premise is potentially problematic, given the presence of third gender categories in many societies (Hollimon 1992:86, 1997:188; Hudson 1976:269, 1990:98). The fit between mortuary patterns at Coweeta Creek and ethnohistoric evidence about leadership in Cherokee communities of southern Appalachia nevertheless lends support to the interpretations put forth here.

Grave goods with men, women, and children, of course, would not have been visible to the community after their placement in the ground. They probably did reflect their contributions to the community during their lifetimes. Thus, there are two male elders with a quiver of seven arrows, in one case, and a rattlesnake gorget and carved stone pipe, in the other. Turtle-shell rattles buried with two different adult women probably represent their status as prominent dancers and ritual leaders. Perhaps the children buried with shell mask gorgets received them as gifts from close clan relatives, because these children may not have lived long enough to make their own marks upon their community. There is not a group of graves whose mortuary artifacts clearly set them apart as hereditary elites within the community, although clearly some people achieved prominence and prestige.

The resting places of certain men, women, and children would not have been forgotten. Some were placed within the council-house space, where significant ritual events would have brought many residents of this and other towns together. Some were placed in the ground close to houses in the village and probably close to those of their own households.

Even though neither the council house nor houses in the village were built specifically as monuments to the dead, they would have served as landmarks for the graves of prominent ancestors. Prominent town leaders were buried in and beside the council house, and adult men are indeed common in graves in this architectural space at Coweeta Creek. My interpretation is that significant household leaders would have been honored with burial close to their houses, publicly communicating their status as leaders of the clans represented by households at Coweeta Creek. This mortuary pattern is visible at the archaeological site representing the historic Cherokee towns of Chota and Tanasee (Sullivan 1995:120), which date to the middle of the eighteenth century. It may have precedents in much earlier towns in southern Appalachia (Sullivan 1987:27), and further study of this phenomenon is warranted.

Gender roles and identities communicated through mortuary ritual became embedded in the built environment of the town at Coweeta Creek; its layout likely paralleled the gender ideology prevalent within the community. Women commonly achieved status through their power within clan kin groups whose local members formed households at Coweeta Creek; clans formed one major social domain in this and other towns in the region. Men often achieved prominence as leaders in the town centered at Coweeta Creek; many of their activities were symbolically related to the architecture of the council house. Thus, there were complementary pathways to prestige in the town at Coweeta Creek. This gender ideology likely contributed to an egalitarian, or perhaps heterarchical, political culture in this part of the upper Little Tennessee River Valley.

The next chapter, by Lynne Sullivan, explores the nature of gender distinctions communicated through mortuary ritual at a town in eastern Tennessee that predates the seventeenth century. Her paper and this chapter, about a protohistoric town in southwestern North Carolina, recommend further archaeological study of gender and power in native communities of the southern Appalachians during the late prehistoric and protohistoric periods.

Author's Note

Many thanks to Hope Spencer, Trawick Ward, Steve Davis, Bennie Keel, Keith Egloff, Brian Egloff, Vin Steponaitis, Stephen Williams, David Moore, Lynne Sullivan, Brett Riggs, David Hally, Margie Scarry, Gerald Schroedl, Tiffiny Tung, Mintcy Maxham, Bram Tucker, Joe Herbert, Tom Hargrove, Randy Daniel, Patrick Livingood, Jane Eastman, Brian Billman, Tom Maher, Tim Mooney, Mark Rees, Rob Beck, Greg Wilson, Pat Lambert, Patricia Samford, Theda Perdue, Amber VanDerwarker, Kathy McDonnell, and anonymous reviewers for their many contributions to this chapter. Thanks to the NSF Graduate Research Fellowship Program for support during graduate school. Thanks to the UNC Research Laboratories of Archaeology for access to their rich archaeological collections. Any problems with this paper are my responsibility.

Notes

1. Patricia Lambert identified the sex and age at death of individuals in the burials at Coweeta Creek and many other sites in western North Carolina as part of the NAGPRA inventory of collections at the RLA (Davis et al. 1996).

2. Tom Maher and the late Tim Mooney photographed grave goods from this and many other sites in western North Carolina for the NAGPRA inventory of archaeological collections at the RLA (Davis et al. 1996).

3. Archaeologists Trawick Ward and Stephen Davis (1999:236–37) have argued that smoking changed from a ritual event to a widespread cultural practice during and after the colonial trade had reached deeply into the lives of native people in northern and central North Carolina.

4. Marvin Smith and Julie Barnes Smith (1989:14–16) have shown that engraved shell masks may have been closely related to warfare and hunting ritual in many different areas in late prehistoric southeastern North America.

5. Thanks to Stephen Davis (1990) for help in identifying the raw material of these arrowheads as Knox black chert.

6. Thanks to Randy Daniel (1998) for the suggestion that the raw material for this triangular point might represent rhyolite or other metavolcanic material from the Piedmont region.

⋊ 5 ⋊

Those Men in the Mounds

Gender, Politics, and Mortuary Practices in Late Prehistoric Eastern Tennessee

Lynne P. Sullivan

The men were somewhat specialized among themselves in their political, religious, and military roles, and they ranked themselves serially with respect to each other. Except for kinship roles, the women were relatively undifferentiated.

Charles M. Hudson (1976:260)

The politics of kinship are fundamental to understanding the organization of many Mississippian communities.

R. B. Lewis (1996:153)

The social and political dynamics of ranked societies, including the roles of elites and the nature of their political power, are topics of considerable debate among archaeologists investigating the late prehistoric (i.e., Mississippian) chiefdoms of the southeastern United States (e.g., Anderson 1994; Barker and Pauketat 1992; Blitz 1999; Emerson 1997; Hally 1996; Knight 1990; Knight and Steponaitis 1998; Milner 1998; Muller 1997; Pauketat 1994; Scarry 1996; Welch 1991; Williams and Shapiro 1990). The degree to which elite status and leadership roles were inherited or achieved, the means by which leaders maintained and manipulated power, and how dissension, factionalism, and resistance influenced the rise (and fall) of chiefs all are at issue.

Ongoing research is delineating the specifics of chiefdom development in southeastern subregions. As the historical trajectories of individual areas are mapped out, we are beginning to see considerable variation within the larger region. For example, some subregions, such as the Black Warrior River Valley in Alabama, witnessed a long-term consolidation of chiefly power at the Moundville site (Knight and Steponaitis 1998; Welch 1996), while other areas, such as eastern Tennessee, never or perhaps only very briefly coalesced into a large, centralized chiefdom (Boyd and Schroedl 1987; Hally 1994b; Hally, Smith, and Langford 1990). In this latter area, many smaller chiefly polities dotted the landscape, (Hatch 1987); at times, some may have become allied, consolidated, or even vanquished, as leaders competed for followers and attempted to turn circumstances to their own advantage.

The study of mortuary practices has proved an important tool for identifying elite individuals, including presumed leaders, and for inferring the composition of elite groups (J. A. Brown 1981, 1995; O'Shea 1984; Peebles and Kus 1977). Many studies of Mississippian mortuary programs interpret as elites those burials associated with prestige goods and interred in public places, such as mounds and/or public buildings. The majority of such individuals are adult males (e.g., Anderson 1996; Hatch 1974; Peebles 1974), a circumstance typically interpreted as implying that men were the political leaders and wielded more political power than women in these societies. Such interpretations are reinforced by accounts of early chroniclers, especially those of the Mississippi Valley (e.g., Tregle 1975), who detail the political activities of, and offices held by, men (see, for example, Scarry 1992; M. T. Smith and Hally 1992). On the other hand, in some areas of the Southeast, women sometimes are mentioned as holding chiefly office (Trocolli 1999), with the chiefdom of Cofitachequi in present-day South Carolina as the oft-cited example (DePratter 1994).

Southeastern tribes are not necessarily portrayed as having political structures dominated by men when ethnohistorical research is geared to recognize gender bias in firsthand accounts of historic native societies. Furthermore, all southeastern groups were (and are) not the same in how or how much political influence and power women wield. For example, Sattler (1995) discusses variation in the degree of political influence of women among eighteenth- and early nineteenth-century Muskogee (Creek) and Cherokee, which he describes as representing "the two extremes regarding gender status in the Southeast" (Sattler 1995:216). He notes that Cherokee women held offices as clan leaders, controlled agricultural production, and were much more politically influential than women among their Creek neighbors.

I argue that gender-related differences observed in Mississippian mortuary programs in eastern Tennessee correlate with gender-specific differences in political leadership and in how men and women acquired prestige. Mortuary data from the Dallas phase (ca. A.D. 1200–1600) Toqua site suggests gendered political spheres similar to those of the historic Cherokee in which women wielded considerable political influence. This finding does not necessarily indicate ethnic continuity between the prehistoric chiefdoms of the Upper Tennessee Valley and the historic Cherokee, nor does it imply similar gender and power relationships for all Mississippian groups. This research does suggest that a long-standing "balance of power" of the genders may relate to the history of chiefdom development characteristic of this southeastern subregion.

Politics, Gender, and "Public versus Domestic" Contexts

The ability to wield political power, influence, and authority is entwined with an individual's social rank and prestige. Elevated social rank often carries with it the potential to affect political decision making, but actual use of this potential is contingent upon culturally constructed and sanctioned contexts. Such contexts may include the way(s) social rank is determined, the particular social institutions to which one's elite status (and presumed prestige) is attached, as well as an individual's age and gender. The means and ability to express political power thus may vary according to contexts and historical circumstances. Different venues for political expression do not inherently imply different degrees of power, influence, or authority, or dominance of one group over another. When evaluating the political roles and effectiveness of various groups, one must be aware of the possibilities of multiple venues and for different groups to have more or less power depending upon circumstances and contexts, as well as different ways to affect decision making.

The concept of "heterarchy" (Crumley 1995; Levy 1995) is appropriate to this discussion, as it allows for multiple lines of empowerment in different contexts and circumstances (Nelson 1997:148). Crumley (1995:3) defines heterarchy as "the relation of elements to one another when they are unranked or when they possess the potential for being ranked in a number of different ways." Rather than a strictly hierarchical arrangement of men over women, gender may well have been a heterarchical context in some prehistoric southeastern societies, in the sense that men may have exercised more influence and power in some contexts, and women in others. As Miller (1993:4) states: "Assessing the existence of sex and gender hierarchies demands that we look more closely than the level of 'society'. . . . Sensitivity to subgroup and context-based variation existing within more general patterns provides a richer picture of sex and gender hierarchies."

Crumley (1995:3) further observes that "power can be counterpoised rather than ranked" (see also Sillitoe 1985). An arrangement that afforded power and influence to women in one context and to men in another may have created a set of checks and balances on political power and action. Among the Cherokee, for example, such a balance of power relates to decisions concerning intersocietal conflict (i.e., war) (Sattler 1995:222). Although the men controlled the war organization, Cherokee women could reject the men's decision to go to war.

Such gender-related distinctions in political influence and prestige, as well as counterposition of power between the genders, receive little consideration in the archaeological literature of the prehistoric Southeast (N. M. White 1999). This state of affairs is all the more unsatisfactory given the Southeast's well-documented matrilineal kinship systems, matrilocal residence, marked sexual division of labor, and historically known female chiefs. A relevant point about chiefdoms, matrilocal domestic organization, and women's status is made by Harris (1993:66). He states that in "chiefdoms which typically engage in warfare with distant enemies . . . external warfare enhances rather than worsens the status of women since it results in avunculocal or matrilocal domestic organization." According to Harris, this residence pattern comes about because when a man is gone from the village for long periods of time, the woman he can trust most with his possessions is his sister, since she shares a common interest in property. "Where matrilocality prevails . . . women tend to take control of the entire domestic sphere of life [but] . . . the effects of matrilocality on women's status extend beyond the domestic sphere. As men transfer the responsibility for managing the cultivation of their lands to female kin, women come to possess the means for influencing political, military, and religious policies" (Harris 1993:67–68).

Nelson (1997:131) notes that an early debate in feminist cultural anthropology was whether or not most cultures were divided "into domestic spheres and public spheres, gendered female and male, respectively." Friedl (1967) made the important observation that "women's status may be low in the public domain of most societies, but it may be high, even dominant, relative to males in the domestic domain" (Miller 1993:7). Furthermore, the valuation of "public" over "domestic" is a direct influence of western European ideology and historical traditions that may have no relevance in nonwestern cultures (MacCormack 1980; Mathews 1985;

Rosaldo 1980; Rothstein 1982; Sudarkasa 1981). To be useful, public/ domestic and male/female dichotomies must be situated within broader conceptual schemes that organize particular cultures (Mukhopadhyay and Higgins 1988:481). The public sphere does not always contain and dominate the domestic sphere, nor is domestic always devalued relative to public. Various cultures define "domestic" and "public," and associate these spheres with femaleness and maleness, in different ways. Considering the public and domestic spheres as separate and distinct worlds fails to recognize that they are aspects of the same cultural tradition (Bujra 1979; Yanagisako and Collier 1987). As Hendon (1996:46–47) notes, the stereotypical domestic unit, "the household[,] is, in effect, politicized in that its internal relations are inextricable from the larger economic and political structure of society. . . . Domestic action and relations . . . are of larger political and economic significance precisely because they are not separable from the relationships and processes that make up the 'public domain'. . . . Household relations and actions are not isolated from society as a whole nor do they merely react passively to changes imposed from outside."

These cross-cultural findings allow archaeologists to envision "women in many past cultures" not only "as acting publicly, with earned prestige or legitimate power" (Nelson 1997:132) but as influential and powerful actors and producers within households and domestic kin units. Such interpretations have been damped in the Southeast because of a focus on the public political arena, which early (male) observers describe in many southeastern societies as mainly a male one (Gearing 1962; Hudson 1976; Swanton 1946). Women's relative invisibility in this public sphere does not necessarily mean they lacked prestige or power (Mukhopadhyay and Higgins 1988), and it is not a new idea that women's political participation often takes the form of influence "behind the scenes" (see, e.g., Friedl 1967; Lamphere 1974) (Albeit these "male scenes" may well have been "behind the female scenes" in certain contexts.)

Nonetheless, a higher regard for public positions of authority held by men and the assumption that these public roles correlate with male dominance pervades the early accounts of southeastern societies and has, by extension, influenced archaeological thinking. The presumption of male dominance through political leadership for all Mississippian societies, based on the predominance of male burials in southeastern platform mounds (i.e., public structures), is, I suggest, an example of how such Eurocentric constructs have been adopted in archaeological interpretation. The following brief review of pertinent ethnohistoric information provides several important lessons for considering the archaeological record of the late prehistoric Southeast.

Politics and Gender in Historic Native Societies of the Southeast

"Each culture must select a sex-role plan—that is, a template for the organization of sex role expectations. . . . Such plans help men and women orient themselves as male and female to each other, to the world around them, and to the growing boys and girls whose behavior they must shape to a commonly accepted mold" (Sanday 1981:3). Hudson (1976:260) states that in the native societies of the Southeast, "the roles of men and women were so different that the two sexes were almost like different species." There were differences among southeastern native societies as to how elite status, political influence, and prestige were allocated that had bearing on the degree of political influence of women. In general, social institutions separated men and women, set them upon separate tracks, and contextualized how and when in their lives men or women could expect to be politically influential.

In many southeastern societies, as males matured, they progressed through a series of age grades that related to social roles within the society (Gearing 1962:18). Young men also received war ranks and were expected to participate in war parties. "One of the main preoccupations of Southeastern Indian men was the acquisition of war names and titles" (Hudson 1976:325). The war organization, an almost exclusively male domain, was the realm in which men were best able to achieve prestige. In most societies, the warriors were divided into ranks correlating with war-earned achievements. As men progressed through the ranks of the war organization, they collected symbols of prestige as public recognition of their prowess and bravery. Numerous sources mention the use or presentation of objects to men in recognition of their achievements as warriors, in conjunction with bestowal of titles (Hudson 1976:325–26; Swanton 1946:696). This specific mode of advancement was by and large a male-dominated trajectory. By age fifty to sixty, a male ceased going to war. Instead, he might assume an important role in guiding the community and serve as an advisor and councilor. Among the Cherokee, for example, the elder age status "beloved man" carried much prestige and influence (Gearing 1962:18).

Gender bias in early ethnohistoric accounts leaves us with little information on the life trajectories of women. Although men often moved through a strict hierarchy of social and political prestige, partially based on age, there is not such a clearly defined pattern for females. Nonetheless, household matriarchs would have ties of obligation over their progeny. These ties are an important source of women's prestige and power that correlate with an increase in women's status with age in many cultures (J. K. Brown and Kerns 1985), especially in matrilineal societies such as those of the Southeast. Crown and Fish (1996) note several cross-cultural studies reporting that postmenopausal women often acquired increased prestige and/or special status, and sometimes participated with men in political and religious activities from which younger women were excluded. They (Crown and Fish 1996) also find that the prestige of Classic-period Hohokam women increased with age, as reflected in burial patterns.

Such general life trajectories for men and women were common to many southeastern groups, but the accompanying contexts that determined elite status were quite variable. Inheritance and achievement both were ways in which elite status could be gained, but the degree to which each of these methods was followed varied among societies. The Muskogee (Creek) and Cherokee examples offered by Sattler (1995) illustrate these points. Although these groups share many similar cultural traditions (including matrilineal descent and matrilocal residence), leadership positions and prestige depended more upon inheritance among the Creek than among the Cherokee. Sattler (1995) also relates differences in women's access to political office and their degree of political influence to these distinctions in determining elite status and leadership positions. His data pertain to the eighteenth and early nineteenth centuries, although he notes that many of the practices and beliefs continue to the present, as he has observed in field studies in Oklahoma.

Creek sociopolitical organization included a local chiefdom (*italwa*), headed by a hereditary chief (*mikko*). These local chiefdoms were subsumed into larger, regional chiefdoms under a paramount chief. Cross-cutting Creek society were exogamous clans and phratries, grouped into moieties that tended to be endogomous within *italwa*. Clans were headed by male elders (*achulaki*), but most other leadership positions were held by members of the *mikko*'s clan or dispensed by this clan to others as patronage. Of the thirty-four clans, only three (that of the *mikko* and two others) held the majority of offices; these clans, then, formed an elite. Heredity, through clan membership, thus was an important factor in determining who was of elite status in Muskogee society, although some offices, particularly in the war organization, could be achieved through individual accomplishment. Furthermore, women did not hold political office or serve as clan heads and thus lacked direct, formal access to power. In general, women in Creek society were not viewed by men as valued political advisors (Sattler 1995).

Elite status in Cherokee society was much less dependent upon ascription. With the exception of the position of town chief (*uku*), which was clan-specific, increased rank of individuals was based mainly on achievement, including an individual's age. Cherokee towns were more autonomous than the Creek *italwa*. Households and lineages represented seven exogamous, matrilineal clans which were not ranked relative to each other, but the clan of the *uku* may have been slightly superior. Senior women of the clans held positions of "Beloved Women" and had considerable influence in beginning or ending wars and in the fate of prisoners; their counsel was highly valued by the male leaders (Sattler 1995).

According to Sattler (1995), a major difference in Cherokee women's power, as compared with Muskogee women, was that Cherokee women maintained control of agricultural production. Although fields were "owned" by the matrilineal clans in both groups, Creek women in the historic period farmed only small garden plots near the houses, while the men worked larger fields away from the settlements and controlled the resulting produce. In contrast, Cherokee women controlled both the land and the produce.

Economic roles of women are directly related to female rank, so much so that some researchers view economics as a primary variable affecting female status (Mukhopadhyay and Higgins 1988). Sattler (1995) points out that since generosity is a requisite of high rank and political power, control of agricultural produce was an important means for Muskogee men to wield political influence. Such control also would have been a factor in Cherokee women's relatively high level of political influence. Marxist theorists link control over the means of production to increased power and status of women (Leacock 1981).

The most important aspect of Sattler's work for archaeological interpretations is that it shows that we should expect neither that men and women had equivalent roles nor that women had equal power in all southeastern groups. Within and among different groups, there likely were different venues for men and women to become politically influential, exert power, and achieve prestige. Also, the range of statuses and political influence available to women was not necessarily the same in every subregion or cultural context. In short, the archaeological presumption that the predominance of male burials in Mississippian mounds always denotes male political dominance is too simplistic to fit the potential range of variation indicated by the ethnographic record.

Mortuary Practices and Mississippian Sociopolitics

Until recently, most studies of the social dimensions of mortuary practices focused on ascertaining aspects of hierarchical relationships. Delineating the degree to which ascription defined elite status was an important research objective for initial studies of Mississippian mortuary programs (J. A. Brown 1971; Goldstein 1980; Hatch 1974, 1976; Peebles 1974) as researchers sought to understand the archaeological correlates of chiefdoms and institutionalized authority (Peebles and Kus 1977). The individuals interred in and around mounds, often with elaborate arrays of funerary objects, were recognized as the archaeological manifestation of chiefly elites. These individuals became the focus of attention because they were the potential "redistributors," ideologues, faction leaders, and controllers of sumptuary goods, trade, and/or surplus, among other possible venues of political power and prestige.

The demographics of elite burials are an important consideration in determining whether heredity was a significant criterion for elite status. The presence of infants and young children in elite burial programs is prima facie evidence of inherited status, since these individuals would not have been able to achieve high status based on their own abilities (J. A. Brown 1981). James Brown (1981:30) also points out that "any statistically significant departure from a 'normal' age/sex curve points to differential recruitment of a particular age and sex category into specific status groups." Many burial populations associated with Mississippian mounds include some women and children, but predominantly comprise adult males. Such demographics are interpreted as indicating that heredity was a factor in gaining elite status, due to the presence of women and children, but not the only factor. Achievement of elite status apparently also was an option, and accounts for the "extra" males in elite burial programs (see, for example, Peebles 1974). Why this option was open only to males is a topic that is not addressed in the literature.

Models of Mississippian sociopolitics thus typically propose elite status as being based on a combination of heredity and achievement. High rank was a privilege of birth for a small segment of a population and consequently included women and children as well as adult males. Persons outside of this kin group also could attain elite status through personal achievement. This latter venue presumably was open mainly to adult males. These models of Mississippian society pose adult males as the wielders of political power because they are the predominant members of the identified elite groups; they are buried in mounds. These interpretations fit well with the accounts of early European explorers who describe, with very few exceptions, male chiefs, councilors, war leaders, and statesmen as the leaders of southeastern groups (Feinman and Neitzel 1984). Viewed along this particular axis, men do indeed appear to dominate the social and political hierarchies of Mississippian societies, but this view may well be one through the blinders of our Eurocentric notions of "public" and "domestic."

As we have seen from cross-cultural information, the reason men predominate in this public dimension may well be that it is a gendered dimension. Ethnohistoric information from the Southeast suggests that one possible venue through which women were empowered politically was as leaders of "horizontal" social dimensions, such as households, kin groups, or clans. The search for horizontal social dimensions in mortuary practices has proved a more difficult objective than identifying the "vertical" dimension of rank (O'Shea 1984). O'Shea (1984) provides a detailed discussion, but basically the problem is that markers for such groups are not readily identifiable in the archaeological record. This problem may further add to the invisibility of women as active players on the political landscape.

While we cannot readily identify clan groups in southeastern mortuary populations, we can look more closely at mortuary programs for gender dimensions. One assumption of modern archaeological analyses of mortuary practices is that the social persona, or overall status composite of an individual, is symbolized in funerary behavior (J. A. Brown 1981:28). Gender obviously is one component of a social persona. Bivariate analyses of artifact associations with the biological sex of skeletons often are used to identify suites of artifacts that correlate with males as opposed to females. One must be careful to distinguish between biological sex and the culturally constructed concept of gender (Miller 1993:4–7; Nelson 1997:15), but for the majority of a population, gender roles do tend to correlate with an individual's biological sex. General inferences about cultural constructions of gender in prehistory thus can be made by examining patterning in mortuary treatments as it pertains to biological sex.

From the cross-cultural and ethnohistoric evidence discussed above, we can pose several hypotheses about prestigious and politically influential women in late prehistoric chiefdoms of the Southeast. First, if women generally were on a "slow track" in terms of achievement of prestige—as compared with men, whose warrior experience allowed them to increase their status at an earlier age—mortuary treatments for males and females should show differences that correlate with age. Although increased age should signal increased prestige for both sexes, male burials should show evidence that men generally gained prestige at an earlier age than women. This patterning would not preclude the possibility that some women achieved higher rank at an earlier age by participating in other activities, nor would it preclude both males and females having access to elite status because of inheritance.

A corollary to such a trend pertains to older females in a population. Based on the ethnohistoric models, in those native southeastern societies in which women have considerable political power, the most prestigious and powerful women are the matriarchs, who served as heads of households, and the senior women of matrilineal clans. Older adult women are the likeliest candidates for matriarch status because they have had the most time to develop their power bases and to outlive potential rivals. The mortuary treatments of older women are likely to differ from those of their male cohort but should flag these women as prestigious individuals, perhaps of rank equal to older men. In other words, if women gained prestige on a different "track" than men, it is quite possible that by the time women reached maturity, the prestige differences with men may have evened out.

Differences in the public versus domestic spheres of males and females also may have influenced the mortuary practices for the genders. The concern of Mississippian peoples with spatial arrangements is well-known (see, for example, Goldstein 1980; Knight 1998; Sullivan 1987). Hudson (1976:260) notes that spatial segregation was a component of gender relations in many southeastern groups: "men and women kept themselves separate from each other to a very great extent. . . . They seem, in fact, to have preferred to carry out their day-to-day activities apart from each other. During the day the women worked with each other around their households, while the men resorted to their town house or square ground." At council meetings, a great deal of attention was paid to the seating arrangement of the various social and political positions (Gearing 1962:24; Hudson 1976:203–20; Swanton 1946:174–241). Spatial distinctions in burial locations for the genders could "mask" prestigious women, because mounds and public areas are presumed to be the most prestigious places of interment for both sexes regardless of how prestige was earned. Different patterns of burial location for "elders" of both sexes may indicate differences in how prestige is symbolized for members of different gender groups.

Rodning's (1999a) study of Qualla phase mortuary practices demonstrates that such research, when attuned to the potential of separate gender dimensions, can recognize women as active players in a sociopolitical landscape. The Qualla phase of the Appalachian Summit is assumed by many archaeologists to represent the archaeological record of the Cherokee in that area from the fifteenth to eighteenth centuries. Rodning's (1999a) analysis of mortuary practices at the Coweeta Creek site shows differential patterning based on the biological sex of skeletons. Burials associated with a large public structure (i.e. a communal, nonresidential structure or "townhouse") are predominantly adult males, while the majority of women are buried in association with houses. Differences in grave associations between the sexes mainly are of kind rather than quality, although there are males in the townhouse group and adult females in the village who are interred with distinctive suites of objects.

Rodning (1999a) interprets these patterns as representing the male and female roles of town and clan leaders, respectively. The locations of the burials correlate with the architecture that represents these two dimensions of community political leadership: the townhouse, which represents the Cherokee "male" domain of town leadership in the realms of trade, diplomacy, warfare, and ceremony; and the households, which represent the Cherokee "female" domain of kinship groups and, in particular, clan leadership. Males and females gained prestige and the ability to affect political decision making through these different venues, and, as Rodning (1996) notes, "these alternative avenues . . . would have complemented each other rather than representing vertically differentiated dimensions of a social hierarchy."

The Chota-Tanasee site, a Cherokee town in the Little Tennessee River Valley dating to the eighteenth century (Schroedl 1986b), also shows similar mortuary patterns (Rodning 1996; Schroedl and Breitburg 1986; Sullivan 1995). Although after European contact the Little Tennessee River Valley was home to the Overhill Cherokee, the relationship of the prehistoric and protohistoric Mississippian occupants of this valley (and, indeed, the rest of the Upper Tennessee River Valley) to the Cherokee is a long-debated issue (Schroedl 1986a). My intent is not to enter into this debate here but instead to examine whether the political status of women in the Mississippian societies of this area is more similar to the ethnographic model offered by the Cherokee or to that of the Muskogee, based on the work of Sattler (1995) and Rodning (1996). We turn to the Mississippian-period, Dallas phase of the upper Tennessee River Valley to examine these ideas.

The East Tennessee Case

The Dallas phase, originally defined by Thomas Lewis and Madeline Kneberg (1946; T. M. N. Lewis, Kneberg Lewis, and Sullivan 1995), is the major Mississippian complex in the upper Tennessee River Valley and dates to A.D. 1300–1600 (Schroedl, Boyd, and Davis 1990). Much of the current thinking about Dallas phase sociopolitical organization rests on Hatch's (1974) regional study of Dallas mortuary practices, which used data from nineteen sites. Hatch (1974:112–13) noted gender-specific differences in burial locations and the kinds of artifacts associated with the sexes, which led him to "hypothesize the general tendency in Dallas sites for adult males to be of a different status than are females of all ages." His study found significant correlations of mound interment with adult males. Burials also occur in village contexts, and the majority of individuals interred in these contexts are female. Hatch posited that these differences had to do with differing statuses of men and women, but he did not further explore the nature of these differences (nor, in some cases, would the data have been sufficient to do so). Hatch assumed, like most other researchers examining hierarchical organization in Mississippian chiefdoms, that the data indicate that men mostly outranked women.

After Hatch's study, research was completed at the Toqua site, a Dallas town in the Little Tennessee River Valley with two mounds. The occupation of the Toqua site spans the entire Dallas phase (Lengyel, Eighmy, and Sullivan 1999). A mid-eighteenth-century Cherokee component also is present at the site. Scott and Polhemus's (1987) study of the social dimensions of Dallas mortuary practices at Toqua produced similar results to those of Hatch, in that the majority of the mound population consists of adult males, several of whom were interred with large sets of prestige goods. They propose that "while there is an indication of ascribed status at Toqua, this is not a dominant means of social ranking. Status at Toqua has both ascribed and achieved characteristics which appear to exist simultaneously" (Scott and Polhemus 1987:398–99). They also offer this intriguing observation: "Although there is no clear evidence of a paramount chief at Toqua, there is a group of high status individuals within the site. . . . [The mortuary program suggests] a model of two social levels comprised of high status lineage elders and commoners. The presence of an apical class of adult males in the mounds was not uniquely set apart from females or other high status burials in the village" (Scott and Polhemus 1987:397–98).

A complete reexamination of the Dallas mortuary data is beyond the scope of this chapter, but we can look more closely at the data from one site, Toqua, to investigate differences in women's and men's statuses. A cautionary note about this preliminary analysis is that it is necessary, for the sake of sample size, to treat the Dallas phase occupation at Toqua as a static unit. Changes in statuses of the genders undoubtedly occurred over the several-hundred-year span of this phase. The research results thus show only very general patterns.

Mortuary Patterns and Gender at the Toqua Site

Parham's (1987) demographic study of the Toqua skeletal series provides relevant information. The Toqua sample includes 439 individuals from the Dallas phase. Male life expectancy was slightly longer than that of females: 20.80 years, as opposed to 18.62 years. Female mortality increased between ages fifteen and twenty-five and that of males between twenty and twenty-five (fig. 5.1a). Parham (1987:443) attributes the increase in female mortality to childbearing and notes that the twenty to twenty-five age bracket for males may represent "prime years for participation in warfare and hunting activities." After age thirty, life expectancies for the sexes are parallel (fig. 5.1b).

Parham (1987) assumed that the mound population represents the highest-status individuals at Toqua and compared the age and gender distributions of the skeletal populations in the mounds to those in the village. He found that the mortality rate for younger males (under age thirty) in the Toqua mounds is considerably higher than that of the male village burials. He suggests this difference may be due to greater participation in hunting and warfare by those males in the mound population. Such skills would have allowed these males to achieve sufficient prestige for mound interment.

Parham also found that mortality was considerably higher for younger females (under age twenty) in the mound population than for those in the village. He interprets these differences as implying that high-status females (i.e., those interred in the mound) were marrying younger than their lower-status (i.e., village) counterparts and encountering greater difficulties in childbirth due to their younger age. He (Parham 1987: 548) further relates the apparent shorter life span of the mound females, as compared with the males, to the possible sacrifice of these younger women upon the death of their high-status husbands—an idea based on Blakely's (1977) work.

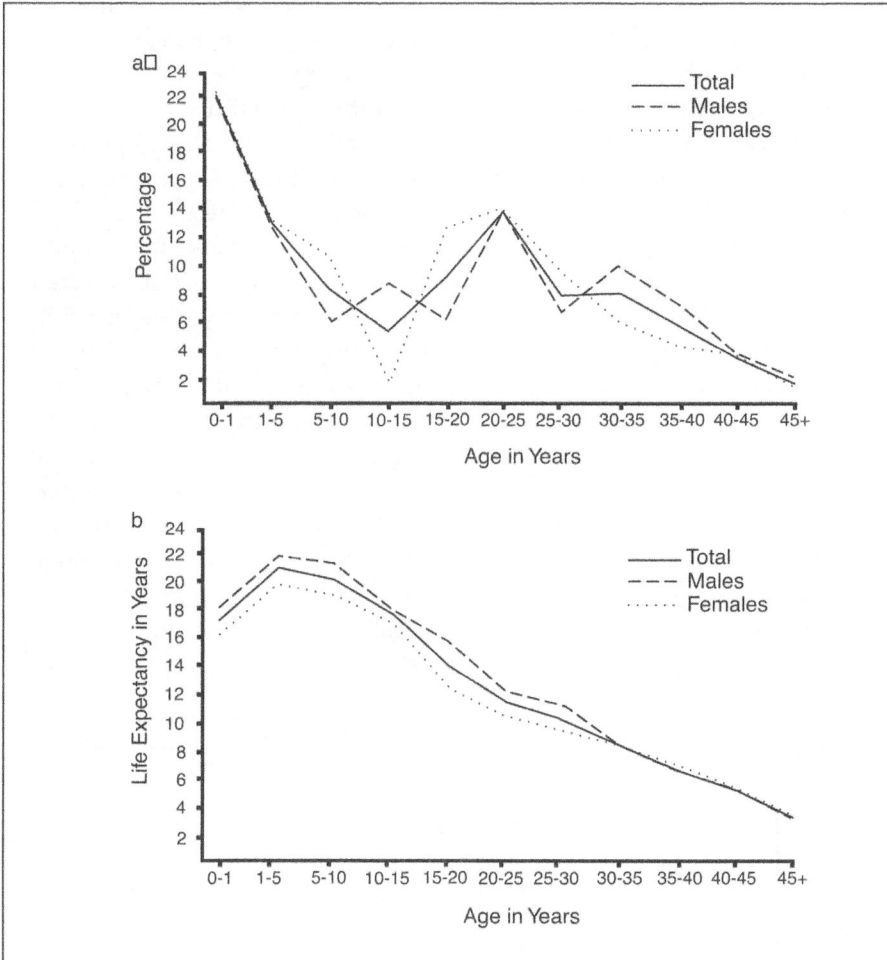

Fig. 5.1. Demographics of the Toqua burial population (from Parham 1987:447–51).

Parham's analysis is a classic example of what Nelson (1997:133) calls the "double standard" in archaeological interpretation—a mindset that causes a male in a "rich" burial to be interpreted as a leader, while an equally prominent female burial is seen as a leader's wife. The differences Parham observed in age-group representations in the Toqua mounds and village can be interpreted in another way: The distributions of male and female burials in the mound and village may well relate to the different life trajectories of men and women and the different ways in which they achieved prestige.

Simple comparisons of age cohorts by burial locations (mound versus village) and sex show patterns similar to those observed by Parham (figs. 5.2 and 5.3) and illustrate important differences in the distributions of males and females. Data are drawn from Polhemus (1987: appendix D). Of the total adult population (older than fifteen years) that could be assigned both sex and age (n = 150), fifty-three individuals (35 percent) were interred in the mounds. Thirty-three individuals (62 percent) in the mound population are male, and twenty (38 percent) are female.

Young males (ages twenty to twenty-nine) are the most likely candidates for mound burial. The percentages of male individuals interred in mounds steadily rise from age fifteen through twenty-nine (fig. 5.2). After a peak in mound interment at age twenty-five to twenty-nine, the percentages of males buried in the mound decrease until the oldest age bracket (forty and above), when the percentage of males buried in the mound again rises. The pattern of age representation for females in the mound is quite different. In sharp contrast to the male pattern, the percentages of females in the age fifteen though twenty-nine brackets steadily decrease, then increase for females in their early thirties. The percentage of females between the ages of thirty-five and thirty-nine buried in the mound equals that of men. But the eldest females, those age forty and older, are not represented in the mound at all.

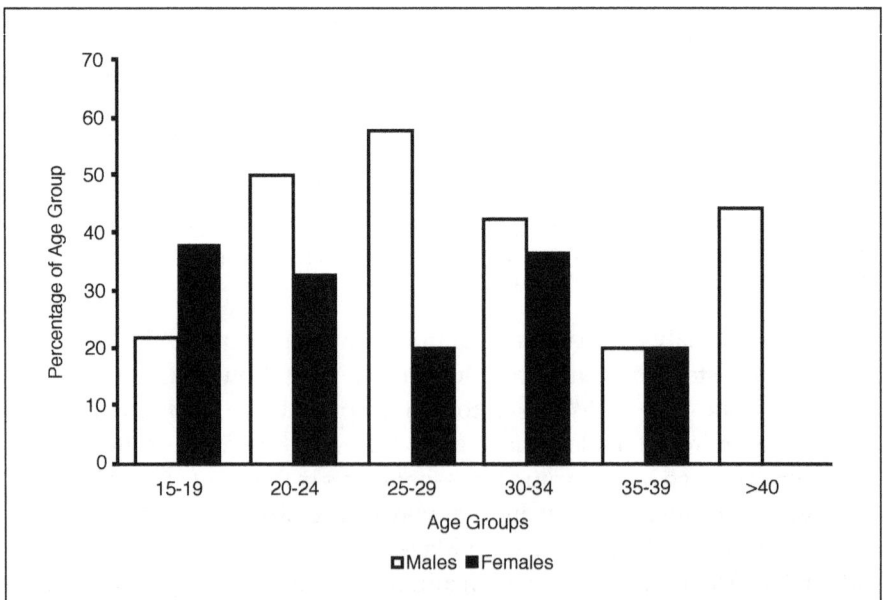

Fig. 5.2. Adult mound interments at Toqua by age cohort and sex.

The patterns for village interments mirror those of the mounds (fig. 5.3). Very young males (ages fifteen to nineteen), women in their late twenties, males and females in their late thirties, and women over forty are the most likely candidates for village burial. Individuals of both sexes aged thirty to thirty-four years more often were buried in the village than in the mounds, but the representation of males and females is nearly equal in both burial locations. All females in the age forty and older cohort are interred in the village.

As Parham suggests, a possible explanation for the increasing representation of young adult males in the mounds is their participation in the war organization. Being a warrior in nearly every southeastern society earned men prestige at relatively young ages. A "benefit" of such prestige could well have been mound interment. If females did not have the same access to this method of prestige enhancement, it makes sense that their representation in the mounds would not increase during the young adult years.

The representation of older men in the mounds may relate to the transition from warrior to roles of older men. Gearing (1962) discusses such a transition among the Cherokee and points out that few men were equally competent warriors and statesmen. It would take time for those men

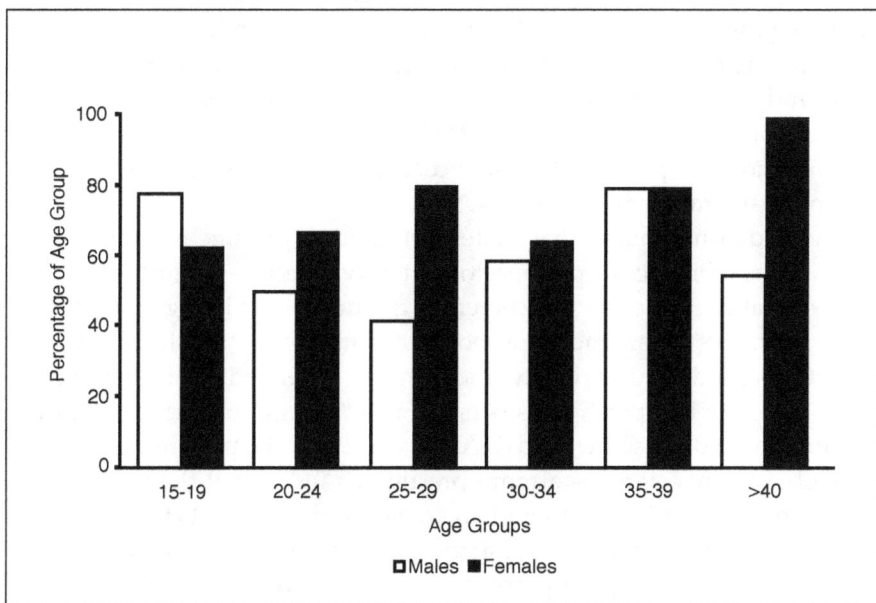

Fig. 5.3. Adult village interments at Toqua by age cohort and sex.

having the latter qualities to become recognized as such. Perhaps the relatively low percentages of men in their thirties who merited mound burial may reflect this phenomenon. Those who had appropriate talents as elders were recognized in death with mound burial.

If we were to rely strictly on mound burial as an indicator of prestige, we would have to conclude that women in the Toqua population actually lost prestige with age. Except for a rise in representation of the early thirties age group, over all, female representation in the mounds declines with age. This pattern is exactly the opposite of what one would expect if mound burial had equal meaning for both men and women. After a marked increase in the early thirties, female representation in the mound declines, with none of the eldest women in the population receiving mound burial.

As Scott and Polhemus (1987) note, there is evidence at Toqua (as in most Mississippian burial populations) that achievement-based prestige is entwined with inheritance of social rank and corresponding prestige. The presence of young children and infants in the Toqua mound population attests to ascription as a factor in determining rank (J. A. Brown 1981). Interment of young females in the mound probably has more to do with their inherited status than with their own accomplishments, as they would not have had time to achieve increased rank. But why are the oldest females in the population not buried in the mounds? Based on cross-cultural and ethnographic research, these "grandmothers" of the community should be among its most accomplished and beloved members and the women most likely to be politically influential. If we rely on mound burial as the sole symbol of "elite status," with its corresponding connotations for power and influence, the eldest women are eliminated from consideration as high status.

An additional data set that relates to individual prestige as symbolized in mortuary practices—presence of funerary objects—suggests another interpretation. Funerary objects reflect gestures of the living toward the deceased. A tenet of studies of mortuary practices is that, in general, a prestigious individual will have more energy expended on his/her grave than a non- or less-prestigious person. Such "energy" may take the form of amount of disposed wealth (J. A. Brown 1995). The presence of funerary objects thus signifies a more prestigious individual than someone with no such offerings (although in archaeological contexts the possibility of perishable items as grave associations must be kept in mind).

A graph depicting the percentage of individuals with at least one funerary object in each adult age cohort shows that the percentage of females buried with objects steadily increases from age fifteen through thirty (fig. 5.4). At the same time that younger adult women are being excluded from mound interment, they are becoming more and more likely to be buried in the village with some type of grave offering. The percentage of males interred with at least one object also rises with age, but not as sharply as for women (fig. 5.4). During the male "role transition" period of the fourth decade of life, the percentage of males buried with objects does not increase at the same rate as that of the women. Both sexes show a marked drop in percentages interred with objects in the oldest age bracket, an interesting phenomenon that is investigated further below.

Taken together, these trends point to an alternate burial program for women—burial in the village in the location of their houses—as they become older and presumably increasingly responsible for managing households (fig. 5.5). Mound interment for men is consistent with an increase in prestige during the younger adult years, when males would have been active in the war organization (fig. 5.6). In fact, it is males of this age group who are the main source of the discrepancy between male

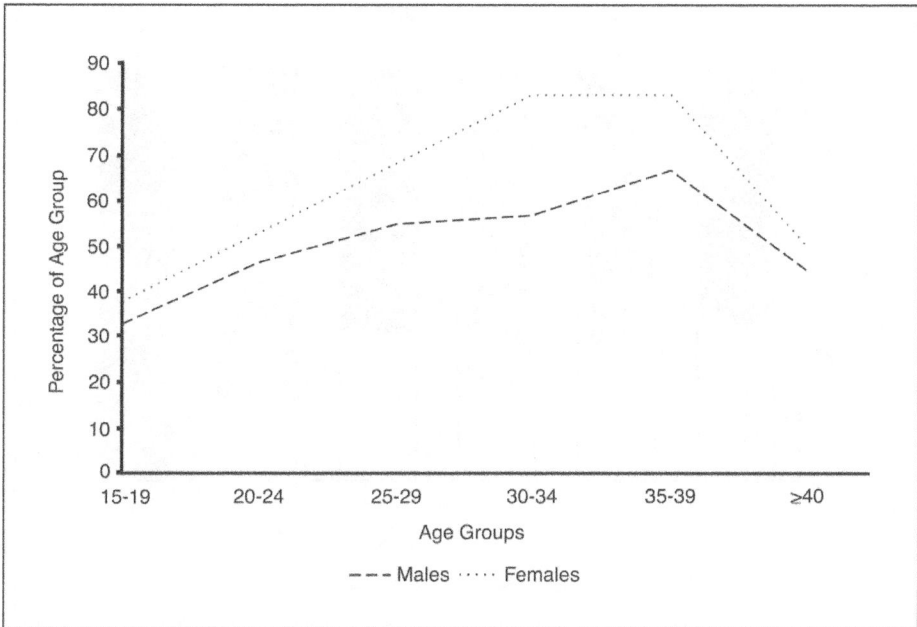

Fig. 5.4. Adult individuals associated with funerary objects at Toqua by age cohorts and sex.

and female representation in the mounds. After age thirty, there is much less difference in the representation of the sexes in the mounds, with the exception of the very oldest members of the population. The general trend is for women to be less likely candidates for mound burial as they age. This trend does not correlate with decreased likelihood of being buried with grave offerings. These patterns suggest that village burial for women does not necessarily correlate with decreased prestige or social standing. In fact, burial in a house may be as much of a material "accouterment" for a female as are some symbolically charged objects interred with males.

The existence of a separate mortuary program for women does not, in and of itself, indicate that women were in positions to influence the political decisions of men. However, it does show that mortuary programs at Toqua are indeed gendered, and that the spatial dimensions of these programs correlate with the spheres of influence and life trajectories we would expect for men and women based on cross-cultural comparisons and ethnographic analogy with historic southeastern groups. We cannot assume that women had little or no political power simply because they are not well represented in mounds. On the other hand, most females and

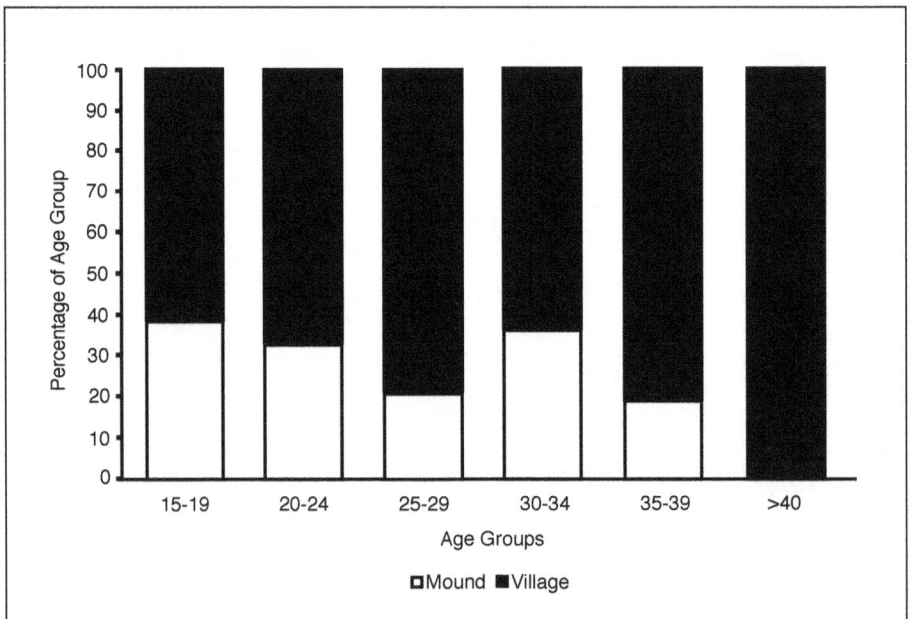

Fig. 5.5. Locations of graves of adult females at Toqua by age cohort.

many males were buried in household contexts. Males interred in the "female" sphere of the household presumably were not of appropriate status or rank to be interred in a mound, if mound burial indeed mainly symbolizes male leadership. We can hypothesize that if there were female leaders at the Toqua site and their appropriate places of interment were in the houses that represent the kin groups they led, we can expect differentiation in mortuary treatments among females in house contexts. That is, not all older females likely were leaders, nor were all female leaders treated in similar ways. The degree of differentiation would be comparable to that observed among the males in the mound (i.e., male "leaders") and those in the village (i.e., male "nonleaders").

In order to explore this idea more thoroughly, we will examine one age cohort in detail. This group is the eldest, age forty and above. This cohort is particularly interesting because there is a dichotomy of the sexes in burial location and because the percentages of individuals interred with funerary objects, for both sexes, distinctly decrease. Data on mortuary treatments are available for seventeen individuals: eleven males and six females (Polhemus 1987). These individuals represent 11 percent of the total adult population (over fifteen years of age) for which sex, age, and

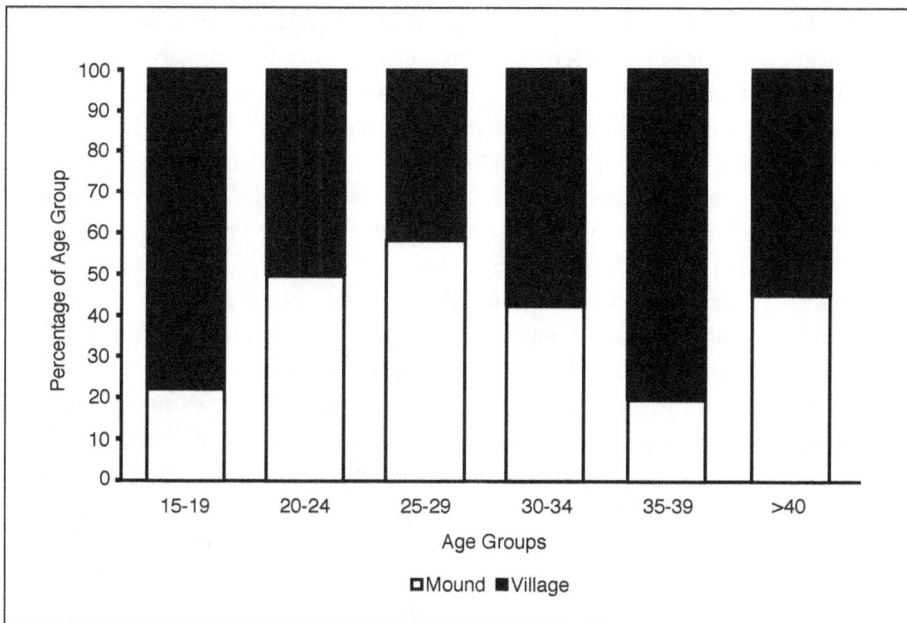

Fig. 5.6. Locations of graves of adult males at Toqua by age cohort.

mortuary treatments could be determined (n = 150). Four individuals
(24 percent) of the over-forty group were buried in the mound. All are
male. Viewed in another way, 36 percent of the oldest males are interred
in the mound, 64 percent of these males are buried in the village, and 100
percent of the females are interred in the village. Mound interment obviously was not an appropriate mortuary treatment for elderly females at
Toqua. In contrast, mound burial was suitable for about one-third of the
elderly males.

The associations of funerary objects with the elderly group indicate
differentiation within this cohort, but there is little difference between
the sexes as to presence or absence of funerary objects. Some individuals
of each sex were treated differently from others. Five of the males (45
percent) and three of the females (50 percent) were interred with objects,
suggesting that this aspect of the mortuary program was not appropriate
for everyone. Of the four elderly males in the mound, two (50 percent)
were interred with objects, as compared with three (43 percent) of the
seven elderly males in the village. The females with grave associations
were, of course, all in the village.

The kinds of objects interred with the dead do show considerable differences between the sexes (table 5.1). Most of the objects appear to relate
to the division of labor: The males have woodworking tools (celts and
adzes—some are "ceremonial" as opposed to usable for woodworking),
hunting and/or war implements (projectile points and possibly paint—
graphite), a pipe, and a few miscellaneous tools and objects of personal
adornment, including marine shell beads and an ear pin. The women have
culinary tools (pots and mussel-shell spoons), some miscellaneous tools
and jewelry (marine-shell ear pins, beads, and a gorget), and some animal
bones which may represent either food offerings or special "bundles"
(see below). The males, on average, have 1.82 kinds of items each, with
the four in the mound averaging 2.75 kinds of objects and the seven in
the village averaging 1.29 objects. In contrast, the females average three
kinds of items, comparable to the men in the mound.

The mortuary treatments of this elderly cohort indicate differentiation
among individuals as well as between the sexes, but the differences between the sexes do not appear to relate to prestige or rank. The mortuary
treatments of the more prestigious females in this group (i.e., those with
funerary objects) are comparable to those of the prestigious males (i.e.,
those men in the mounds). If the oldest males in the mounds at Toqua
were leaders in the male sphere of public politics, it is just as likely that
three of the oldest females interred in their houses were leaders in the
female sphere of matrilineal kin groups and matrilocal households.

Table 5.1. Mortuary goods from Toqua associated with individuals over the age of forty

Burial number	Sex	Age	Burial location	Mortuary goods
55	M	42.5	mound	none
63b	M	40	mound	none
103	M	40	mound	projectile points, celt, shell beads, graphite, mica, bone spear point, worked bone
136	M	40	mound	celt, shell beads, shell pin
109	M	42.5	village	none
177	M	47.5	village	none
209	M	42.5	village	none
243	M	50	village	celt, pipe, adze
372	M	40	village	none
419	M	45	village	celt, pipe, adze, projectile points, biface, bone bead, flakes
440	M	40	village	bone bead
169	F	45	village	shell spoon, pottery jars, shell beads, freshwater shells, small animal bones
180	F	42.5	village	none
217	F	42.5	village	shell bead, pottery jars, shell pins, niad, deer and bird bone
263	F	50	village	none
413	F	42.5	village	none
416	F	40	village	shell pin, projectile point, niad

Powerful Women and Chiefly Politics

The data from east Tennessee suggest that in examining and interpreting prestige and political power as symbolized in Mississippian mortuary practices in this particular region, we have fallen into our own cultural trap. Since women mainly are buried in "domestic" space, and more men are buried in "public" space than are women, we took these data to mean that women were inferior in prestige and power. These interpretations are too simplistic and are devoid of appropriate cultural context.

Gendered life cycles and division of labor and gendered burial programs can account for most of the perceived "inferiority" of women in the Toqua data set. Mounds, with their public political connotations,

symbolize the male sphere of community leadership and foreign relations. In contrast, the houses represent the female sphere of everyday
life, family, and kin. These complementary spheres of men and women
involve different social institutions: individual settlements and/or localities (towns), on one hand, and kinship groups that cross-cut communities, on the other.

The simple existence of gendered spheres implies neither political
dominance nor equality. Further analyses employing thoughtful comparisons along gender axes could suggest patterns of control and/or
reciprocity pertaining to resources, social groupings, and/or ideology.
The preliminary comparisons offered here using the Toqua data suggest
no clear patterns of political dominance along gender lines. There is a
link between inherited status and town leadership, reflected in the presence of children and young females in the mound-burial population,
but the most prevalent means of attaining high social rank appears to be
through individual achievement. The most likely venue for the majority
of the adult males in the mounds to achieve prestige worthy of mound
burial was through their prowess as warriors and statesmen. Most of
the females in the mound may well be there due to inherited status, but
a cadre of women also gained increased status through achievement.
These latter women are represented in house burials, which likely are
distinguished archaeologically by associated funerary objects with contexts and meanings we do not yet understand.[1]

The gender patterns observed in the Toqua data are strikingly similar to those observed by Rodning (1996, 1999a) for Cherokee town sites
and are not incompatible with Sattler's (1995) characterization of eighteenth-century Cherokee sociopolitical organization. Female leaders, as
senior members of clans, were very influential in Cherokee politics. It is
appropriate that such women were interred in household contexts, because their prestige and political influence in these matrilineal societies
derived from, and was based in, the social context of households and
kin groups. Mortuary practices at the Ledford Island site, a Mouse Creek
phase (Late Mississippian/protohistoric) town in the Hiwassee River
Valley of southeastern Tennessee, exhibits similar patterns (Sullivan 1986,
1987, 1995), but the poor bone preservation precludes age definitions of
most individuals in the "public" plaza cemetery.

As noted above, during late prehistory many small chiefly polities
dotted the landscape in eastern Tennessee. The Toqua site likely was the
center of one such polity (Polhemus 1987). Mississippian polities in

eastern Tennessee never or perhaps only very briefly coalesced into a large, centralized chiefdom (Hally 1994b; Hally, Smith, and Langford 1990). If they did so at all, it was perhaps in response to influence from Lamar-tradition centralized chiefdoms to the south (see Williams and Shapiro 1990).

Mortuary practices at "Lamar" sites on the Savannah River are summarized by Anderson (1996:188) as follows: "[P]roportionally far more females than males were found in the village areas than the mounds, and . . . the burials in the village area typically had a much lower incidence of grave goods. Mound burial appears to have been restricted to high-status adults, typically males." If we were to look again at Lamar mortuary data, would we find patterning similar to Toqua? What about Moundville, Etowah, or Cahokia? Would the Cherokee model compare favorably with these data sets, or would perhaps the Muskogee model offered by Sattler (1995) be more compatible?

Do the upper Tennessee River Valley and adjacent Appalachian Summit regions differ from other southeastern subregions by virtue of maintaining a long tradition of active political influence by women? Such a balance of power with male leadership (including the war organization) would be a significant factor in the sociopolitical dynamics of this subregion. As Sattler (1995:229) notes, "complementarity of the roles and statuses [of the genders] implies very different relations of power and mechanisms for its acquisition and expression than does structural inequality and subordination." The implications for gendered politics and how such engendered spheres of influence may relate to factionalism, resource control and allocation, and other aspects of how power was manipulated are fascinating to consider. Perhaps those men in the mounds thought so, too.

Author's Note

Thanks go to Jane Eastman and Chris Rodning for inviting me to participate in this publication project, for their helpful comments on the various drafts, and their patience and good humor as I missed deadlines. I am very grateful to Tim Pauketat and Vin Steponaitis for listening to my ideas while they were even more half-baked, and to Tim for providing very useful comments on the draft manuscript. Although these colleagues greatly improved the quality of the paper, they are not to be blamed for its failings. Those belong to me.

Notes

1. Marine-shell pins are associated with two of the elderly females with funerary objects (Burials 217 and 416). The third (Burial 169) had in association two collections of objects, including various animal bones, which were "concentrated behind the back in two clusters which may represent bags or other containers. Such collections are found associated with several other burials at Toqua and appear to be restricted to older females" (Scott and Polhemus 1987:420).

Piedmont Siouans and Mortuary Archaeology on the Eno River, North Carolina

Elizabeth Monahan Driscoll, R. P. Stephen Davis Jr.,
and H. Trawick Ward

Gender was a meaningful aspect of past mortuary ritual, and interpreting gender in archaeologically visible mortuary patterns demands more than knowledge about the biological sex and age at death of interred individuals. Gender roles are often actively created, negotiated, and reinforced through mortuary ritual. By examining the material remains of burials and individuals and evidence of other aspects of burial ritual, archaeologists can learn a great deal about the gender roles within past communities. This chapter reviews mortuary patterns at the Fredricks site, the early eighteenth-century settlement of Occaneechi Town, located in the Piedmont of North Carolina. The people who occupied Occaneechi Town were under considerable stress from European-introduced diseases, and they were also recently dislocated from their previous homes in Virginia. Historic records indicate that several disparate groups came together in the Piedmont at the time the site was occupied, due to their diminishing numbers and increasingly embattled existence. We examined mortuary patterns at the site with an eye toward discerning possible cultural differences among the burials, especially in the realm of gender.

The Fredricks site was discovered in 1983 by archaeologists from the University of North Carolina's (UNC) Research Laboratories of Archaeology and was excavated between 1983 and 1986 (fig. 6.1). It represents

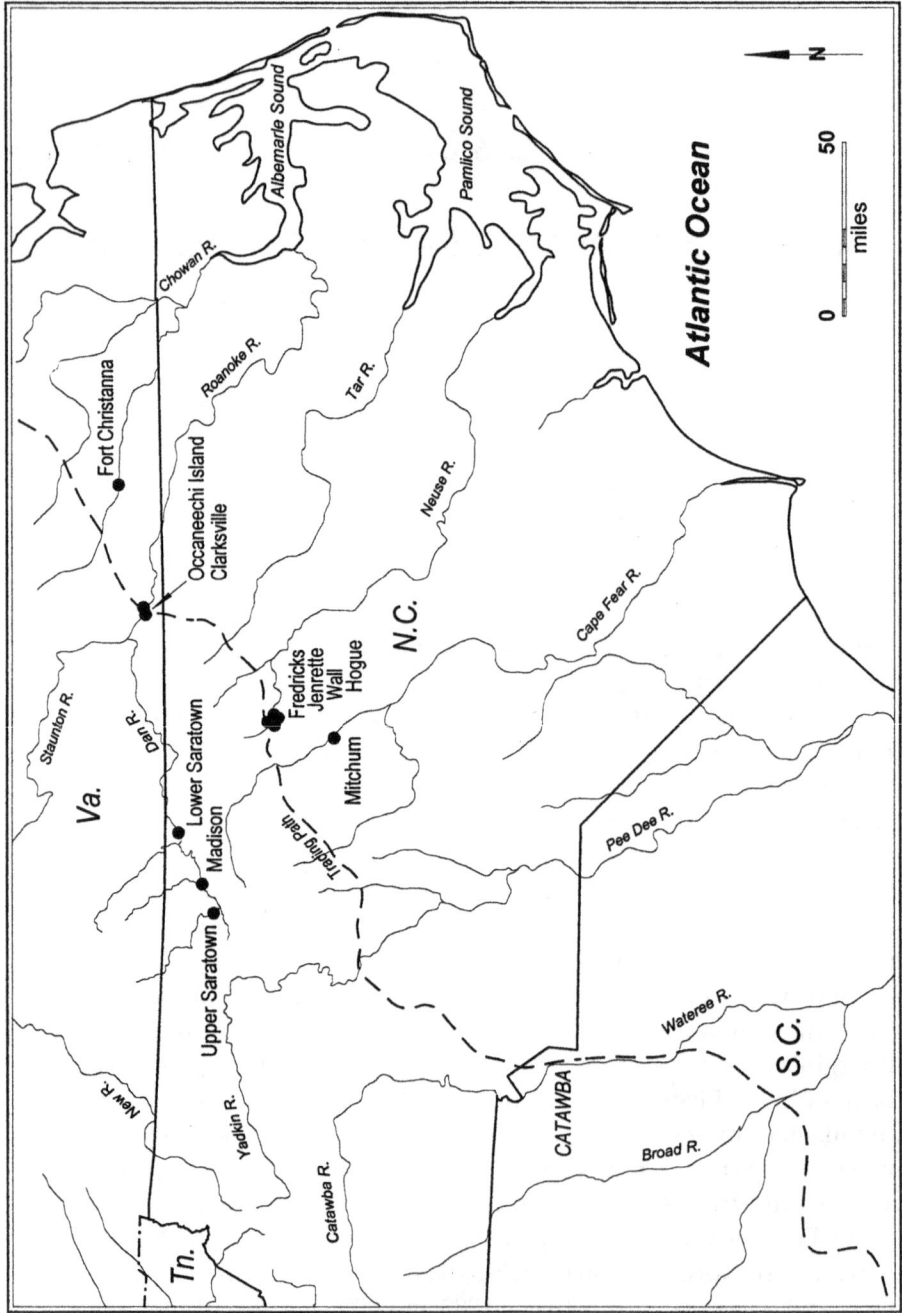

Fig. 6.1. Fredricks and other sites mentioned in the text.

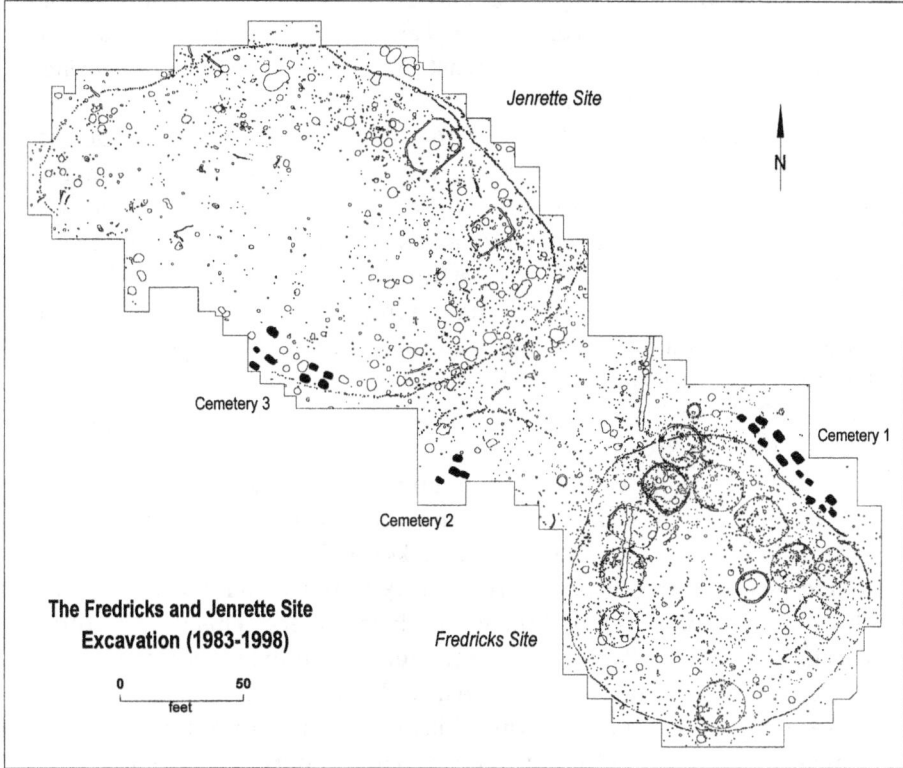

Fig. 6.2. Excavation plan of the Fredricks and Jenrette sites showing the three cemeteries.

Occaneechi Town, a settlement of the Occaneechi tribe on the north bank of the Eno River, near present Hillsborough, North Carolina, which was visited by John Lawson in 1701 (Lefler 1967). Archaeological excavations revealed a small village about one-fourth of an acre in size which consisted of about a dozen houses of bower construction, arranged in a circle around an open plaza where a large sweat house stood. A stockade of small saplings surrounded the village, and a cemetery containing thirteen graves was located along the stockade at the northeast side (Davis et al. 1998; Dickens, Ward, and Davis 1987; Ward and Davis 1988) (fig. 6.2).

The Fredricks cemetery represents a unique mortuary feature in the North Carolina Piedmont. At other excavated late prehistoric and contact-period village sites, including Wall, Upper Saratown, and Mitchum, burials are more randomly scattered and located within or just outside dwellings. At Wall, a fifteenth-century site located directly to the east of

Fredricks, all of the burials were placed within or in the vicinity of the houses. The individuals were all flexed and placed in shaft-and-chamber pits with their heads to the southeast. At Upper Saratown, 111 burials have been excavated, and they also were found either within or near houses (Navey 1982; Ward 1987). Other Piedmont Siouan sites, such as Madison, Clarksville, and Mitchum, reflect similar spatial arrangements and indicate a Siouan mortuary pattern during the late prehistoric and contact periods. The first cemetery excavated at Fredricks was immediately conspicuous by its departure from this pattern. Because the historic record indicates that depopulation from European diseases caused various Piedmont ethnic groups to form amalgamated communities, it has been hypothesized that the Fredricks cemetery represents the resting place of Occaneechis who had joined the previous local residents of this bend in the Eno River (Ward 1987).

In 1989, a second cemetery, containing four graves, was discovered (fig. 6.2). It, too, was located outside the stockade, between Fredricks and the newly discovered Jenrette site, a Shakori village dating to the middle to late seventeenth century. During the 1995 and 1996 field seasons, archaeologists found yet another Fredricks cemetery. This burial group was located west of the other two cemeteries, within and adjacent to the stockade surrounding the slightly earlier Jenrette site.

Recently, we have begun to question our earlier assumption regarding cemeteries as representing spatially separated burials associated with ethnically distinct social groups. Could they not just as easily reflect deaths from different epidemics and a recognition of the contagiousness of Old World diseases (Ward and Davis 1993:416)? In this chapter, we will explore this question by examining several dimensions of mortuary behavior, including grave associations, burial pit structure, and body positioning, along lines of age and sex. It is our hope that behavioral differences or similarities within and among the Fredricks burial groups will shed light on the advent of cemetery interments in the North Carolina Piedmont during the contact period.

The Fredricks site excavation was part of the Siouan Project of the Research Laboratories of Archaeology. This project has sought to reconstruct patterns of culture change among the Native American groups of the Piedmont in northern North Carolina and southern Virginia (Dickens, Ward, and Davis 1987). Archaeologists have conducted research at several sites, including Fredricks, Wall, Jenrette, Hogue, Upper Saratown, Lower Saratown, and Mitchum. Initial investigations focused on the watersheds of the Dan, Eno, and Haw rivers, which together comprise the heartland of the Piedmont Siouans during the contact period. Research at the Fredricks site, discussed in this chapter, has led to many conclusions about the nature and impact of European contact and interaction on the Occaneechis and other Siouan peoples.

Elsewhere, scholars have written comprehensive descriptions of the histories of the Occaneechis and their Piedmont neighbors, which we summarize here (see Cumming 1958; Dickens, Ward, and Davis 1987; Merrell 1987, 1989; Rights 1957). When European explorers began surveying the Piedmont in what is now Virginia and North Carolina, they encountered several Native American tribes who spoke related languages (now recognized as Eastern Siouan [J. Mooney 1894; Speck 1935]) and who descended from a common cultural background. These groups practiced comparable subsistence strategies of foraging and farming, and their societies were organized along kinship lines and according to relatively egalitarian rules of social reciprocity.

As traders and colonists spread across the Piedmont and as interactions among Native Americans and European Americans became more direct and more intense, the Occaneechis became prominent entrepreneurs among these Siouan groups. The Occaneechis controlled the supply side of the deerskin trade, and their language became a *lingua franca* across the Piedmont. One of their villages, on an island in the Roanoke River, was located at a natural ford where the Great Trading Path from Virginia to Georgia crossed the river. From this location, the Occaneechis attained a pivotal role in the fur trade. It was here that John Lederer visited them in 1670 (Cumming 1958). Although not as populous as other groups in the area, their fierce and pugnacious reputation and their willingness to back it up with warfare and intimidation seem to have reinforced the Occaneechis' role in the trade network.

This prominence ultimately led to armed hostilities with Nathaniel Bacon's Virginia frontier militia in 1676. First enlisting the Occaneechis as allies to defeat a group of Susquehannocks he had pursued into their region, Bacon then attacked the Occaneechis (Billings 1975:267–69). This battle so reduced the numbers of the Occaneechi that they were unable to defend their village on the Roanoke and retreated southward. They relocated on the Eno River, near present Hillsborough, North Carolina. There John Lawson, an English surveyor, found them in 1701 (Lefler 1967:61). By this time, warfare, disease, and alcohol had virtually destroyed the Occaneechi and many other Piedmont tribes (Dickens, Ward, and Davis 1987). During the first three decades of the eighteenth century, remnants of these once-autonomous Siouan groups either gathered together for protection near Fort Christanna in Virginia or joined the Catawba in South Carolina.

Merrell (1987) has described four stages of interaction between Europeans and Native Americans in the Piedmont. During the first era, between 1525 and 1625, interactions between Europeans and Native Americans involved mostly indirect contacts. European material culture was carried inland by Native American groups from the coastal regions. In addition, Spanish explorers traveled through the western Piedmont of North Carolina between 1539 and 1541 (Hudson, Smith, and DePratter 1984) and again between 1566 and 1568 (Beck 1997; Hudson 1990), and some Native Americans may have traveled to the South Carolina low country to satisfy their curiosity about the strange new people. Although Spanish-introduced diseases certainly began to impact some Native Americans at this time (M. T. Smith 1987), particularly those in direct contact with or in close proximity to the Spanish explorers and settlements, these diseases do not appear to have impacted peoples of the northeastern North Carolina Piedmont. Current archaeological and ethnohistoric evidence suggest that significant depopulation from European diseases in this area did not occur until after 1650, and then it resulted from English, not Spanish, contacts (Ward and Davis 1991).

The second stage of interaction began with the defeat of the Powhatan Confederacy in 1622 and again in 1644, eventually leading to the spread of Virginia traders and colonists to lands west of the falls of James River. The first explorers were followed quickly by traders eager to barter with the Native Americans. The increased contact led to clashes between English settlers and Native Americans in the 1650s and 1670s, including Bacon's rebellion and the destruction of the Occaneechis' Roanoke River trading center.

The third stage of interaction saw a dramatic increase in intercultural exchange between natives and colonists. With the strongest native groups defeated, the remaining scattered groups were subject to incessant Iroquois raiding. The most serious problem for the Siouan Piedmont groups were attacks by "Sinnagers," probably warriors of the Seneca and perhaps other western Iroquois tribes. Their war parties regularly attacked Piedmont tribes, taking prisoners and destroying villages. These raids eventually drove the Sara from the Dan River along the North Carolina–Virginia border to South Carolina, where they joined the Catawba. The Occaneechi, Tutelo, and Saponi sought refuge in Virginia, signing a treaty with Lieutenant Governor Spotswood in 1714 and relocating to Fort Christanna on the Meherrin River (Alexander 1972; Lefler 1967:242;

Merrell 1987; L. B. Wright 1966:398). This sanctuary was short-lived, and in 1728 the refugees headed to join the Catawbas in South Carolina. In 1732 they returned to Virginia and began to disperse. Some joined remnants of the Tuscarora in eastern North Carolina, while others merged with their old enemies, the Six Nations (Merrell 1987:26).

The history of the Piedmont Siouans presents a complicated picture of amalgamation and dispersal in the face of various threats and opportunities. Remnants of individual tribes sought to maintain unique cultural identities throughout the process, even when joining with other groups. For example, although the Occaneechi, Saponi, Tutelo, and Stuckanock resided in a single village at Fort Christanna and were considered one nation by the Virginians, each group continued to elect its own headman, and each group preserved its own customs (Brock 1885:88; Merrell 1987; L. B. Wright 1966:315–16). One of the questions we seek to answer here is whether the community at the Fredricks site represents such an amalgamation of distinct ethnic groups whose identities were expressed through mortuary ritual.

In this chapter, we draw from the mortuary patterns at Fredricks to learn more about the social and political arrangements of the Occaneechi residents of the site. The practices underlying these archaeologically visible mortuary patterns include rituals performed before, during, and after the actual burial of an individual. Because archaeologists usually can observe only the manner in which the dead were disposed and the spatial relationships between burials and other architecture, they often compare the material culture of burials of members of different age and sex groups to answer questions about social status, gender, and group affiliation. Methods for such comparisons begin with the "assumption that an individual's treatment following death bears some predictable relationship to the individual's state in life and to the organization of the society to which the individual belonged" (O'Shea 1984:3).

The first archaeological studies to evaluate systematically the relationship between mortuary patterns and social structure sought to prove that such relationships were relatively straightforward (J. A. Brown 1971). Binford (1971) assessed the relationship between an individual's "social persona" (Goodenough 1965) and the dimensions of this social persona that were recognized in differential mortuary treatment. Each individual has a number of social identities, such as father, brother, and husband. Together, these identities constitute an individual's social persona (Goodenough 1965). Binford (1971) searched the Human Relations Area Files (Murdock 1967) for funerary distinctions based on the following social identities: age, sex, social position, and social affiliation. He found that sex, social position, and social affiliation were the most common factors symbolized but that there were major differences in mortuary behaviors of mobile foragers, shifting agriculturalists, settled agriculturalists, and pastoralists.

Saxe (1970) further expanded the notion of social persona and the significance of social role in mortuary treatment. Saxe applied componential analysis based on the work of Goodenough (1965) on the concepts of role and persona, stating that "(d)eath calls forth a fuller representation of ego's various social identities than at any time during life" (Saxe 1970:6). Therefore, archaeologists are not merely excavating individuals but rather a "coherent social personality" (Saxe 1970:4).

The spatial dimension of mortuary ritual—how graves are arranged across a site—can also be a sensitive social barometer. For example, cemeteries may contain individuals of equal rank, and several cemeteries within a site may reflect the sociopolitical hierarchy of a group. In more-egalitarian societies, burials segregated in cemeteries may express strong lineage affiliations, the presence of corporate groups, or the presence of kinship structures such as clans (Bartel 1982; Howell and Kintigh 1996; Peebles 1974; Saxe 1971; Tainter 1978).

The initial assumptions in mortuary analysis came under considerable criticism in the early 1980s, at the same time as the processual archaeology in which they were rooted came under intense scrutiny (Trigger 1989) and for similar reasons. Processual archaeology often fails to take into account the importance of ritual and symbolism in society (Hodder 1982; Shanks and Tilley 1982). This is especially important in mortuary analysis since disposal of the dead is a ritually dominated practice (Hodder 1982). Hodder (1982) argues that the entire funeral rite, and not merely the physical disposal of the dead, is the appropriate frame of reference for generalizations about social organization.

However, mortuary practices can mask rather than express real social relationships and realities. After all, it is the peers of a deceased person who perform mortuary rituals. The survivors may reinforce their own position by demonstrating their relationship to the dead (Huntington and Metcalf 1979). Or it may be in their interest to downplay the wealth or position of the dead (Shanks and Tilley 1982). This may lead to "masked rank," where internal tensions resulting from social inequality are neutralized by the appearance of egalitarianism in mortuary (and other) ritual (Trinkaus 1995). In this way, ritual can reflect cultural notions of how things *should be*, not how they actually *are*. Ritual is an idealized expression of power relations, and in these expressions the dead are sub-ject to manipulation by the living (Parker Pearson 1982).

Conkey and Spector (1984), in their seminal article on gender and archaeology, point out that our interpretations of the past are often col-ored by our perceptions of relationships between men and women. This is an especially important point to keep in mind when using mortuary remains to reconstruct past activity patterns, sociopolitical organization, and gender roles. We can determine the sex, health, and diet of an in-dividual from his or her skeletal remains. Using that information and knowledge about the mortuary context and other aspects of the site, we can reconstruct social categories. But we must always be conscious that we are attempting to use *biological* and *physical* remains to reconstruct aspects of *social* and *cultural* identities, and we must be aware of our assumptions.

A gendered perspective can be especially enlightening for mortuary studies in archaeology. By dividing a group of related burials into gen-der categories based initially on biological sex and age at death, we can learn about the meaning these categories held for people. For example, shell ornaments are commonly associated with subadult burials in the Southeast (Thomas 1996). We can speculate about the meaning of such symbolism, but without considering children as a separate category this pattern would be obscured. By looking at burials of young women and comparing them with older, postmenopausal women, we can learn how their status may have differed in life. We may also learn about gender roles by comparing males and females of similar ages. The importance of a gendered perspective to mortuary studies cannot be overemphasized. The patterns revealed through sorting by both age and sex add tremen-dously to our understanding of past social interactions. Incorporating health and diet information sorted by gender criteria also helps to point out arrangements that might be masked through ritual practices. What is obscured by ritual is as important and interesting as what is revealed. The present case study of the mortuary dimensions at Fredricks clearly demonstrates the importance of a gendered approach.

Summary of Skeletal Analysis

We begin the process of interpretation with the information gathered from the biological remains of the individuals interred at the Fredricks site. Biological sex, age at death, and pathology of the thirteen individu-als buried in Cemetery 1, excavated between 1983 and 1985, were studied by Patricia Lambert using standard osteological and osteometric proce-

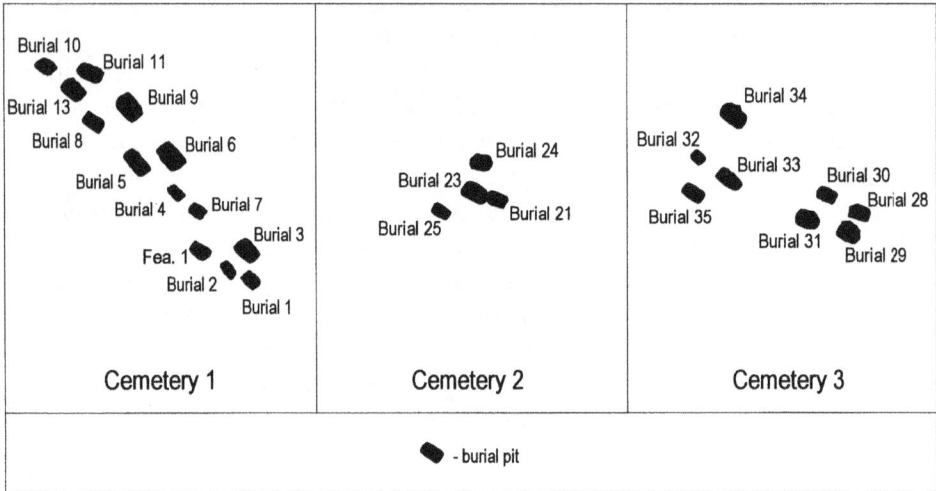

Fig. 6.3. Maps of Cemeteries 1, 2, and 3 at Fredricks, showing individual burial designations.

dures (W. M. Bass 1987; T. D. White 1991). After 1985, human remains no longer were removed from the ground but were analyzed *in situ*. Several researchers, including Elizabeth Monahan Driscoll, performed the *in situ* analysis of age, sex, and pathology on the twelve individuals buried in Cemeteries 2 and 3. Different researchers have reported estimates of age at death in different ways (fig. 6.3).

All three cemeteries were similar in age and sex composition (table 6.1). Each contained a preponderance of subadults and a mix of male and female adults (fig. 6.4). Young adult males (aged eighteen to twenty-five years) were conspicuous by their absence in each cemetery. There is a difference between the average age of the females in Cemeteries 1 and 3. Taking the median of the age estimate for each female, we found that the two females (aged approximately nineteen and thirty years old) in Cemetery 1 averaged twenty-four years old, ten years younger than the three females in Cemetery 3, who averaged about thirty-three years old at death (aged approximately thirty-five, thirty, and thirty-five years old). The adult males were similar in age in both Cemeteries 1 and 3.

Pathology was examined for the individuals in Cemeteries 1 and 3. Cribra orbitalia, porotic hyperostosis, linear enamel hypoplasia, caries percentage, and periostitis were all recorded where possible. Each tooth was examined for evidence of caries. The percentage of teeth present which had at least one carious lesion was calculated for each individual.

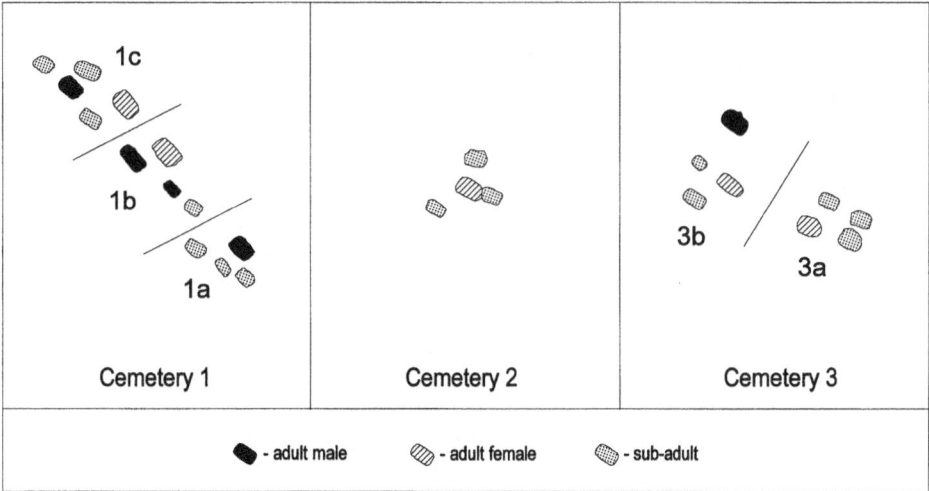

Fig. 6.4. Maps of Cemeteries 1, 2, and 3 at Fredricks, showing burial groups and age/sex determinations.

Caries rates were considered by age and sex for Cemeteries 1 and 3. Caries information was not recorded for Cemetery 2, where human remains were poorly preserved. The percentages of carious-lesion prevalence vary widely. The percentage of carious teeth per individual is correlated with age. Therefore, the females in Cemetery 1 should have fewer carious teeth due to the younger age of the two women. The average for the two women in Cemetery 1 is 34 percent, only slightly lower than the average of 40 percent for the three females in Cemetery 3. Part of the problem of comparing caries incidence is that older individuals may have lost more teeth that were carious, skewing the results. The average for the males, however, is also slightly different between the two cemeteries. The four males in Cemetery 1 had an average of 45 percent carious teeth, while the males in Cemetery 3 had an average of only 31 percent carious teeth. Because the ages of the males are similar in both cemeteries, this slight difference in caries percentage may indicate subtle differences in diet between the two groups, but to draw firm conclusions from such small samples is unwarranted.

Linear enamel hypoplasias are furrows in the tooth enamel that form when a young individual suffers a period of growth disruption. This disruption may be due to inadequate nutrition, a period of poor health, or both. The body sacrifices growth to divert its resources to survival. If the individual survives the episode, enamel deposition resumes at a normal

Table 6.1. Age, sex, and mortuary attributes for the Fredricks Cemetery burials

Burial, age, and sex	Mortuary attributes
Cemetery 1 (Group 1a)	
Burial 1 (subadult, 3.5 ± 1 yrs.)	*Garment* (heavily decorated—small shell and glass beads, buttons) *Adornment* (large glass and shell beads, shell gorgets) *Funerary objects* (spoon, hammerstone, iron knives, scissors)
Burial 2 (subadult (7.5 ± 2 yrs.)	*Garment* (heavily decorated—small shell and glass beads, buttons) *Adornment* (large glass, shell, and bone beads) *Funerary objects* (pewter porringer, Fredricks Check Stamped pot, iron knives, Jew's harp, lead shot)
Burial 3 (male, 32 ± 5 yrs.)	*Garment* (lightly decorated—wampum) *Adornment* (none) *Funerary objects* (wine bottle, iron ax, iron knives, scissors, pewter pipe, ember tender, striking flint, iron nails, lead shot, brass buckle)
Feature 1 (neonate?)	*Garment* (undecorated) *Adornment* (none) *Funerary objects* (none)
Cemetery 1 (Group 1b)	
Burial 4 (male, 25 ± 4 yrs.; disarticulated bundle); Burial 4a (neonate, 1 month)	*Garment* (undecorated) *Adornment* (none) *Funerary objects* (pewter porringer, wine bottle, bundled tubular shell beads)
Burial 5 (male, 41 ± 9 yrs.)	*Garment* (undecorated) *Adornment* (none) *Funerary objects* (iron ax, iron knife, kaolin pipes, shell-beaded bag)
Burial 6 (female?, 19 ± 3 yrs.)	*Garment* (lightly decorated—small shell and glass beads) *Adornment* (wire bracelets, large glass beads) *Funerary objects* (dog-lock musket, Fredricks Check Stamped pot, iron hoe, pewter pipe, scissors)

Burial 7 (neonate, <3 months)   *Garment* (undecorated)
                                       Adornment (brass bells)
                                       Funerary objects (none)

Cemetery 1 (Group 1c)

Burial 8 (subadult, 3.5 ± 1 yrs.)   *Garment* (undecorated)
                                       Adornment (none)
                                       Funerary objects (copper kettle, Fredricks
                                       Check Stamped pot, basket, iron knife,
                                       brass spoon, brass buckles)

Burial 9 (female, 30 ± 5 yrs.)   *Garment* (undecorated)
                                       Adornment (none)
                                       Funerary objects (iron hoe, iron knife)

Burial 10 (subadult, 4.5 ± 1.3 yrs.)   *Garment* (heavily decorated—small glass
                                       beads)
                                       Adornment (large glass beads, brass bells)
                                       Funerary objects (Fredricks Check Stamped
                                       pots, plain pot, small celt, iron hoe)

Burial 11 (subadult, 17 ± 3 yrs.)   *Garment* (lightly decorated—small glass
                                       beads)
                                       Adornment (large glass beads, buckles)
                                       Funerary objects (cord-marked pot, iron
                                       knife, lead shot, Jew's harps, bone-handled
                                       punch/awl[?], tin box, wire C-bracelet)

Burial 13 (male, 40 ± 5 yrs.)   *Garment* (undecorated)
                                       Adornment (none)
                                       Funerary objects (pewter porringer, kaolin
                                       pipe, iron knives)

Cemetery 2

Burial 21 (subadult, 10–15 yrs.)   *Garment* (lightly decorated—small glass
                                       beads)
                                       Adornment (large glass beads, brass bells)
                                       Funerary objects (cylinder-shaped iron ob-
                                       ject)

Burial 23 (female, 20–35 yrs.)   *Garment* (undecorated)
                                       Adornment (none)
                                       Funerary objects (none)

Burial 24 (subadult?)   *Garment* (undecorated)
                                       Adornment (none)
                                       Funerary objects (none)

Burial 25 (subadult)   *Garment* (undecorated)
                                       Adornment (none)
                                       Funerary objects (Fredricks Check Stamped
                                       pot, pewter pipe)

Cemetery 3 (Group 3a)   *continued*

Table 6.1 *(continued)*

Burial, age, and sex	Mortuary attributes
Burial 28 (subadult, 1.75 yrs. ± 7 months)	*Garment* (heavily decorated—small glass and shell beads) *Adornment* (large glass beads, brass bells) *Funerary objects* (kaolin pipe)
Burial 29 (subadult, 12 ± 2.5 yrs.)	*Garment* (lightly decorated—small shell beads) *Adornment* (large shell beads, brass ornaments) *Funerary objects* (iron knife, iron scissors, brass Jesuit ring, brass thimble)
Burial 30 (subadult, 1.5 ± 0.5 yrs.)	*Garment* (undecorated) *Adornment* (shell gorget) *Funerary objects* (iron knife, scissors, brass Jesuit[?] ring)
Burial 31 (female, 30–39 yrs.)	*Garment* (undecorated) *Adornment* (none) *Funerary objects* (Fredricks Check Stamped pot)
Cemetery 3 (Group 3b)	
Burial 32 (subadult, 3 ± 1 yrs.)	*Garment* (undecorated) *Adornment* (none) *Funerary objects* (chipped-stone projectile point, iron knife)
Burial 33 (female, 25–35 yrs.)	*Garment* (undecorated) *Adornment* (none) *Funerary objects* (iron knife, kaolin pipe)
Burial 34 (male, 40+ yrs.)	*Garment* (undecorated) *Adornment* (none) *Funerary objects* (plain pot, chipped-stone projectile points, iron ax, iron knife, scissors, clay pipe, ember tenders, gunflints, sheet brass object, glass button)
Burial 35 (subadult, 6 ± 2 yrs.)	*Garment* (undecorated) *Adornment* (large shell and glass beads, shell gorgets) *Funerary objects* (Fredricks Check Stamped pot, iron ax, iron knife, brass spoon, polished stone discoidal)

rate, leaving behind a gap that permanently marks the period of slower growth. Most of the individuals in Cemeteries 1 and 3 were evaluated for linear enamel hypoplasias. Of the individuals in Cemetery 1 who could be scored, nearly all had at least one hypoplastic line, except one child (Burial 8, aged approximately three and a half years). Two infants and one other child (Burials 1, 4a, and 7) could not be scored. The individuals in Cemetery 3 displayed a similar pattern. Again, one young child (Burial 32, aged approximately three years), showed no lines, likely having died before they could form.

The other pathological indicators evaluated could not be scored reliably in over half of the individuals in the two cemeteries, making their usefulness dubious. The overall pattern of health and nutrition indicators from the skeletal remains portrays individuals who had a fairly significant disease load and relatively high infant and child mortality. Unfortunately for this study, the European diseases that annihilated the majority of Native Americans in the Southeast, including smallpox, chicken pox, measles, influenza, diphtheria, cholera, bubonic plague, typhus, and scarlet fever, do not leave markers on the skeletons of the victims (Dobyns 1983; Ortner and Putschar 1981). Therefore, while we can speculate on the causes of death of such a large percentage of the estimated population of Occaneechi Town, we cannot pinpoint the diseases. Evidence of traumas on the skeletal remains include a healed broken arm for Burial 2 and possible scalping marks on the Burial 4 cranium. Additionally, a flattened piece of lead shot was found resting against the left fibula of Burial 9, indicating a likely gunshot wound.

In summary, there are no patterns of health or nutrition indicators that would indicate that inclusion in a specific cemetery was due to social status, if status carried any social buffering from disease or food shortages. Overall, the assemblage of individuals paints a picture of a population under acute disease stress.

Burial Groupings

Next, we consider the spatial organization of burials at the site. One of the more interesting features of the Fredricks site cemeteries is that graves are clustered spatially into groups of four or five individuals. Cemetery 1 contains three such groups, Cemetery 2 is comprised of a single group, and Cemetery 3 contains two groups (fig. 6.4). Even more intriguing is the similarity among the groups in terms of age and sex composition. Each group consists of a young adult female, sometimes an older adult male, and several subadults. The spatial separation and the age and sex composition of each group suggest that they represent households or families. Given the age ranges estimated for the female in each cluster, it is biologically possible that the children were born to that female.

There are two exceptions to the pattern described above. In Cemetery 1, Group 1a does not contain an adult female. Group 1b in Cemetery 1 contains a young adult female, an older adult male, a subadult, and the bundled remains of a young adult male. The occurrence of a few infant bones with the bundled young adult male suggest that they were buried or curated elsewhere prior to reburial in the cemetery. Perhaps this is an indication that young adult males were treated differently after death and usually buried elsewhere. Alternatively, the general absence of young adult males from the burial population may reflect their involvement in the fur trade—a lifestyle that would have kept them away from the village for long periods and perhaps made them less susceptible to villagewide epidemics. It also is possible that increased exposure to disease through trade led to death away from the village. Perhaps, given the violent history of the Occaneechi prior to their relocation to North Carolina, young males were largely absent in the living population as well. They may have been killed in the conflicts, or some may not have joined the older men, women, and children on their flight south. It seems unlikely that this situation would have persisted, however, given the nature of the settlement as a trading outpost.

If these groups of burials can be interpreted correctly as family units, then they suggest that several households experienced episodes of multiple death—a situation expected to result from exposure to highly lethal epidemics. The presence of four older subadults within the cemeteries supports the likelihood that Occaneechi Town suffered from European-introduced or other disease epidemics. This age group usually has the lowest mortality in a population not experiencing a significant infectious-disease load. Thus, normally we would not expect to see this proportion in the burial population in the absence of such epidemics (Weiss 1973).

How should we interpret multiple cemeteries comprising separate family or household groups? It is possible that each cemetery represents a kin group burial area. However, the morphological characteristics of the burial pits and the differential distribution of certain artifact types (discussed below) suggest differences greater than what might be expected between related kin groups. Given that Occaneechi Town was occupied at a time of widespread depopulation across much of the Piedmont, during which refugees from decimated villages came together to form new communities (see Lefler 1967:61–62, 232), it seems more reasonable to view each cemetery as representing a distinct but culturally similar ethnic group that maintained its own mortuary tradition.

Funerary Objects

Items intentionally buried with an individual during a mortuary ritual constitute an important source of information about that person's identity within his or her society. By examining the patterned distribution of such items by age and sex and across space, we hope to provide some preliminary insights into the Fredricks burial population at four levels:

1. Individuals (examined as gender categories of adult males, adult females, and subadults).
2. Burial groups (possibly reflecting family units).
3. Cemeteries (mortuary manifestations of ethnicity or of specific disease episodes).
4. The entire burial population (a corporate group that may have been ethnically diverse).

Of the twenty-five burials within the three cemeteries, twenty were accompanied by nonperishable grave goods (fig. 6.5). This prevalence of mortuary items is in sharp contrast to those preceding groups in the region who often buried their dead clothed in beaded garments but with few accompanying grave goods. In most cases, funerary objects found

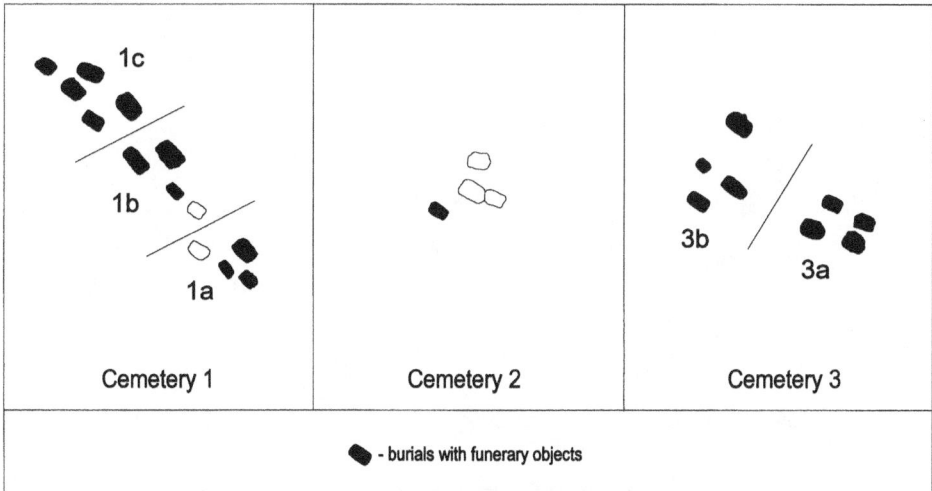

Fig. 6.5. Maps of Cemeteries 1, 2, and 3 at Fredricks, showing the distribution of funerary objects.

with the Fredricks burials were items of European manufacture, and, collectively, they display a wealth in trade goods that has not been found archaeologically elsewhere in the Piedmont (see table 6.1).

The occurrence of identical artifact types and styles within all three cemeteries, including a Fredricks Check Stamped pot in at least one burial in each cemetery, indicates that they are roughly contemporaneous and further differentiates these burials from the other scattered shaft-and-chamber graves which can be attributed to the slightly earlier habitation of the Jenrette village. Within all three cemeteries, funerary objects tend to occur in clusters on the burial pit floor, and in several instances the presence of preserved organic material suggests that mortuary goods were placed in skin or cloth bags, or baskets.

Funerary objects found in cemetery burials include iron knives, metal scissors, iron axes and hoes, clay and pewter smoking pipes, ember tenders, lead shot, gunflints, a musket, pewter porringers, wine bottles, a brass kettle, spoons, and clay pots. Over one-third of the individuals wore garments that were decorated with glass beads, shell beads, or buttons. Almost one-half wore necklaces of large glass or shell beads or were adorned with shell or brass ornaments (fig. 6.6).

By examining the distribution of funerary objects, several gender-specific patterns can be seen (fig. 6.7). First, subadults were most likely to be buried clothed in garments decorated with beadwork or adorned with necklaces, anklets, or bracelets. All four individuals buried in heavily decorated garments were subadults, and three of five individuals in

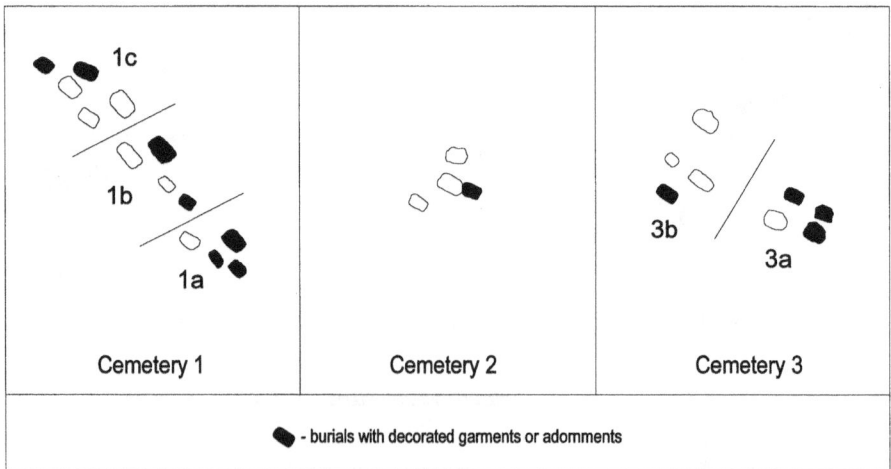

Fig. 6.6. Maps of Cemeteries 1, 2, and 3 at Fredricks, showing the distribution of decorated garments or adornments.

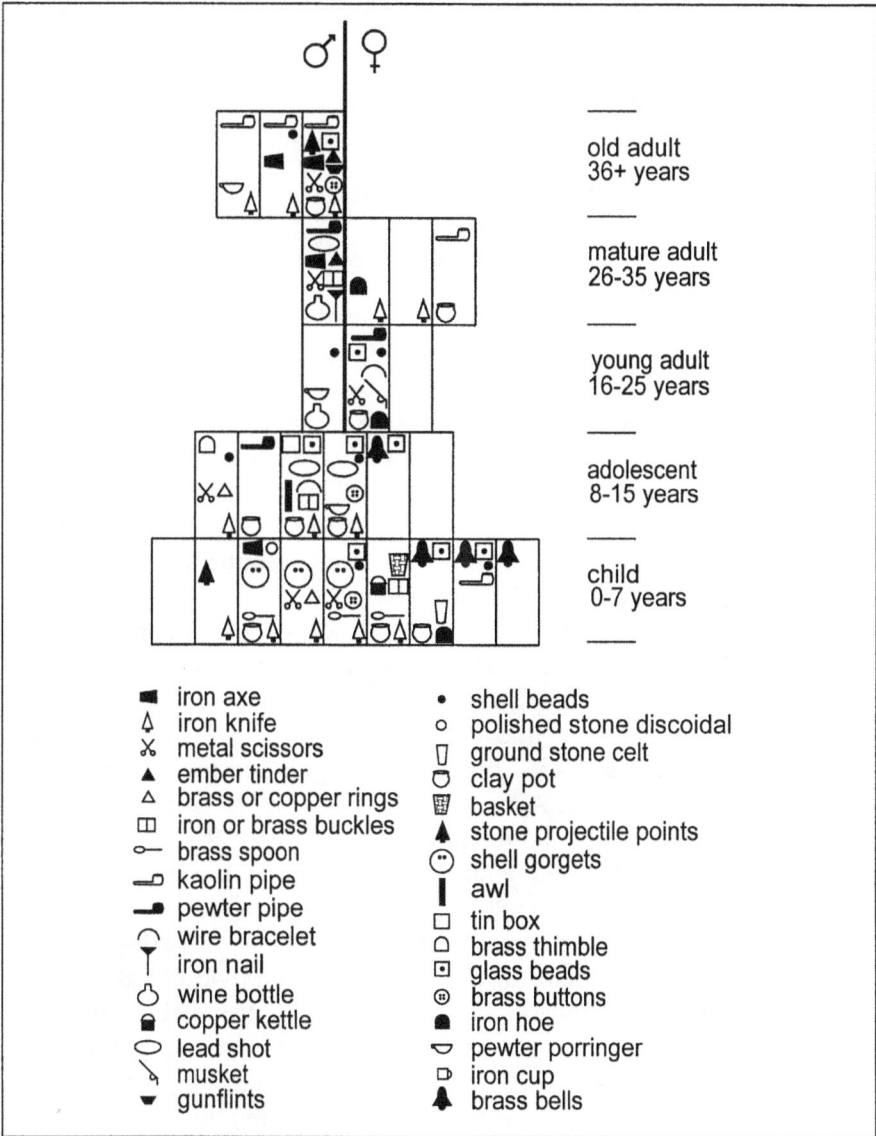

♂ ♀

old adult
36+ years

mature adult
26-35 years

young adult
16-25 years

adolescent
8-15 years

child
0-7 years

◼ iron axe	• shell beads
⬙ iron knife	○ polished stone discoidal
✕ metal scissors	⋃ ground stone celt
▲ ember tinder	⥾ clay pot
△ brass or copper rings	▥ basket
▥ iron or brass buckles	▲ stone projectile points
⌒ brass spoon	☉ shell gorgets
◡ kaolin pipe	❙ awl
⬤ pewter pipe	☐ tin box
⌒ wire bracelet	⌂ brass thimble
ⵏ iron nail	⊡ glass beads
◯ wine bottle	⊕ brass buttons
◖ copper kettle	◼ iron hoe
◡ lead shot	▽ pewter porringer
↘ musket	⌓ iron cup
▼ gunflints	▲ brass bells

Fig. 6.7. Chart showing the distribution of funerary objects, decorated garments, and adornments by age and sex.

lightly decorated garments also were subadults. Likewise, ten of the eleven individuals adorned with necklaces or other ornaments also were subadults. Metal spoons, which occurred in three separate burial groups, were associated exclusively with subadults. These were sometimes decorated and worn as ornaments.

Certain other classes of funerary objects were associated with adult males or females but usually did not accompany subadults. Only two of the eight individuals with smoking paraphernalia were subadults, while four of the five adult male burials had clay or pewter pipes. Large metal implements likewise were distributed differentially among adult female and male burials and may reflect gender-specific activities in the Occaneechis' daily lives. Iron axes were found in three of the five adult male burials and in one subadult burial, while iron hoes accompanied two of the five adult females and one subadult.

European-made containers and native-made clay pots also appear to be differentially distributed. Of the nine burials with clay pots, six were subadults, two were adult females, and only one was an adult male. The pot associated with the adult male was one of the few vessels found that was not Fredricks Check Stamped. Conversely, two of the three pewter porringers and both wine bottles were found in adult male graves. Such a pattern might reflect the very different ways (by local manufacture and through the fur trade) in which these two types of containers could have been acquired by women and men, respectively.

Firearms and related items do not show an age- or sex-specific distribution. The one musket found is associated with a young adult, probably female, individual. This individual had been tentatively identified in the field as a young adult male, and identified as an adult male aged between twenty-five and thirty-five years at death by a previous researcher (Ward 1987; H. H. Wilson 1987). A recent reanalysis of these skeletal remains leads us to believe that the individual was younger than the original estimate and may have been female. The individual (Burial 6) died at a young age (about seventeen to twenty-two years), and it can be difficult to be certain of sex in young adults. However, comparison of the size and morphology of this skeleton with the rest of the individuals at the site leads us to believe that the individual was more likely female than male.

The reevaluation of Burial 6 as possibly a young woman poignantly raises the subject of gender and assumptions of gendered roles and activities. When the individual was thought to be a male, the automatic assumption was that this individual probably acquired the weapon through trade interactions in which he was likely to have been an active participant. However, once we realized that the individual could have been a young woman, we had to reevaluate our assumptions. It forced us to ensure that our explanations of how this weapon came to be included in this burial were based on ethnohistory and other evidence and not on our own assumptions of what a man or a woman would be doing with a musket. Approaching this interpretation with a gendered perspective brings up additional interesting questions to consider. If the burial was that of a young woman, was she involved with trading? Did she participate in raids or hunt with it? What is the symbolism of this grave inclusion? These are all questions we may not have considered if we simply assumed the gender roles of men and women in this group.

Four subadult burials contained varying quantities of lead shot or gunflints. Most adult males had one or two iron knives; however, almost half of all adult females and more than half of the subadults also were buried with knives. Scissors likewise are not strongly associated with males, females, or subadults.

It is possible to detect spatial patterns in funerary accompaniments not only among the three cemeteries but also among the six burial groups within those cemeteries. As a simple comparative exercise, each burial group was characterized based on the occurrences of funerary objects representing twelve separate artifact classes, and then each group was compared to every other group (see table 6.2). It was found that the three groups within Cemetery 1 (Groups 1a, 1b, and 1c) and one of the Cemetery 3 groups (Group 3b) were very similar to one another in terms of burial goods. The other Cemetery 3 group (Group 3a) appears somewhat less closely related, while the Cemetery 2 group shares few common traits with the other groups.

Whereas most burials in Cemeteries 1 and 3 contained funerary objects, only one of the four Cemetery 2 burials was accompanied by artifacts and another wore a garment lightly decorated with glass beads. These artifacts—a Fredricks Check Stamped pot and a pewter pipe—do indicate that Cemetery 2 is culturally and chronologically associated with the two other cemeteries. It is noteworthy that two of the four burials within Group 3a contained brass Jesuit rings (see Wood 1974). While such artifacts are much more common on seventeenth-century sites in the Northeast, they have not been found in North Carolina except at Fredricks. Their presence in the Eno River Valley may reflect a historical and perhaps cultural relationship between the Susquehannock and the Occaneechi (Ward 1987:89–90). Moreover, these rings serve to distinguish the individuals comprising Group 3a from the other cemetery burials.

Burial Pit Morphology

The morphology and fill characteristics of the burial pits, as well as the occurrences of other pit features possibly associated with the burial ritual in Cemetery 3, indicate some differences among the three cemeteries

Table 6.2. Comparison of pairs of burial groups within the Fredricks Cemeteries based on artifact content

Burial group pair[a]	Garment[b]	Adorn[c]	Funerary[d]	Pot[e]	European container[f]	Large iron[g]	Firearms[h]	Knife[i]	Scissors[j]	Smoking[k]	Spoon[l]	Other metal[m]	Total no. shared attributes[n]
2-3a	–	–	–	X	–	–	–	–	–	–	–	–	1
2-3b	–	–	–	X	–	–	–	–	–	–	–	–	1
1a-2	–	–	–	X	–	–	–	–	–	X	–	–	2
1c-2	–	X	–	X	–	–	–	–	–	–	–	–	2
1b-2	X	X	–	X	–	–	–	–	–	X	–	–	4
1c-3a	X	–	X	X	–	–	–	–	–	X	–	X	5
1a-3a	X	X	X	X	–	–	–	–	X	–	–	X	6
1b-3a	–	–	X	X	–	–	–	X	X	X	–	X	6
3a-3b	–	–	X	X	X	–	–	–	X	X	–	X	6
1b-3b	–	–	X	X	–	X	X	–	X	X	–	X	7
1a-1b	–	–	X	X	X	X	X	–	X	X	–	X	8
1b-1c	–	X	X	X	X	X	X	–	–	X	–	X	8
1c-3b	–	–	X	X	–	X	X	X	–	X	X	X	8
1a-1c	X	–	X	X	X	X	X	X	–	–	X	X	9
1a-3b	–	X	X	X	–	X	X	X	X	X	X	X	10

a. "X" indicates that a pair of burial groups shares the same attribute state.
b. Similar amount of garment decoration in burials.
c. Adornment items present in some burials.
d. Smiliar frequency of burials with funerary objects.
e. Clay pot present in some burials.
f. European-made container present in some burials.
g. Large iron tool present in some burials.

h. Firearms-related objects present in some burials.
i. Iron knife present in some burials.
j. Scissors present in some burials.
k. Smoking-related items present in some burials.
l. Spoon present in some burials.
m. Other metal object present in some burials.
n. 0 = no similarity, 12 = completely similar.

which may be related to ethnicity. While all the graves were rectangular in outline and the bodies were usually deposited in a loosely flexed position with the heads oriented to the southeast, pit depths below the base of the plow zone varied greatly. The graves in Cemetery 1 averaged 2.3 feet in depth, while those in Cemetery 2 averaged 2.0 feet deep, and those in Cemetery 3 were only 1.4 feet deep (almost a foot shallower than those in Cemetery 1).

The most striking characteristic of the deep burial pits in Cemetery 1 was a refuse-rich fill which was deposited in the tops of several of the graves, particularly those in Group 1a at the southeastern end of the cemetery. Similarly, the graves in Cemetery 2 also were topped with a dark, organically enriched fill. While some of the graves in Cemetery 3 (Group 3a) contained upper zones of dark fill, others (such as those in Group 3b) hardly could be distinguished from the yellow subsoil clay surrounding the pits.

A unique feature of Cemetery 3 was the presence of six pit features aligned with and interspersed among the graves (fig. 6.8). These shallow, basin-shaped pits ranged from three to five feet in diameter and usually were less than a foot deep. All contained fill zones rich in refuse, particularly animal bones. Before excavation, it was sometimes difficult to distinguish these features from burial pits.

We believe that the association of refuse, particularly food refuse, with burials reflects feasting behavior that was a part of the mortuary ritual (Ward 1987). If this is the case, then a different form of this ritual was practiced when burials were placed in Cemetery 3 than was the case for Cemeteries 1 and 2. In addition to depositing the refuse from the mortuary feasts in some of the graves, special pits also were used for this purpose in Cemetery 3 but not in either of the other cemeteries. This distinction, when considered with the unusual shallowness of the graves in Cemetery 3, suggests a somewhat different pattern of mortuary behavior. This difference, though not great, is on a scale that would be expected between ethnically distinct but culturally related tribal groups, such as the Siouans of the Piedmont during the seventeenth and early eighteenth centuries.

The distinctiveness of Cemetery 3 is indicated further by the presence of Jesuit-related artifacts in two of the burials. Based on this evidence, it can be argued that the people buried in this cemetery probably had contacts with Iroquois groups to the north who were directly in contact with the Jesuit missions. The lack of evidence in Cemeteries 1 and 2 of similar contacts further suggests ethnic differences between the people buried in

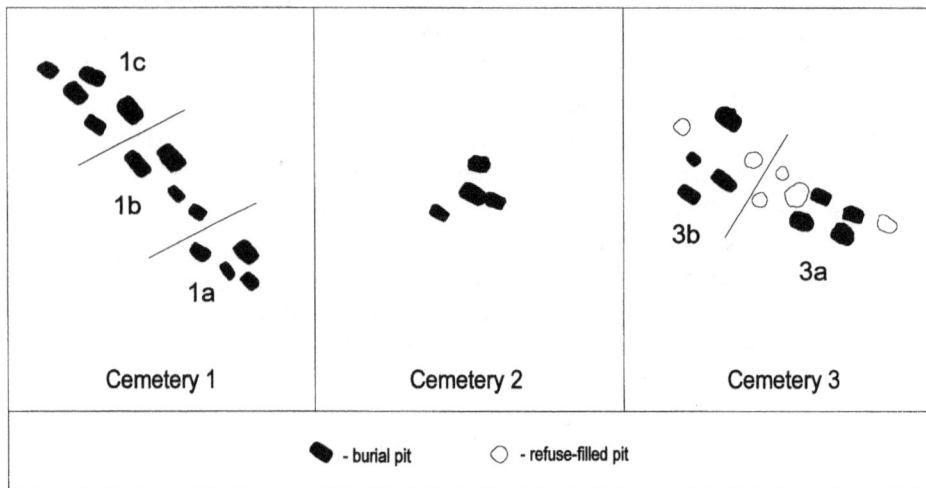

Fig. 6.8. Cemeteries and associated refuse-filled pits at Fredricks.

them and the individuals buried in Cemetery 3. Perhaps the Cemetery 3 individuals were the first Occaneechi arrivals from the Roanoke Valley, where in 1676 they were living near the Susquehannocks (Billings 1975: 267–69).

Conclusions

Archaeological research conducted since 1986 at the Fredricks site and adjacent Jenrette site has shed much new light on the community known historically as Occaneechi Town and on its treatment of the dead. Most obviously, the twelve additional burials found in Cemeteries 2 and 3 indicate a mortality rate far higher than the one estimated from the initial 1983–86 excavation. Given our estimate—based on site size and architectural remains—that Occaneechi Town probably was occupied for less than a decade by only fifty to seventy-five people, the present burial sample accounts for a substantial portion of that population. It seems likely that epidemic diseases affected this group, resulting in several episodes of multiple deaths.

Some of the insights we have gained, such as the recognition of multiple cemeteries and corresponding evidence for subtle differences in mortuary ritual, bear out earlier predictions and are consistent with the archaeological expectations of an ethnically diverse population. Others, like the detection of six separate burial groups that have similar numbers of individuals, and similar age and sex profiles, suggest that these cemeteries alternatively may represent individual families. More research is needed to establish which explanation is more accurate, but perhaps both are correct. Perhaps these related Siouan groups shared the idea that cemeteries should be organized by kinship groups but differed in other aspects of the mortuary ritual, such as feasting-refuse disposal and the types of mortuary items to include in the burials.

Besides consideration of the spatial organization of cemeteries, other patterns in the mortuary data were identified. One such pattern is the near absence of younger adult males in the burial population. This pattern is puzzling, but it may be explained by increased mobility of young males during the deerskin trade and warfare of the seventeenth century.

Finally, the nonperishable artifacts that accompany the burials in all three cemeteries indicate that each population shared much of the same material culture. These mortuary items further suggest that the gender-based choices made for those individuals in death—reflected in the decoration of their clothing, the adornment of their bodies, and the objects placed in their graves—were similar for all three cemeteries.

Authors' Note

Archaeological excavations at the Fredricks and nearby Jenrette sites were undertaken as an archaeological field school by the Research Laboratories of Archaeology with financial support from the National Geographic Society, the National Science Foundation, and the University of North Carolina at Chapel Hill. We wish to thank the dozens of students who participated in the excavations, and we particularly want to acknowledge Patricia M. Lambert and Marianne E. Reeves, who assisted Elizabeth Monahan Driscoll with the *in situ* analysis of human remains found during the Jenrette site investigations. We also gratefully recognize the helpful comments of the editors, Jane M. Eastman and Christopher B. Rodning, both of whom helped supervise the fieldwork at Fredricks and Jenrette. Chris also drafted figure 6.7.

∘⟨ 7 ⟩∘

Auditory Exostoses

A Clue to Gender in Prehistoric and Historic Farming Communities of North Carolina and Virginia

Patricia M. Lambert

The purpose of this chapter is to explore the use of auditory exostoses as a source of information on gender roles in late prehistoric and early historic indigenous communities of North Carolina and southern Virginia (fig. 7.1). Auditory exostoses are bony outgrowths of the external auditory meatus. They most commonly appear as rounded protuberances within or along the margins of the canal. A lesion that until recently was most extensively studied in and best known from archaeological human skeletal series (e.g., Frayer 1988; Gregg et al. 1981; Hrdlička 1935; Kennedy 1986; Manzi, Sperduti, and Passarello 1991), auditory exostoses remain a somewhat puzzling skeletal anomaly. Many hypotheses have been proposed to explain the etiology of these ear lesions (see Hrdlička 1935), including heredity, on the one hand (e.g., Berry and Berry 1967; Blake 1880), and several environmentally induced causes, on the other. Explanations invoking environmental causation include mechanical pressures associated with body modification, such as ear ornamentation (Seligman 1864) and cranial deformation (Hrdlička 1935:68–72), and activity-related stimuli, such as swimming (Starachowicz and Koterba 1977), subsistence diving (Frayer 1988; Kennedy 1986), and bathing (Ascenzi and Balistreri 1975; Manzi, Sperduti, and Passarello 1991). The

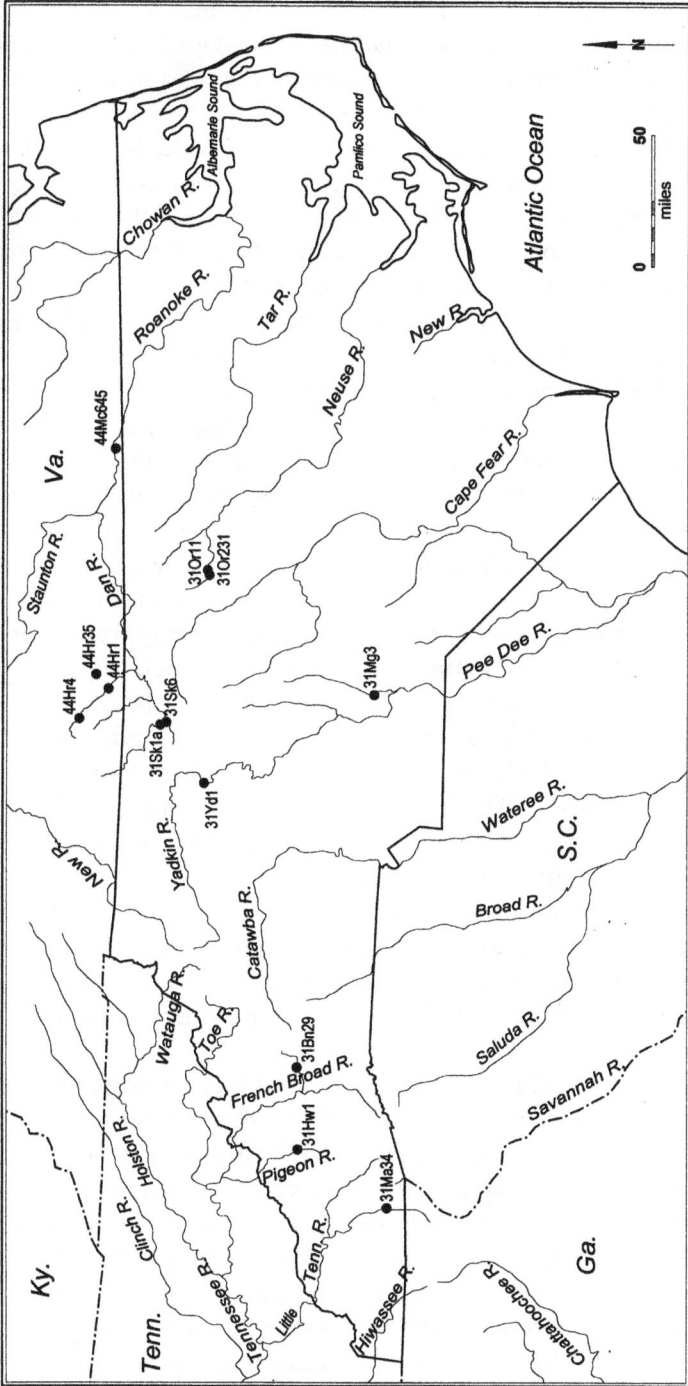

Fig. 7.1. Map of archaeological sites included in the North Carolina/Virginia study sample.

prominence of explanations from the environmental school of thought is indicative of the general view that heredity plays little or no role in the formation of these lesions, a view supported and further explored in this chapter.

The more common occurrence of auditory exostoses in males than in females has long been recognized in the anthropological literature (see Hrdlička 1935:27), which would appear to recommend them as a source of sex-specific information on ancient populations. If it could be shown that these lesions form in response to genetic instructions, they might provide a useful marker of sex and heredity (some type of sex-linked trait), but they would be of little value in the study of gender. However, Gail Kennedy's (1986) extensive latitudinal survey of auditory exostosis prevalence in archaeological skeletal series (eighty samples, each containing more than thirty individuals) provides convincing evidence for the role of the physical environment in their formation. According to this study, auditory exostoses are most common in individuals from archaeological sites located within the latitudinal range of 30° to 45° north and south of the equator, particularly in coastal samples from these latitudinal zones. The association between ear growths and geography appears to be one of habitual cold water exposure. Recent clinical research concerning the prevalence of auditory exostoses in surfers (Chaplin and Stewart 1998; Deleyiannis, Cockcroft, and Pinczower 1996; Ito and Ikeda 1998; Umeda, Nakajima, and Hoshioka 1989; Wong et al. 1999) and professional divers (Ito and Ikeda 1998; Karegeannes 1995) strongly supports this hypothesis. Clinical observations further suggest that sex differences in the frequency of auditory exostoses have more to do with sex differences in level of participation in aquatic activities than in biological differences in susceptibility to the lesions. As women become more prominent in the male-dominated sport of surfing, for example, they are beginning to exhibit the same ear changes (surfer's ear) previously associated with male surfers.[1]

According to the cold water hypothesis, auditory exostoses form when cold water infiltrates the ear canal, causing inflammation of the soft tissue lining the ear canal and stimulating periosteal new bone formation (bone hyperostosis) along the tympanic ring at the tympanomastoid and tympanosquamos sutures (Fowler and Osmon 1942; Hutchinson et al. 1997; Kennedy 1986; Wong et al. 1999). Extrapolating from this physiological model, archaeological researchers have argued that subsistence activities involving underwater diving were responsible for auditory exostoses in ancient skeletal series (e.g., Arriaza 1995; Frayer

1988; Hrdlička 1935; Kennedy 1986; Standen, Arriaza, and Santoro 1997; but see Hutchinson et al. 1997). The greater frequency of these bony ear growths in males relative to females, then, can be understood to reflect gender-specific behaviors that brought males more often than females into contact with chilly waters. Credence to this argument comes from rare cases such as Tasmania, where women are known to have been responsible for fishing, a task usually relegated to men, and where females correspondingly show a higher frequency of auditory exostoses (Pietrusewsky 1981).

Auditory Exostoses in the Southeast

A high frequency of ear lesions in human skeletal series from the Southeast was first noted over one hundred years ago (Blake 1880; see Hrdlička 1935:4). Some years later, Hrdlička (1935) researched the prevalence of auditory exostoses in skeletal samples from Arkansas, Louisiana, and Virginia, but was unable to isolate a single mode of causation in his extensive treatise on the subject. A number of the environmentally induced causes described above could have been responsible for lesions in this region. Ear ornamentation as a cultural practice, for example, is known from a number of different cultures in the Southeast (Swanton 1946) and could explain excessive bone formation of the ear canal in some cases. On the other hand, proponents of the "cold water" hypothesis have argued that the exploitation of riverine resources explains the high frequency of auditory exostoses in southeastern skeletal series (Kennedy 1986). Although cold water exposure has emerged in recent years as a prominent explanation for these lesions, this finding does not preclude the possibility that other stressors caused or contributed to the formation of auditory exostoses in ancient populations (see DiBartolomeo 1979). Several hypotheses relevant to the explication of gender roles in the Southeast are explored in the following discussion.

Materials and Methods

Data on 577 external auditory meatuses representing 335 individuals are included in this study. These remains derive from thirteen archaeological sites in the Piedmont and mountain regions of western North Carolina and southern Virginia (fig. 7.1; table 7.1). Most were collected by the Research Laboratories of Archaeology (RLA) at the University of North Carolina at Chapel Hill during their long history of archaeological field research in the region (see Coe 1995; Ward and Davis 1993, 1999). Three of the four Virginia samples (Leatherwood Creek [44Hr1],

Philpott [44Hr4], and Stockton [44Hr35]) were collected during amateur salvage excavations in the upper Dan River basin and are also curated at the RLA facility. Most derive from small- to medium-sized agricultural communities of the later prehistoric (A.D. 1000–1500) and early European contact (A.D. 1500–1710) periods (Davis et al. 1997; Dickens, Ward, and Davis, 1987; Ward and Davis 1993, 1999); a few may predate slightly this period (see table 7.1).

All individuals with at least one complete auditory canal were scored for appositional lesions of the external ear. Discrete bony masses of the external ear canal were categorized as auditory exostoses (fig. 7.2).[2] Bony thickening within or around the margins of the canal that lacked surficial definition was systematically noted, but this generalized hyperostotic

Table 7.1. Samples scored for pathological lesions of the ear canals

Site	Time period (A.D.)	Unsexed juveniles <20 yrs.	Adults (18+ years)			
			Males	Sex Females	unknown	Total
Mountains (North Carolina)						
31Bn29	1250–1450	3	13	13	3	32
31Hw1/2	1350–1450	0	2	6	3	11
31Ma34	1600–1700	9	24	11	2	46
Northern Piedmont (North Carolina/Virginia)						
44Hr1	1200–1400	4	1	4	0	9
44Hr4	1300–1450	1	3	2	0	6
44Hr35	1300–1450	2	7	10	0	19
44Mc645	800–1200	5	10	4	1	20
31Or11	1400–1500	1	3	0	0	4
31Or231	1690–1710	5	4	2	0	11
31Sk1	1450–1620	4	2	3	1	10
31Sk1a	1670–1710	6	13	14	2	35
31Sk6	1690–1710	4	1	0	0	5
31Yd1	800–1200	4	11	11	1	27
Southern Piedmont (North Carolina)						
31Mg2/3	1200–1500	18	33	40	9	100
Total		66	127	120	22	335

response was classified as "amorphous thickening" rather than as an auditory exostosis. Canals were scored according to the most severe lesion present, so that in cases where auditory exostoses and thickening were both observed, the recorded observation was "auditory exostosis." The size and location of auditory exostoses were evaluated for a subset (n = 37) of affected individuals for which more detailed data were recorded. Lesion size was estimated according to a qualitative, three-level scale (small, medium, large) based on visual assessment of the degree of occlusion of the auditory canal (see fig. 7.2). The location of auditory exostoses was described as posterior, anterior, or both, relative to a line envisioned to bisect the canal in the coronal plane.

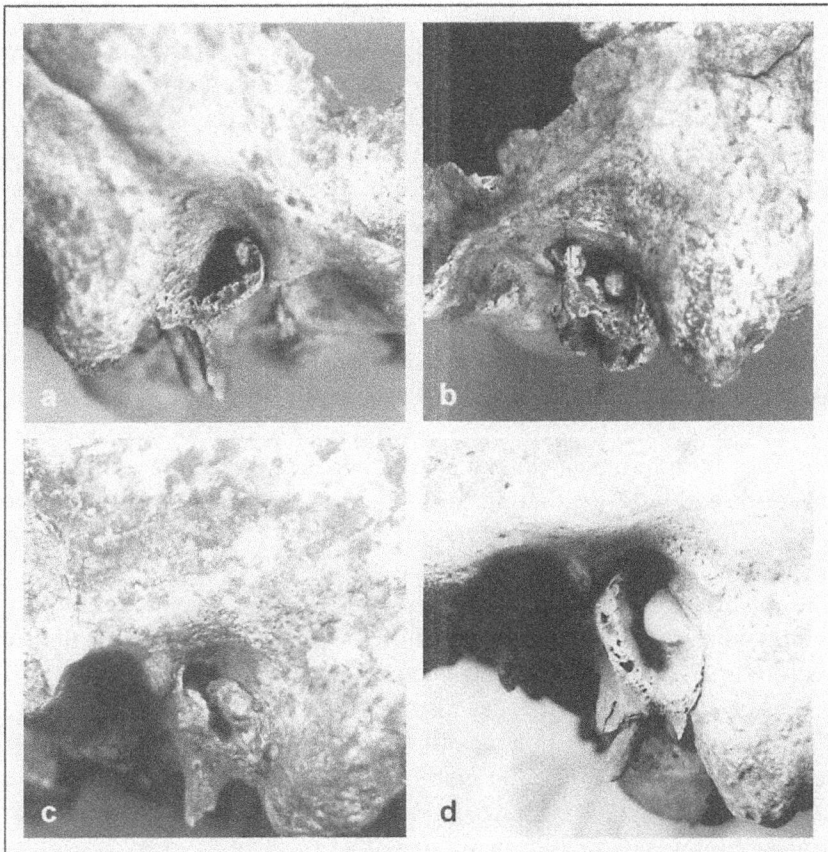

Fig. 7.2. Auditory exostoses in the North Carolina/Virginia study sample: *a*, Burial 37, 31Bn29; *b*, Burial 104, 31Sk1a; *c* Burial 26, 31Ma34; *d* Burial 3, 44Hr35.

Age and sex were determined according to standard osteological criteria (see Buikstra and Ubelaker 1994; T. D. White 1991). Sex determinations were made with reference to pelvic criteria whenever the ox coxae were available for analysis. When these bones were missing, sex was determined from cranial morphology and long-bone metrics.

Results

Auditory exostoses are fairly common in the skeletal collections from North Carolina and Virginia. A total of 13.1 percent of the 335 individuals sampled for this study have at least one auditory exostosis (table 7.2). Another 5.1 percent of the sample shows signs of amorphous bony thickening in or around the auditory canals without evidence for discrete bony growths. The total number of individuals with hyperostotic bone lesions of the external auditory meatus is thus 18.2 percent. This is a somewhat deceptive figure, however, because rates of occurrence vary considerably by site. Auditory exostoses are altogether absent from seven samples and occur in 2.9 to 52.6 percent of individuals in the other seven (table 7.2). They are absent in early agriculturalists (A.D. 800–1200), most common (18.8 percent affected) in agriculturalists from the later part of the prehistoric period (A.D. 1200–1500), and show some evidence for decline (9.3 percent affected) in early contact period populations (A.D. 1500–1710).

Several noteworthy patterns are evident in the distribution of auditory exostoses. Lesions most commonly are bilateral in distribution, affecting both right and left sides in 68 percent of affected individuals with two preserved canals. Most of these bony growths are located along the posterior margin of the ear canal (61.8 percent) or are present on both posterior and anterior margins (16.4 percent); only 21.8 percent of the lesions are restricted to the anterior margin of the canal. Both are patterns documented by Hrdlička (1935) in his extensive treatise on the subject. The majority of auditory exostoses are small (63 percent), presenting minimal occlusion of the external auditory canal, but large growths are present in 25.9 percent of affected canals.

The age distribution of auditory exostoses in the North Carolina/ Virginia sample (table 7.3) corresponds to that observed in many other regions of the world (e.g., Frayer 1988; Hrdlička 1935; Hutchinson et al. 1997; Kennedy 1986; Manzi, Sperduti, and Passarello 1991). The ear canals of infants and children are free of lesions. Auditory exostoses increase in frequency with age and are most common in individuals in their fifth decade of life (59 percent of males and 50 percent of females from

Table 7.2. Distribution of appositional lesions of the auditory canals

Site	External auditory canals free of lesions		Amorphous thickening in/around ear canals		Auditory exostoses		Total
	n	%	n	%	n	%	
Mountains							
31Bn29[a]	20	62.5	1	3.1	11	34.4	32
31Hw1/2[a]	5	45.4	3	27.3	3	27.3	11
31Ma34[a]	32	69.5	5	10.9	9[d]	19.6	46
Northern Piedmont							
44Hr1[b]	8	88.9	1	11.1	0	0.0	9
44Hr4[b]	3	50.0	2	33.3	1	16.7	6
44Hr35[b]	9	47.4	0	0.0	10	52.6	19
44Mc645[b]	20	100.0	0	0.0	0	0.0	20
31Or11[c]	4	100.0	0	0.0	0	0.0	4
31Or231[b]	11	100.0	0	0.0	0	0.0	11
31Sk1[b]	10	100.0	0	0.0	0	0.0	10
31Sk1a[c]	34	97.1	0	0.0	1	2.9	35
31Sk6[c]	5	100.0	0	0.0	0	0.0	5
31Yd1[b]	27	100.0	0	0.0	0	0.0	27
Southern Piedmont							
31Mg2/3[a]	85	85.0	6	6.0	9	9.0	100
Total	274	81.8	17	5.1	44	13.1	335

a. Frontal-occipital cranial deformation predominates.
b. No cranial deformation.
c. Occipital deformation present in some individuals.
d. Includes one individual with bony bar spanning ear canal from posterior to anterior margins.

samples with at least one auditory exostosis). There is also an association between age and the size of the lesions: 92 percent of individuals with large growths are thirty or more years of age. When auditory exostoses are analyzed together with the evidence for amorphous thickening, the process of their formation is suggested (fig. 7.3). Amorphous thickening without auditory exostosis is most common in individuals between the ages of ten and thirty years and appears to presage the appearance of well-defined bony lesions; older individuals more often exhibit the full-blown lesion. These findings are consistent with modern clinical studies of auditory exostoses in surfers and divers, which show a strong positive correlation between the frequency and severity of auditory exostoses and the number of years spent participating in aquatic activities (Chaplin and Stewart 1998; Deleyiannis, Cockcroft, and Pinczower 1996; Karege-annes 1995; Wong et al. 1999). These data support morphological and histological evidence (Hutchinson et al. 1997) that auditory exostoses are accretionary in nature, increasing in size and definition with age (see Manzi, Sperduti, and Passarello 1991).

The sex distribution of auditory exostoses is also similar to that observed in many regions of the world (e.g., Hrdlička 1935; Kennedy 1986; Manzi et al. 1991; Wong et al. 1999), with lesions differentially affecting adult males (table 7.4). In the North Carolina/Virginia sample, auditory exostoses are twice as common in males as in females, a statistically significant difference (Pearson's Chi Square = 6.598; $p = 0.01$) very similar

Table 7.3. Percentage of individuals with pathological ear conditions by age group

Age group (yrs)	n	External auditory canals free of lesions	Amorphous thickening in/around ear canals	Auditory exostoses[a]
0–4.99	33	100.0	0.0	0.0
5–9.9	13	100.0	0.0	0.0
10–14.9	11	100.0	0.0	0.0
15–19.9	24	87.5	8.3	4.2
20–24.9	23	78.3	8.7	13.0
25–29.9	36	80.6	8.3	11.1
30–34.9	23	82.6	4.4	13.0
35–39.9	36	72.2	5.6	22.2
40–44.9	39	64.1	5.1	30.8
45–49.9	25	80.0	0.0	20.0
50+	3	66.7	33.3	0.0
Total	266	81.6	4.9	13.5

a. None of 21 additional juveniles (0–15 years) excluded from study sample because of incomplete or dirt/PVC-filled canals showed signs of auditory exostoses.

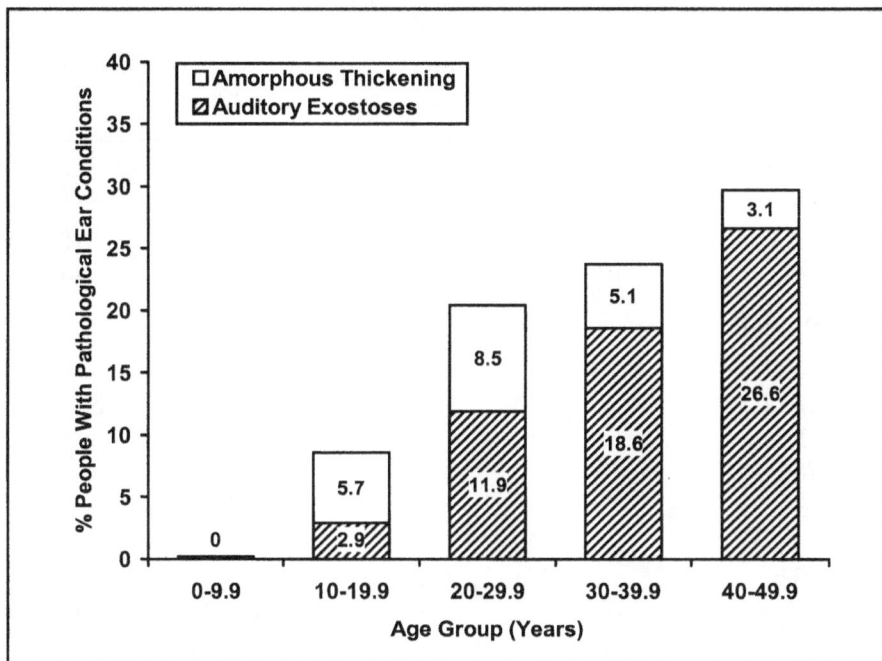

Fig. 7.3. Age distribution of appositional lesions of the external auditory canal.

in magnitude (F:M = 0.45) to that observed by Hrdlička (1935:28) in his study of sixty-five crania from Virginia (0.47). In individual site samples, they are more common in males in five of seven collections.

Discussion

A number of environmentally based hypotheses proffered to explain the formation of auditory exostoses are consistent with archaeological data from North Carolina. The frequency of lesions varies geographical-ly, which suggests regional variation in the frequency of activities or practices resulting in auditory exostoses (fig. 7.4). Auditory exostoses are most common in mountain samples and least common in those from the North Carolina Piedmont. Sex differences in lesion frequency, on the other hand, are most pronounced in the southern Piedmont sample. These differences, particularly in light of temporal differences in lesion frequency, strongly support the hypothesis that auditory exostoses were environmentally induced in this Southeast region. The greater preva-lence of these lesions in men further argues for gender differences in body modification, work, ritual, or play that differentially exposed males

Table 7.4. Sex distribution of auditory exostoses

Site	Males		Females	
	+/-	% affected	+/-	% affected
Mountains				
31Bn29	5/8	38.5	5/8	38.5
31Hw1/2	1/1	50.0	0/6	0.0
31Ma34	7/17	29.2	1/10	9.1
Northern Piedmont				
44Hr1	0/1	0.0	0/4	0.0
44Hr4	0/3	0.0	1/1	50.0
44Hr35	7/0	100.0	3/7	30.0
44Mc645	0/10	0.0	0/4	0.0
31Sk1	0/2	0.0	0/3	0.0
31Sk1a	1/12	7.7	0/14	0.0
31Sk6	0/1	0.0	0/0	-
31Yd1	0/11	0.0	0/11	0.0
Southern Piedmont				
31Mg2/3	7/26	21.2	2/38	5.0
Total	28/99	22.0	12/108	10.0

to inflammatory ear conditions. Although it is possible that the observed lesions were caused by a number of different conditions (see Hutchinson et al. 1997), their complete absence in some samples and high frequency in others (table 7.2) would argue for the dominance of a single mode of causation. The evidence for, and gender implications of, different hypotheses for the formation of these lesions in the Southeast are explored below.

Ear Ornamentation

Mechanical trauma associated with ornaments that pierce and pull the skin and cartilage of the external ear was posited early on as a possible explanation for auditory exostoses (Seligman 1864; see also Hrdlička 1935: 66). According to this model, it is the mechanical irritation of the osteogenic tissue lining the canals that stimulates bone production. Seligman (1864), for example, argued that the practice of heavy ear adornment

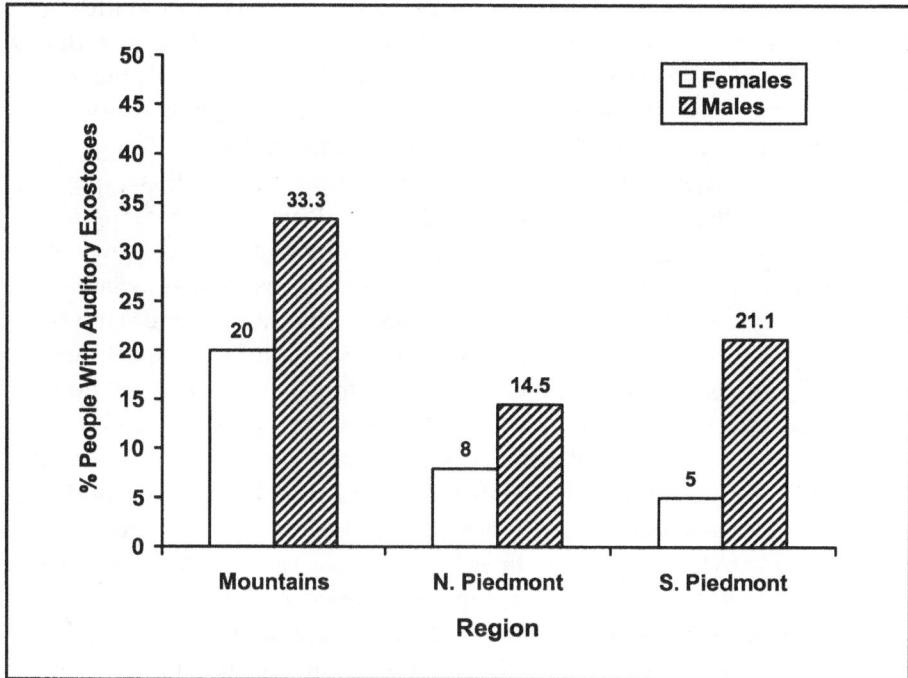

Fig. 7.4. Geographic variation in the frequency of auditory exostoses.

at puberty led to the formation of these lesions in ancient Peruvians. Numerous accounts of ear adornment for both men and women are documented in the ethnohistoric record of the Southeast (Swanton 1946), including those specific to peoples of North Carolina and Virginia: "Barlowe observed that the wife of a North Carolina coast noble, Granganimeo, wore in her ears 'bracelets [i.e., strings] of pearls hanging down to her middle . . . and those were of the bignes of good pease. The rest of her women of the better sort had pendants of copper hanging in either eare, and some of the children of the kings brother and other noble men, have five or six in either eare'" (Burrage 1906:232, in Swanton 1946:510). Swanton (1946:511) also relates an account of ear adornment among men in this region: "When men of the Piedmont country went to war they wore in their ears feathers, the wings of birds, rings, copper, wampum, and probably at an earlier date roanoke." The ear ornaments described in these historic accounts appear to have been relatively substantial in size, and would have involved a considerable amount of tissue, particularly that in proximity to the posterior margin of the canal. Although ear ornaments were not recovered from all sites with affected individuals, they have been recovered from some (Davis et al. 1996; Rodning, this volume). The data are thus not inconsistent with the hypothesis that ear ornaments, through mechanical trauma, caused the auditory exostoses observed in burials from these southeastern communities.

One of the most important archaeological implications of this hypothesis is that affected individuals should be those habitually making use of, and presumably buried with, ear ornaments. Given that the greatest frequency of lesions is found in adult males, ear ornament associations should similarly show a male bias. The archaeological evidence is mixed in this regard. In the Coweeta Creek (31Ma34) sample, all sexed individuals with ear ornaments are males (Rodning, this volume), but none of these are affected with auditory exostoses. On the other hand, two adult females—one from Warren Wilson (31Bn29) and one from Stockton (44Hr35)—are the only individuals with clear ear ornament associations at these sites, and both have auditory exostoses. Most affected individuals, however, do not appear to have been wearing ear pins or disks at the time of burial. It is possible that some of the piercing ornaments used by these people were fashioned of organic materials (such as the feathers described above) that did not survive the ravages of time. It is also possible that jewelry was removed before burial, although the presence of beads and other items of adornment with some individuals (Davis et al. 1996) argues against this hypothesis. Overall, the available archaeological evidence does not appear to support trauma associated with ear adornment as an exclusive or important cause of auditory exostoses, nor does it seem to explain the pronounced sex bias observed in the distribution of these lesions.

Cranial Deformation

As Hrdlička (1935) noted many years ago, there is a curious but incomplete relationship between auditory exostoses and frontal-occipital cranial deformation. In the North Carolina/Virginia sample, auditory exostoses are particularly common in crania from Warren Wilson, a fourteenth-century mountain village in western North Carolina, where all but one scorable vault exhibits this mode of cranial deformation. Fifty percent (nine of eighteen) of the vaults from this site with frontal-occipital deformation exhibit ear growths, including similar numbers of males and females. Of all head forms, crania with frontal-occipital deformation are most commonly associated with both auditory exostoses and amorphous thickening (fig. 7.5). These data suggest that bony ear lesions in individuals from this and other sites with cranial deformation could be the result of mechanical forces imposed on the cranial bones by artificial manipulation during the growth years (see also Hrdlička 1935).

However, the demographics of auditory exostoses do not support mechanical stimulation as an exclusive explanation for lesions. If the mechanical processes of deformation were responsible for this pathological bone formation, then ear lesions should begin to appear in childhood, and they are virtually absent in juveniles under eighteen years of age (table 7.3; see also Hrdlička 1935). In addition, one of the highest frequencies of auditory exostoses occurs in a sample from the northern Piedmont (44Hr35) with no evidence of cranial deformation (table 7.2). In this sample, all seven males and three of ten females are affected.

The exact nature of the relationship between cranial deformation and auditory exostoses, thus, is unclear. Correlation is not causation, so the apparent association could be meaningless. On the other hand, many of the individuals with posteriorly deformed vaults have antero-posteriorly narrowed lumina (ear channels), an abnormality noted previously

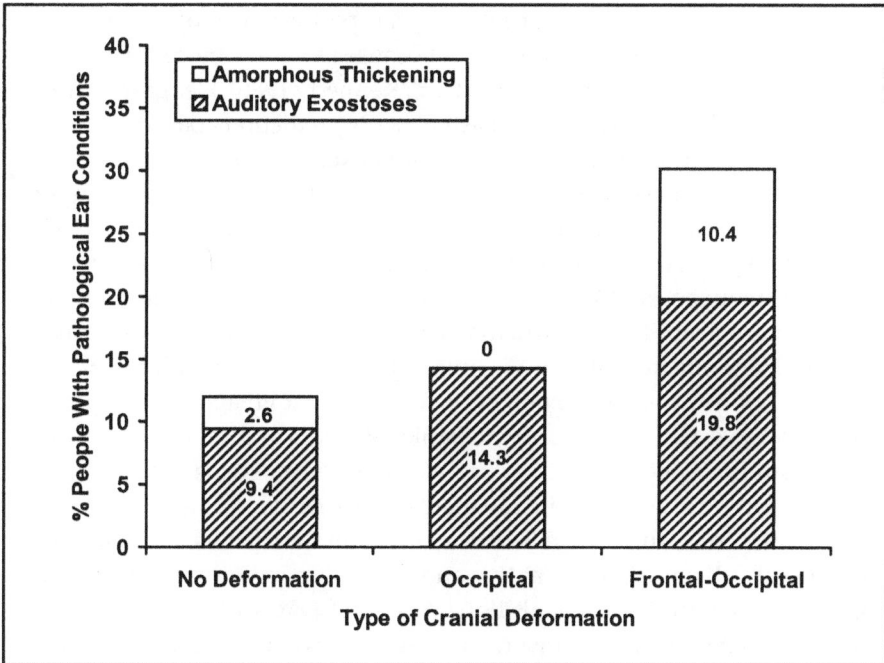

Fig. 7.5. Relationship between appositional lesions of the external auditory canal and cranial deformation.

in association with frontal-occipital deformation (see Bachauer 1909, in Hrdlička 1935:9), and it is possible that these shape changes altered the external ear environment, predisposing them to inflammatory conditions. However, although males are slightly more likely than females to exhibit cranial deformation in the sample as a whole (F:M = 0.91), the relatively equal practice of cranial deformation among people of all ages and both sexes does not suggest that, as a cultural marker of sex or gender, cranial deformation was responsible for the pronounced sex bias in auditory exostoses.

Cold Water Immersion

As discussed previously, the predominant view of etiology in the case of auditory exostoses in archaeological skeletal series is one of cold water exposure due to subsistence-related diving activities (Kennedy 1986). This argument encompasses both riverine and ocean resource acquisition as it has been applied to the Southeast as well as to other temperate regions as far afield as Chile and the former Yugoslavia (e.g., Arriaza 1995; Frayer 1988; Kennedy 1986; Standen, Arriaza, and Santoro 1997). A clear sex-based division of labor in the performance of subsistence activities is implied by this argument because males are more commonly affected than females in most cases (e.g., Kennedy 1986). Geographically, this explanation is certainly consistent with predictions based on Kennedy's (1986) latitudinal survey of auditory exostosis prevalence because the North Carolina/Virginia skeletal samples described in this chapter all derive from archaeological sites located between latitudes 35° and 37° north. However, the creeks and rivers in close proximity to sites with the highest frequencies of these lesions, although potentially cold enough, are not very deep. This is particularly pertinent in the case of Stockton, a small village site in southern Virginia with an unusually high frequency of auditory exostoses (52.6 percent): "Unlike most villages of this phase which were established along the banks of rivers and major tributaries that form the upper Dan River basin, the Stockton site is located in an upland setting . . . near the headwaters of Leatherwood Creek" (Davis et al. 1997:1). To be sure, there is direct faunal and artifactual evidence for the use of fish and shellfish at this and other sites in both mountain and piedmont regions (Davis et al. 1997; Ward and Davis 1999), but it seems unlikely that in waters that were in most cases no more than waist deep, the collection of riverine foods would have been viewed as a male task to be performed systematically underwater.

This is not to say, however, that cold water immersion cannot be invoked as a reasonable explanation for the bony ear lesions observed in indigenous peoples of this region. Ritual bathing played an important role in many aspects of life in southeastern societies (Alexander 1972; Hudson 1976; Swanton 1946), and it may well have provided the primary physiological stimulus for these lesions. A recent study of ancient Roman skeletons (Manzi, Sperduti, and Passarello 1991), for example, found very pronounced differences in the frequency of auditory exostoses between males and females as well as among different social classes. Auditory exostoses were much more common (31.3 percent) in middle-class males than in male laborers (6.9 percent) but virtually absent in middle-class females. According to the authors, the differences likely are explained by the habitual use by middle-class males (but not by their wives or male laborers) of *thermae*, a graded sequence of thermal baths ranging from hot to cold. They also note that the *frigidarium* (cold pool), an important feature of the men's bathing regime, appears to have been lacking in the women's regime, which may also explain the absence of auditory exostoses in female skeletons (Manzi, Sperduti, and Passarello 1991).

Evidence that such an explanation is tenable for the Southeast comes from historic accounts of indigenous healing and purification practices. Ritual sweating, which appears to have culminated with a plunge into frigid waters, is a form of bathing that figures prominently in these accounts. For example, Swanton notes the following account by Beverley (1705:49–51) of the sweating ritual among the Indians of Virginia:

> They [the men] take great delight in Sweating, and therefore in every Town they have a Sweating House, and a Doctor is paid by the Publick to attend it. They commonly use this to refresh themselves, after they have been fatigu'd with Hunting, Travel, or the like, or else when they are troubl'd with Agues, Aches, or Pains in their Limbs. . . . [T]he Doctor, to raise a Steam, after they have been stewing a little while, purs cold Water on the Stones, and now and then sprinkles the Men to keep them from fainting. After they have sweat as long as they can well endure it, they sally out, and (tho it be in the depth of Winter) fortwith plunge themselves over Head and Ears in cold Water, which instantly closes up the Pores, and preserves them from taking cold. (Swanton 1946:784–85)

An account by John Fontaine, an eighteenth-century European visitor to the Saponi town near Fort Christanna, also describes the sweating ritual as well as details concerning the appearance of sweat houses: "Between the town and the river side there are several little huts built with wattles in the form of an oven with a small door in one end of it. These wattles are plaistered without side with clay very close, and they are big enough to hold a man. They call those houses sweating houses" (Alexander 1972:97). Archaeological features suggestive of sweat houses have been identified in mountain village sites (Dickens 1976:56; Ward and Davis 1999:163) as well as on the northern Piedmont (Davis et al. 1997; Dickens, Ward, and Davis 1987.) Given that not only excessive cold but also excessive heat may be associated with inflammatory conditions of the external ear (Hutchinson et al. 1997), it seems reasonable that the cultural practice of "sweating" as described above could have been particularly important in producing the high frequency of auditory exostoses observed in the study sample. Indeed, the traumatic effect on the ear canals of the cold water finale may have been heightened by the long period of heat exposure that preceded it.

If ritual sweating is invoked as an explanation for auditory exostoses in the North Carolina/Virginia sample, then sex differences in the frequency of these lesions can offer insights into gender differences in the ritual behavior of men and women in some late prehistoric and early historic villages. As indicated previously, males are twice as likely as females to exhibit auditory exostoses overall (table 7.4). This is in keeping with many historic accounts of sweating practices among indigenous southeastern societies, which suggest that males more commonly incorporated sweating into their various rituals and ceremonies. Hudson (1976) recounts several contexts for sweating among the Creeks that exclusively involved men. For example, LeClert Milfort, a French adventurer, described participating in a sweat as part of his initiation as a Creek war chief: "The next day all the men took off their clothing and went into a circular building used as a sweat house, where the heat and steam was so intense Milfort was afraid he would not be able to endure it. They remained there about half an hour, and then to Milfort's consternation all ran to plunge into a river a short distance away" (Hudson 1976:327). Creek candidates for priesthood also sweated as a part of the initiation ceremony: "After four days of instruction, the young men went into a makeshift tent. They put hot stones on the ground and poured water over them, making clouds of steam. After they had been sufficiently steamed, they immersed themselves in the cold water of the creek" (Hudson 1976: 339). Sweating was even used to treat men suffering the potential ill effects of exposure to menstruating women: "If a menstruating woman

carelessly came into contact with a man, the Southeastern Indians believed that the man would develop pain in his lower legs, nosebleed,
headache, and severe depression. If a Creek man fell ill with this, he was
treated with a decoction of *miko hoyanidja*, which he drank, bathed in,
and used to make steam in a sweat bath" (Hudson 1976:343). Extrapolating from these Creek accounts to the larger Southeast culture area
(see Swanton 1928), ritual sweating would appear to have figured more
prominently in male roles than it did in female roles—at least during the
historic period.

This is not to say that women did not participate in the sweat, only
that they may not have done so with the regularity that men did. It is
possible that women sometimes were excluded or more commonly chose
to abstain from such activities, perhaps during menstruation and pregnancy. Various accounts do suggest, however, that as a treatment for ill-
ness, sweating was employed by both males and females: "for when they
[Saponi] have any sickness they get 10 or 12 pebble stones which they
make very hot in a fire and when they are red hot they carry them in
those little huts and the sick man or woman goes in naked and they shut
the door upon them and there they sit and sweat until they are no more
able to support it and then they go out naked and immediately jump
into the water over head and ears" (Alexander 1972:97). Perhaps less habitual use of sweating facilities, rather than abstention, reduced wom-
en's exposure to the environmental stimuli that induce inflammatory
ear conditions, which in turn resulted in a lower incidence of auditory
exostoses.

Other bathing rituals also may have contributed to the observed frequency and distribution of auditory exostoses. Among the Cherokee, for
example, the act of "going to water" played a central role in divination,
healing, purification, and spiritual cleansing; this ritual often involved
immersion in cold, running water (Hudson 1976; J. Mooney 1890; Anne
Rogers, personal communication 1999). According to Hudson (1976:345):
"Bathing in fresh water was believed to be especially purifying when
performed just at day-break, when the red sky of dawn was reflected
in the water. An especially good season for bathing was autumn, when
fallen leaves in the water imparted to it their medicinal virtues." The
close of the Green Corn ceremony was accompanied by river bathing, as
was the ball game (Hudson 1976:374, 414; Swanton 1946:675, 681). Once
again, cold water exposure would have been likely to result in ear lesions
in cases of habitual practice.

Broader Implications of the Bathing Hypothesis

Bathing involving cold water immersion appears to have played a prominent role in indigenous communities throughout the Southeast. Given the growing body of clinical research supporting a cold-water etiology for these lesions, it is likely that many (if not most) of the auditory exostoses observed in prehistoric and historic skeletal series from North Carolina and Virginia formed as a result of sweating practices and other bathing rituals that regularly exposed bathers to cold water. If this argument is correct, then age and sex differences in the prevalence of auditory exostoses can provide some interesting insights into levels of participation in ritual bathing and in the various activities in which it played a central role. Clinical studies indicate that bony obstruction of the ear canal begins to appear after five to seven years of participation in cold water activities (Chaplin and Stewart 1998; Deleyiannis, Cockcroft, and Pinczower 1996; Umeda, Nakajima, and Hoshioka 1989). One recent study also suggests that the severity of the osseous response is positively correlated with frequency of exposure (Deleyiannis, Cockcroft, and Pinczower 1996; but see Chaplin and Stewart 1998). The age distribution of ear lesions in the North Carolina/Virginia sample thus suggests that sustained participation in rituals involving cold water immersion began in early adolescence and continued unabated into old age.

Sex differences in the frequency of auditory exostoses further suggest that these ritual ablutions were most prominent in the performance of male-dominated social roles. This does not always appear to have been the case, however. At the late prehistoric site of Warren Wilson in the mountains of North Carolina, males and females have comparable rates of auditory exostoses, which may reflect more equal participation of both sexes in behaviors that exposed ear canals to thermal trauma. Perhaps bathing practices were more commonplace and less ritualized at this time and place. At villages where the male sex bias is most pronounced, on the other hand, the few affected females may have held unique roles or social positions of which greater participation in ritual bathing was just one manifestation. Indeed, social distinctions may explain why only some individuals of both sexes are affected with auditory exostoses. However, it is also possible that affected women were those suffering more commonly from complaints for which cold water immersion was part of the prescribed cure or that they constituted a minority of women who simply enjoyed the bracing qualities of a cold bath and chose to participate in bathing behaviors more commonly or actively expected of men. Variation in the way the bathing act was performed also may have contributed to the observed patterns (e.g., Swanton 1946:714).

Geographic variation in the frequency of auditory exostoses may be evidence that the habitual practice of cold water immersion, within or outside of the sweating ritual, was infrequent or foreign to one or both sexes. However, caution is warranted with regard to this interpretation. Recent clinical studies suggest that regional differences in water temperature can influence both the prevalence and severity of auditory exostoses (Chaplin and Stewart 1998; Umeda, Nakajima, and Hoshioka 1989), so it may be that colder water temperatures in the Blue Ridge Mountains and on the Virginia Piedmont at least in part explain geographic (and apparent temporal) variation in the observed frequency of affected individuals. Nonetheless, the pronounced sex bias evident in some samples from all regions still suggests that cultural differences in behavior were more important than differences in water temperature in the formation of these bony ear lesions.

Concluding Remarks

Auditory exostoses in human skeletal remains from North Carolina and Virginia show an age and sex distribution strikingly similar to that observed in archaeological skeletal series from elsewhere in the world (e.g., Hrdlička 1935; Kennedy 1986). The lesions tend to be bilateral, to appear in adulthood, and to affect adult males differentially. As elsewhere, the evidence from this region does not support a genetic origin for auditory exostoses but rather suggests several behaviors that could have caused these appositional lesions to form. These include ear ornamentation and cranial deformation, which could have stimulated bone formation mechanically, and activities performed or conducted in cold water, which would have induced an inflammatory response ultimately leading to periosteal bone buildup in the canals. The explanation that appears to tie in best with bioarchaeological and clinical research on auditory exostoses and also with ethnohistoric information on what men and women were actually doing in these southeastern societies is that of ritual bathing. Thermal trauma is well documented as a cause of otitis externa and of the bony lesions described as "surfer's ear" in the clinical literature. That auditory exostoses affected more males than females in five of seven samples is evidence that men in these societies more commonly engaged in bathing rituals that exposed their ears to thermal trauma. Like the women of ancient Rome, these southeastern women may have eliminated cold water from the bathing regime or perhaps may have found themselves simply too busy to engage regularly in prolonged social engagements such as ritual sweating.

Author's Note

I thank Jane Eastman and Chris Rodning for their invitation to participate in this volume and in the symposium organized for the 1996 Southeast Archaeological Conference in Birmingham, Alabama, on which it is based. I would also like to thank Clark Larsen for his help and guidance with the larger bioarchaeological project from which these data derive, and R. P. Stephen Davis Jr. for making figure 7.1 and providing information on the dating of various collections. Funding for this research was provided by the Research Laboratories of Archaeology, University of North Carolina at Chapel Hill.

Notes

1. Robert T. Scott, M. D., personal communication, 1999. Dr. Scott, of Santa Cruz, California, has been examining the ear canals of surfers, swimmers, sailboarders, and divers since 1976. He has observed thousands of exostoses in participants in these aquatic sports. He is currently president of DOC'S PROPLUG, Inc., a company that manufacturers vented ear plugs for water-sports participants.

2. Histological analysis was not conducted during this investigation, so it was not possible to differentiate auditory exostoses from the pedunculate growths identified as osteomatas by Hutchinson and colleagues (1997). However, the lesions observed in these skeletal series were not pedunculate and frequently were bilateral in distribution, which would appear to identify them as auditory exostoses rather than as osteomatas.

⋊ 8 ⋉

Concluding Thoughts

Janet E. Levy

I am honored to be able to conclude this volume on the study of gender in the prehistoric southeastern United States. As I write this, it is now nine years since I was given the opportunity to comment on the first symposium about gender presented at the Southeastern Archaeological Conference in Jackson, Mississippi, in 1991; some of those contributions have since been published as well (Galloway 1997; Kozuch 1993; Sassaman 1993; Trocolli 1999). Since that time, archaeological studies of gender have expanded dramatically in many regions. While archaeological practice in the southeastern United States is frequently considered to be distant from modern innovations in theory (Johnson 1993:xi), gender research gradually has become well established in the area. The richness and diversity of available archaeological, ethnohistoric, and ethnographic data are the foundation for current and, I am confident, future gender research. While the prehistoric record of the Southeast certainly suffers from differential preservation, the data available—including artifacts, ecofacts, architectural remains, human skeletal remains, and a rich ethnohistoric record—provide investigators with a superb base from which to examine these critical topics.

As has been pointed out before, while seeking gender in the archaeological record may well be difficult, it should not be any more difficult than seeking rank, power, specialization, or other topics widely considered to be legitimately within the purview of the archaeologist. It is the necessary assumption of archaeologists that patterned human behavior leaves patterned material remains: distorted, disturbed, partial, incomplete, but nevertheless with some discernible pattern. It would be truly incredible if sex roles and gendered behavior in prehistoric communities were the only sets of patterned behavior that did not leave some patterned material remains.

As is demonstrated in these chapters and elsewhere, gender has relevance to virtually all the "big topics" of archaeology, whether that be a culture-historical archaeology, a processual archaeology, or a postprocessual archaeology: These include subsistence practice (Bridges 1989), seasonality (Thomas, this volume), exchange relationships (Thomas, this volume), ritual (Eastman; Lambert; Rodning, this volume), household economy, rank (Sullivan, this volume), acculturation (Monahan Driscoll, Davis, and Ward, this volume), iconography (Koehler 1997). In the past, the argument was made that an engendered archaeology required conceptual but not methodological innovation. Yet Claassen, in this volume, demonstrates several arenas—in particular, analysis of human skeletal remains and use of ethnographic/ethnohistoric documents—where methodological revision will also be helpful. In this context, it is refreshing to acknowledge the testimony by Monahan Driscoll, Davis, and Ward in their contribution to this volume, in which they discuss how an engendered perspective caused them to reconsider skeletal sexing and the implications of artifact associations.

Archaeology is ultimately the study of variability: variability in the material record as a guide to diversity and variability in prehistoric social and cultural arrangements. Given this essential emphasis on variability, it is particularly valuable to see, in these chapters, analyses that struggle to incorporate gender along with other axes of variability in human social life: in particular, age (e.g., Eastman), but also rank (Sullivan), kinship, and ethnicity (Monahan Driscoll, Davis, and Ward). Human social life is complex, not necessarily in the unfortunately common sense of "complexity" as equivalent to "hierarchy," but in the sense that all humans experience a social world with numerous axes of variation influencing values and behavior.

In fact, the quite real frustrations we meet in attempting to understand prehistoric gender relationships tell us that perhaps we have been overconfident in our reconstructions of other social variables. In this context, I see a valuable contribution in incorporating the concept of "heterarchy" into our analyses of past social relationships. This concept encourages us to investigate lateral social relationships as well as vertical ones and, in fact, denies the intellectual priority given to hierarchy as a sign of social complexity (Crumley 1987). As we begin to consider gender as a significant social variable, it becomes clearer that all social complexity cannot be encompassed within concepts of rank. While Sullivan, explicitly, and Rodning, implicitly, in this volume find that heterarchy illuminates their understandings of late prehistoric societies in the southern Appalachian region, I hope that attention to gender will expand our openness to heterarchy in analyses of the more noticeably hierarchical classic chiefdoms of the Southeast as well (e.g., Levy 1999).

While these fine papers stand on their own, I can use them to ask the question: Where do we go from here? To start with, let me note contributions to another topic area within the larger subject of an engendered archaeology: the sociopolitics of current archaeological practice, with emphasis on the role of women in the profession. This topic has been developed by archaeologists in parallel with investigations of gender in prehistory. While not part of this volume, the foundation of a database for the Southeast now exists as represented in publications by Claassen (1993), Claassen et al. (1999), and N. M. White, Sullivan, and Marrinan (1999). A direction for the future could be the ethnography of gendered excavation practice, as exemplified by Gero's (1996) study of an excavation in South America. Gero's analysis of how unconscious, "taken-for-granted" excavation practice has, in fact, a gendered component suggests a rich field for inquiry, one that speaks particularly to all of us who run field schools where the next generation of Southeastern archaeologists, female and male, are socialized.

In reference to the topics of this volume, it is notable that these papers all focus on very late prehistory, fundamentally the Mississippian cultural period. This is understandable, given the special wealth of both archaeological and ethnohistoric data from this time. There is a small number of engendered studies focusing on earlier periods in the Southeast, for example Claassen (1991), Sassaman (1993), and Watson and Kennedy (1991) on the late Archaic. Claassen reported in her 1996 SEAC paper that little or no engendered research had been conducted on Paleoindian and earliest Archaic periods. It will be a difficult challenge to add an engendered perspective to these early periods given the nature of their databases. But these periods pose difficult challenges for *all* archaeological analysis. Certainly, there were females and males living in these times. Perhaps gender categories were very salient and sex roles very differentiated in those cultures, perhaps not; either way, it raises valuable questions that are worth struggling to answer.

Second, there is relatively little attention given here to long-term culture change. Again, I see this not as a criticism but as a challenge for the future. As we gradually develop an empirical and analytical database for engendering individual case studies, we should keep in mind the core archaeological concern with change through time. A fine model for the Southeast is Patricia Bridges's (1989) study of changing work patterns from Archaic through Mississippian periods, while Sassaman (1993) and Watson and Kennedy (1991) discuss major technological innovations. Gender theorists often decry the dominance of cultural evolutionary models as silencing concerns with agency, power, and gender, among other things (e.g., Nelson 1997:171–73). Yet there should be ways to integrate the concerns of an evolutionary archaeology and an engendered archaeology. For example, Flannery's (1972) model of how state political structures develop from more egalitarian politics through linearization and promotion cries out for the enrichment of a gender perspective. He did not provide such a perspective, but we certainly can do so in the future. The prehistoric narrative of the Southeast is a prime locale for investigating the role of gender in the development of hierarchical polities. Indeed, there is still much more to be said about men, women, and gender in the development of horticulture, pottery, and other technologies, such as metal- and shell-working, in different parts of the Southeast.

Third, I would like to see an integration of gender studies with what some might consider more old-fashioned concerns with ecological adaptation. While Claassen, in this volume, rightly emphasizes the significance of social relations in prehistory, and elsewhere (Claassen 1997) links the study of gender to new theoretical insights about individual agency in the past, the relationships between humans and environment remain important: Every individual, every agent lived in a real environment that, while it did not dictate cultural arrangements, must have had an influence on them. Thus, Watson and Kennedy (1991) consider the proposed environmental changes of the early Holocene in their model of the development of horticulture in the mid-South. The natural environment will have varied influences in the different areas (e.g., coast, piedmont, mountains, alluvial valleys) of the ecologically diverse Southeast. A case worthy of examination is the role of environmental fluctuation, known through tree-ring data, in the cycling of chiefdoms in the Savannah River Valley as documented by Anderson (1994). Given what we know about the gendered division of labor in the Southeast and the iconography of the supernatural world, which incorporates both gendered and environmentally focused images, our understanding of these chiefdoms will be enriched if we integrate our understanding of environmental and social factors.

Finally, we must still grapple with an issue developed by Claassen in this volume: the complex interconnections among sex, sex roles, gender, gender roles, and gender ideology. Claassen, as others have done, warns us against simplistic and, especially, simplistically dualistic analyses of a phenomenon we call "gender" and against equating biological sex and cultural gender. This is a particularly knotty problem in interpreting human skeletal remains, and there are no easy answers to the dilemma; the authors here sometimes do use "gender" when, in fact, they are referring to osteological identifications of sex, for which only two options (male and female) have been provided. Among other things, it would be valuable to clarify cases in which the sex of an adult skeleton cannot be determined with current osteological methods. If this is due to poor preservation, the case is unfortunate but not further illuminating. But if this occurs because a well-preserved skeleton does not clearly match the established osteological criteria for male or female, then there is a potential for further inquiry into sexual dimorphism in the population and its implications for sex roles and gender ideology.

The contributions in this volume demonstrate a rich understanding of sexually differentiated roles—that is, the different statuses and activities of males and females in particular prehistoric societies. This is extremely valuable; it is a worthwhile contribution, in my opinion, simply to improve the cultural historical detail of our narrative of prehistory through a consideration of gendered variability in prehistoric life course. However, a further step, in addition to considering culture change as noted above, is to utilize these data for analysis of gender ideology—that is, the cultural elaboration of intertwined ideas about sex, sexuality, work, and social relations. Concepts of gender may or may not be dualistic in any particular social setting; genders may be dramatically differentiated or culturally insignificant; gender relationships may be complementary, antagonistic, hierarchical, or unimportant. While the ethnohistoric and ethnographic record suggest that gender concepts in the late prehistoric Southeast were certainly important parts of the cultural pattern, we have less immediate insight into the situation in earlier periods. We must also take into consideration the gendered and other biases of ethnohistoric chroniclers and nineteenth-century ethnographers. But the gender arrangements of any particular prehistoric community remain problematic: to be examined, questioned, and evaluated, rather than read back from the early historic records or cross-cultural assumptions. I predict that gender will turn out to have been a significant cultural category in all periods of southeastern prehistory; how that category was expressed, valued, and manipulated will, without doubt, turn out to have changed through time. But all this remains to be demonstrated through the careful assessment of empirical data and theoretical understanding.

So there is a lot of work—difficult work—to do. Acknowledging and researching gender makes our archaeological lives more complicated but also more interesting. This volume and the growing number of other contributions from southeastern archaeologists promise a future of intriguing and illuminating research on the prehistoric human societies of the region. A gendered archaeology will not be about subjects different from those we have tackled before; rather it will be a better archaeology about the questions that have interested us for years. This volume provides us with both illuminating information about several prehistoric communities in the Southeast and a promise for fine research to come.

Author's Note

Many thanks to Jane Eastman and Chris Rodning for inviting me to participate both in the 1996 SEAC symposium and in this edited volume, as well as to Patty Jo Watson, who joined us at SEAC in 1996 and provided her usual elegant editing to this contribution.

References

Alexander, Edward P., editor

1972 *The Journal of John Fontaine. An Irish Huguenot Son in Spain and Virginia, 1710–1719*. Colonial Williamsburg Foundation, Williamsburg, Virginia.

Anderson, David G.

1990 "Stability and Change in Chiefdom-Level Societies: An Examination of Mississippian Political Evolution on the South Atlantic Slope." In *Lamar Archaeology: Mississippian Chiefdoms of the Deep South*, ed. Mark Williams and Gary Shapiro, 187–212. University of Alabama Press, Tuscaloosa.

1994 *The Savannah River Chiefdoms: Political Change in the Late Prehistoric Southeast*. University of Alabama Press, Tuscaloosa.

1996 "Chiefly Cycling and Large-scale Abandonments as Viewed from the Savannah River Basin." In *Political Structure and Change in the Prehistoric Southeastern United States*, ed. John F. Scarry, 150–91. University Press of Florida, Gainesville.

Anderson, David G., David J. Hally, and James L. Rudolph

1986 "The Mississippian Occupation of the Savannah River Valley." *Southeastern Archaeology* 5:32–51.

Arriaza, Bernardo T.

1995 *Beyond Death: The Chinchorro Mummies of Ancient Chile*. Smithsonian Institution Press, Washington, D.C.

Ascenzi, A., and P. Balistreri

1975 "Aural Exostoses in a Roman Skull Excavated at the 'Baths of the Swimmer' in the Ancient Town of Ostia." *Journal of Human Evolution* 4:579–84.

Bachauer, J.

1909 *Anthropologische Studien uber den ausseren Gehorgan*. Inaug.-Diss. Phil. Munchen.

Baden, William W.

1983 *Tomotley: An Eighteenth Century Cherokee Village*. University of Tennessee, Department of Anthropology Report of Investigations 36, Knoxville.

Barker, Alex W., and Timothy R. Pauketat

1992 "Introduction: Social Inequality and Native Elites of Southeastern North

America." In *Lords of the Southeast: Social Inequality and the Native Elites of Southeastern North America,* ed. Alex W. Barker and Timothy R. Pauketat, 1–10. Archeological Papers of the American Anthropological Association 3, Washington, D.C.

Barrett, John, Richard Bradley, and Martin Green
1991 *Landscape, Monuments and Society: The Prehistory of Cranbourne Chase.* Cambridge University Press, Cambridge.

Bartel, Brad
1982 "A Historical Review of Ethnological and Archaeological Analysis of Mortuary Practices." *Journal of Anthropological Archaeology* 1:32–58.

Bartram, William
1928 *Travels of William Bartram,* ed. Mark Van Doren. Dover Publishers, New York.

Bass, Patricia
1991 "The Interpretation of U.S. Rock Art: Is It Time to Move to 'Meta-Rules'?" Paper presented at the 56th Annual Meeting of the Society for American Archaeology, New Orleans, Louisiana.

Bass, William M.
1987 *Human Osteology: A Laboratory and Field Manual,* 3d ed. Missouri Archaeological Society, Columbia.

Beaudry, Mary, and Jacquelyn White
1994 "Cowgirls with the Blues? A Study of Women's Publication and the Citation of Women's Work in *Historical Archaeology.*" In *Women in Archaeology,* ed. Cheryl Claassen, 138–58. University of Pennsylvania Press, Philadelphia.

Beck, Robin A., Jr.
1997 "From Joara to Chiaha: Spanish Exploration of the Appalachian Summit Area, 1540–1568." *Southeastern Archaeology* 16:162–69.

Bender, Donald R.
1967 "A Refinement of the Concept of Household: Families, Co-Residence, and Domestic Functions." *American Anthropologist* 69:493–504.

Berry, A. C., and R. J. Berry
1967 "Epigenetic Variation in the Human Cranium." *Journal of Anatomy* 101:361–79.

Bettinger, Robert, and Jelmer Eerkens
1999 "Point Typologies, Cultural Transmission, and the Spread of Bow-and-Arrow Technology in the Prehistoric Great Basin." *American Antiquity* 64:231–42.

Beverley, Robert
1705 *The History and Present State of Virginia, in Four Parts . . . By a Native and Inhabitant of the Place.* London.

Billings, Warren, editor
1975 *The Old Dominion in the Seventeenth Century: A Documentary History of Virginia, 1606–1689.* University of North Carolina Press, Chapel Hill.

Binford, Lewis R.
1971   "Mortuary Practices, Their Study and Their Potential." In *Approaches to the Social Dimensions of Mortuary Practices,* ed. James A. Brown, 6–29. Society for American Archaeology Memoirs 25, Washington, D.C.

Blake, C.
1880   "The Occurrence of Exostoses within the External Auditory Canal in Prehistoric Man." *American Journal of Otology* 2:81–91.

Blakely, Robert L.
1977   "Sociocultural Implications of Demographic Data from Etowah, Georgia." In *Biocultural Adaptation in Prehistoric America,* ed. Robert L. Blakely, 45–66. University of Georgia, Proceedings of the Southern Anthropological Society 11, Athens.

Blitz, John H.
1993a   *Ancient Chiefdoms of the Tombigbee.* University of Alabama Press, Tuscaloosa.
1993b   "Big Pots for Big Shots: Feasting and Storage in a Mississippian Community." *American Antiquity* 58:80–96.
1999   "Mississippian Chiefdoms and the Fission-Fusion Process." *American Antiquity* 64:577–82.

Borker, Ruth, and Daniel Maltz
1989   "Anthropological Perspectives on Gender and Language." In *Gender and Anthropology: Critical Reviews for Research and Teaching,* ed. Sandra Morgen, 411–37. American Anthropological Association, Washington, D.C.

Bowdler, Sandra
1976   "Hook, Line, and Dilly Bag: An Interpretation of an Australian Coastal Shell Midden." *Mankind* 10:248–58.

Boyd, C. Clifford, Jr., and Gerald F. Schroedl
1987   "In Search of Coosa." *American Antiquity* 52:840–45.

Braun, David P.
1981   "A Critique of Some Recent North American Mortuary Studies." *American Antiquity* 46:398–420.

Braund, Kathryn E. Holland
1993   *Deerskins and Duffels: The Creek Indian Trade with Anglo-Americans, 1685–1815.* University of Nebraska Press, Lincoln.

Breitburg, Emanuel
1990   "Appendix A: Faunal Remains from the 1989 Excavation at the Great Salt Spring Site, Gallatin County, Illinois." In *The Great Salt Spring: Mississippian Production and Specialization,* ed. Jon Muller, 347–69. Report submitted to the United States Forest Service, Shawnee National Forest, Harrisburg, Illinois.

Bridges, Patricia S.
1989   "Changes in Activities with the Shift to Agriculture in the Southeastern United States." *Current Anthropology* 30:385–93.
1990   "Osteological Correlates of Weapon Use." In *A Life in Science: Papers in Honor of J. Lawrence Angel,* ed. Jane Buikstra, 87–99. Center for American Archaeology, Scientific Papers 6, Kampsville, Illinois.

1991   "Skeletal Evidence of Changes in Subsistence Activities between the Archaic and Mississippian Time Periods in Northwestern Alabama." In *What Mean These Bones: Studies in Southeastern Bioarchaeology*, ed. Mary Lucas Powell, Patricia S. Bridges, and Ann Marie Wagner Mires, 89–103. University of Alabama Press, Tuscaloosa.

1994   "Vertebral Arthritis and Physical Activities in the Prehistoric Southeastern United States." *American Journal of Physical Anthropology* 93:83–94.

Brock, R. A., editor

1885   *The Official Letters of Alexander Spotswood, Lieutenant Governor of the Colony of Virginia, 1710–1722, Volume 2*. The Society, Richmond, Collections of the Virginia Historical Society.

Brown, Catherine

1982   "On the Gender of the Winged Being on Mississippian Period Copper Plates." *Tennessee Anthropologist* 7:1–8.

Brown, Ian W.

1980   *Salt and the Eastern North American Indian: An Archaeological Study*. Harvard University, Peabody Museum, Lower Mississippi Survey Bulletin 6, Cambridge.

Brown, James A.

1981   "The Search for Rank in Prehistoric Burials." In *The Archaeology of Death*, ed. Robert W. Chapman, Ian A. Kinnes, and Klavs Randsborg, 123–32. Cambridge University Press, Cambridge.

1990   "Archaeology Confronts History at the Natchez Temple." *Southeastern Archaeology* 9:1–10.

1995   "On Mortuary Analysis, with Special Reference to the Saxe-Binford Program." In *Regional Approaches to Mortuary Analysis*, ed. Lane Anderson Beck, 3–23. Plenum Press, New York.

Brown, James A., editor

1971   *Approaches to the Social Dimensions of Mortuary Practices*. Society for American Archaeology Memoir 25, Washington, D.C.

Brown, Jane N.

1999   "Steadfast and Changing: The Apparent Paradox of Cherokee Kinship." *Journal of Cherokee Studies* 20:28–49.

Brown, Judith K.

1985   "Introduction." In *In Her Prime: A New View of Middle-Aged Women*, ed. Judith K. Brown and Virginia Kerns, 1–12. Bergin & Garvey, South Hadley, Massachusetts.

Brown, Judith K., and V. Kerns, editors

1985   *In Her Prime: A New View of Middle-Aged Women*. Bergin & Garvey, South Hadley, Massachusetts.

Bruhns, Karen Olsen

1991   "Sexual Activities: Some Thoughts on the Sexual Division of Labor and Archaeological Interpretation." In *The Archaeology of Gender*, ed. Dale Walde and Noreen D. Willows, 420–29. Archaeological Association of the University of Calgary, Proceedings of the Chacmool Conference 22, Calgary, Alberta, Canada.

Brumbach, Hetty Jo, and Richard Jarvenpa

1997a "Ethnoarchaeology of Subsistence Space and Gender: a Subarctic Dene Case." *American Antiquity* 62:414–36.

1997b "Woman the Hunter: Ethnoarchaeological Lessons from Chipewyan Life-Cycle Dynamics." In *Women in Prehistory: North America and Mesoamerica*, ed. Cheryl Claassen and Rosemary A. Joyce, 17–32. University of Pennsylvania Press, Philadelphia.

Brumfiel, Elizabeth M.

1991 "Weaving and Cooking: Women's Production in Aztec Mexico." In *Engendering Archaeology: Women and Prehistory*, ed. Joan M. Gero and Margaret W. Conkey, 224–51. Blackwell, Oxford.

1992 "Breaking and Entering the Ecosystem: Gender, Class, and Faction Steal the Show." *American Anthropologist* 94:551–67.

Brumfiel, Elizabeth M., and Timothy K. Earle

1987 "Specialization, Exchange and Complex Societies: An Introduction." In *Specialization, Exchange and Complex Societies*, ed. Elizabeth M. Brumfiel and Timothy K. Earle, 1–9. Cambridge University Press, Cambridge.

Buikstra, Jane E.

1991 "Out of the Appendix and into the Dirt: Comments on Thirteen Years of Bioarchaeological Research." In *What Mean These Bones: Studies in Southeastern Bioarchaeology*, ed. Mary Lucas Powell, Patricia S. Bridges, and Ann Marie Wagner Mires, 172–88. University of Alabama Press, Tuscaloosa.

Buikstra, Jane E., and Douglas H. Ubelaker

1994 *Standards for Data Collection from Human Skeletal Remains*. Arkansas Archeological Survey, Research Series 44, Fayetteville.

Bujra, J. M.

1979 "Introduction: Female Solidarity and the Sexual Division of Labour." In *Women United, Women Divided: Contemporary Studies of Ten Contemporary Cultures*, ed. P. Caplan and J. M. Bujra, 13–45. Indiana University Press, Bloomington.

Burrage, H. S., editor

1906 "Early English and French Voyages, 1534–1608." In *Original Narratives of Early American History*. Charles Scribner's Sons, New York.

Campbell, Thomas N.

1959 "Choctaw Subsistence: Ethnographic Notes From the Lincecum Manuscript." *Florida Anthropologist* 12:9–24.

Carr, Christopher

1995 "Mortuary Practices: Their Social, Philosophical-Religious, Circumstantial, and Physical Determinants." *Journal of Archaeological Method and Theory* 2:105–200.

Carter, Barbara, Robert C. Dunnell, and Laura Newell-Morris

1995 "Gender-linked Differences in Sr/Cr Ratios: Experimental Data from *Mar-*

caca nemestrina." Paper presented at the 61st Annual Meeting of the Society for American Archaeology, Minneapolis, Minnesota.

Champagne, Duane

1983   "Symbolic Structure and Political Change in Cherokee Society." *Journal of Cherokee Studies* 8:87–96.

1990   "Institutional and Cultural Order in Early Cherokee Society: A Sociological Interpretation." *Journal of Cherokee Studies* 15:3–26.

Chaplin, J. M., and I. A. Stewart

1998   "The Prevalence of Exostoses in the External Auditory Meatus of Surfers." *Clinical Otolaryngology* 23:326–30.

Chapman, Jefferson

1985   *Tellico Archaeology: Twelve Thousand Years of Native American History.* University of Tennessee, Department of Anthropology Report of Investigations 43, Knoxville.

Chapman, Robert W.

1981   "The Emergence of Formal Disposal Areas and the 'Problem' of Megalithic Tombs in Prehistoric Europe." In *The Archaeology of Death,* ed. Robert W. Chapman, Ian A. Kinnes, and Klavs Randsborg, 71–81. Cambridge University Press, Cambridge.

1995   "Ten Years After: Megaliths, Mortuary Practices, and the Territorial Model." In *Regional Approaches to Mortuary Analysis,* ed. Lane Anderson Beck, 29–51. Plenum Press, New York.

Chester, Hilary, Nan Rothschild, and Diana Wall

1994   "Women in Historical Archaeology: The SHA Survey." In *Equity Issues for Women in Archaeology,* ed. M. Nelson, S. Nelson, and Alison Wylie, 213–18. Archaeological Papers of the American Anthropological Association 5, Washington, D.C.

Claassen, Cheryl

1991   "Gender, Shellfishing, and the Shell Mound Archaic." In *Engendering Archaeology: Women and Prehistory,* ed. Joan M. Gero and Margaret W. Conkey, 276–300. Blackwell, Oxford.

1992   "Questioning Gender: An Introduction." In *Exploring Gender through Archaeology,* ed. Cheryl Claassen, 1–10. Prehistory Press, Monographs in World Archaeology 11, Madison, Wisconsin.

1993   "Black and White Women at Irene Mound." *Southeastern Archaeology* 12: 137–47.

1996   "Research Problems with Shells from Green River Shell Matrix Sites." In *Of Caves and Shell Mounds,* ed. Kenneth C. Carstens and Patty Jo Watson, 132–39. University of Alabama Press, Tuscaloosa.

1997   "Changing Venue: Women's Lives in Prehistoric North America." In *Women in Prehistory: North America and Mesoamerica,* ed. Cheryl Claassen and Rosemary A. Joyce, 65–87. University of Pennsylvania Press, Philadelphia.

Claassen, Cheryl, Michael O'Neal, Tamara Wilson, Elizabeth Arnold, and Brent
Lansdell
1999 "Hearing and Reading Southeastern Archaeology: A Review of the Annual
Meetings of SEAC from 1983 through 1995 and the Journal *Southeastern
Archaeology*." *Southeastern Archaeology* 18: 85–97.

Clark, John E., and William J. Parry
1990 "Craft Specialization and Cultural Complexity." *Research in Economic Anthropology* 12:289–346.

Clayton, Lawrence A., Vernon James Knight, Jr., and Edward C. Moore, editors
1993 *The De Soto Chronicles: The Expedition of Hernando De Soto to North America
in 1539–1543, Volume I.* University of Alabama Press, Tuscaloosa.

Cobb, Charles R.
1988 "Mill Creek Chert Biface Production: Mississippian Political Economy in
Illinois." Doctoral dissertation for the Department of Anthropology, Southern Illinois University, Carbondale.
1989 "An Appraisal of the Role of Mill Creek Chert Hoes in Mississippian Exchange Systems." *Southeastern Archaeology* 8:79–92.
1996 "Specialization, Exchange, and Power in Small-Scale Societies and Chiefdoms." *Research in Economic Anthropology* 17:251–94.

Cobb, Charles R., and Brian M. Butler
1996 "The Organization of Production for Exchange in a Mississippian Village
and Lithic Workshop." Paper presented at the 61st Annual Meeting of the
Society for American Archaeology, New Orleans.

Coe, Joffre Lanning
1961 "Cherokee Archaeology." In *The Symposium on Cherokee and Iroquois Culture*, ed. William N. Fenton and John Gulick, 51–60. Smithsonian Institution, Bureau of American Ethnology Bulletin 180, Washington, D.C.
1995 *Town Creek Indian Mound: A Native American Legacy.* University of North
Carolina Press, Chapel Hill.

Conkey, Margaret W.
1991 "Contexts of Action, Contexts for Power: Material Culture and Gender in
the Magdalenian." In *Engendering Archaeology: Women and Prehistory*, ed.
Joan M. Gero and Margaret W. Conkey, 57–92. Blackwell, Oxford.

Conkey, Margaret W., and Joan M. Gero
1991 "Tensions, Pluralities, and Engendering Archaeology: An Introduction to
Women and Prehistory." In *Engendering Archaeology: Women and Prehistory*,
ed. Joan M. Gero and Margaret W. Conkey, 3–30. Blackwell, Oxford.

Conkey, Margaret W., and Janet D. Spector
1984 "Archaeology and the Study of Gender." *Advances in Archaeological Method
and Theory* 7:1–38.

Costin, Cathy Lynne
1991 "Craft Specialization: Issues in Defining, Documenting, and Explaining
the Organization of Production." *Archaeological Method and Theory* 3:1–56.

1996   "Exploring the Relationship between Gender and Craft in Complex Societies: Methodological and Theoretical Issues of Gender Attribution." In *Gender and Archaeology,* ed. Rita P. Wright, 111–40. University of Pennsylvania Press, Philadelphia.

Crown, Patricia L., and Suzanne K. Fish

1996   "Gender and Status in the Hohokam Preclassic to Classic Transition." *American Anthropologist* 98:803–17.

Crumley, Carole L.

1987   "A Dialectical Critique of Hierarchy." In *Power Relations and State Formation,* ed. Thomas C. Patterson and Christine W. Gailey, 141–73. American Anthropological Association, Archeology Papers, Washington, D.C.

1995   "Heterarchy and the Analysis of Complex Societies." In *Heterarchy and the Analysis of Complex Societies,* ed. Robert M. Ehrenreich, Carole L. Crumley, and Janet E. Levy, 1–5. Archeological Papers 3. American Anthropological Association, Washington, D.C.

Cumming, William Patterson, editor

1958   *The Discoveries of John Lederer.* University of Virginia Press, Charlottesville.

Damm, Charlotte

1991   "From Burials to Gender Roles: Problems and Potentials in Post-Processual Archaeology." In *The Archaeology of Gender,* ed. Dale Walde and Noreen D. Willows, 130–36. Archaeological Association of the University of Calgary, Proceedings of the Chacmool Conference 22, Calgary, Alberta, Canada.

Daniel, I. Randolph, Jr.

1998   *Hardaway Revisited: Early Archaic Settlement in the Southeast.* University of Alabama Press, Tuscaloosa.

Davis, R. P. Stephen, Jr.

1990   *Aboriginal Settlement Patterns in the Lower Little Tennessee River Valley.* University of Tennessee, Department of Anthropology Report of Investigations 50, Knoxville.

1999   "The Cultural Landscape of the North Carolina Piedmont at Contact." Paper presented at the 56th Annual Meeting of the Southeastern Archaeological Conference, Pensacola.

Davis, R. P. Stephen, Jr., Jane M. Eastman, Thomas O. Maher, and Richard P. Gravely, Jr.

1997   *Archaeological Investigations at the Stockton Site in Henry County, Virginia.* University of North Carolina, Research Laboratories of Archaeology Research Report 14, Chapel Hill.

Davis, R. P. Stephen, Jr., Patricia M. Lambert, Clark Spencer Larsen, and Vincas P. Steponaitis

1996   *Native American Graves Protection and Repatriation Act Inventory of Human Skeletal Remains and Associated Grave Objects.* Manuscripts on file at the Research Laboratories of Archaeology, University of North Carolina, Chapel Hill.

Davis, R. P. Stephen, Jr., Patrick C. Livingood, H. Trawick Ward, and Vincas P. Steponaitis
1998   *Excavating Occaneechi Town: Archaeology of an Eighteenth-Century Indian Village in North Carolina.* CD-ROM. University of North Carolina Press, Chapel Hill.

Davis, R. P. Stephen, Jr., and H. Trawick Ward
1991   "The Evolution of Siouan Communities in Piedmont North Carolina." *Southeastern Archaeology* 10:40–53.

Deleyiannis, F. W., B. D. Cockcroft, and E. F. Pinczower
1996   "Exostoses of the External Auditory Canal in Oregon Surfers." *American Journal of Otolaryngology* 17:303–7.

DePratter, Chester B.
1994   "The Chiefdom of Cofitachequi." In *The Forgotten Centuries: Indians and Europeans in the American South, 1521–1704,* ed. Charles M. Hudson and Carmen Chaves Tesser, 197–226. University of Georgia Press, Athens.

Derevenski, Joanna Sofaer
1994   "Editorial. *Archaeological Review from Cambridge* 13:1–5.
1997a   "Age and Gender at the Site of Tiszapolgár-Basatanya, Hungary." *Antiquity* 71:875–89.
1997b   "Engendering Children, Engendering Archaeology." In *Invisible People and Processes: Writing Gender and Childhood into European Archaeology,* ed. Jenny Moore and Eleanor Scott, 192–202. Leicester University Press, London.

DiBartolomeo, J. R.
1979   "Exostoses of the External Auditory Canal." *Ann. Otol. Rhinol. Laryngol. Suppl.* 88(6 pt. 2 Suppl. 61):2–20.

Dickens, Roy S., Jr.
1967   "The Route of Rutherford's Expedition against the North Carolina Cherokees." *Southern Indian Studies* 19:3–24.
1976   *Cherokee Prehistory: The Pisgah Phase in the Appalachian Summit Region.* University of Tennessee Press, Knoxville.
1978   "Mississippian Settlement Patterns in the Appalachian Summit Area: The Pisgah and Qualla Phases." In *Mississippian Settlement Patterns,* ed. Bruce D. Smith, 115–39. Academic Press, New York.
1979   "The Origins and Development of Cherokee Culture." In *The Cherokee Indian Nation: A Troubled History,* ed. Duane H. King, 3–32. University of Tennessee Press, Knoxville.
1986   "An Evolutionary-Ecological Interpretation of Cherokee Cultural Development." In *The Conference on Cherokee Prehistory,* comp. David G. Moore, 81–94. Warren Wilson College, Swannanoa, North Carolina.

Dickens, Roy S., H. Trawick Ward, and R. P. Stephen Davis Jr., editors
1987   *The Siouan Project, Seasons I and II.* University of North Carolina, Research Laboratories of Anthropology Monograph 1, Chapel Hill.

Dobyns, Henry F.

1983   *Their Number Become Thinned.* University of Tennessee Press, Knoxville.

Dommasnes, Liv Helga

1987   "Male/Female Roles and Ranks in Late Iron Age Norway." In *Were They All Men? An Examination of Sex Roles in Prehistoric Society,* ed. R. Bertelsen et al., 65–77. Arkeologisk Museum i Stavanger.

Drooker, Penelope Ballard

1992   *Mississippian Village Textiles at Wickliffe.* University of Alabama Press, Tuscaloosa.

Dunnell, Robert C., M. Ikeya, P. T. McCutcheon, and S. Toyoda

1994   "Heat Treatment of Mill Creek and Dover Cherts on the Malden Plain, Southeast Missouri." *Journal of Archaeological Science* 21:79–89.

Earle, Timothy K.

1987   "Specialization and the Production of Wealth: Hawaiian Chiefdoms and the Inka Empire." In *Specialization, Exchange, and Complex Societies,* ed. Elizabeth M. Brumfiel and Timothy K. Earle, 64–75. Cambridge University Press, Cambridge.

Egloff, Brian John

1967   "An Analysis of Ceramics from Historic Cherokee Towns." Master's thesis for the Department of Anthropology, University of North Carolina, Chapel Hill.

Egloff, Keith Touton

1971   "Methods and Problems of Mound Excavation in the Southern Appalachian Area." Master's thesis for the Department of Anthropology, University of North Carolina, Chapel Hill.

1992   "The Late Woodland Period in Southwestern Virginia." In *Middle and Late Woodland Research in Virginia: A Synthesis,* ed. Theodore R. Reinhart and Mary Ellen N. Hodges, 187–224. Archaeological Society of Virginia, Special Publication 29, Richmond.

Emerson, Thomas E.

1989   "Water, Serpents, and the Underworld: An Exploration into Cahokian Symbolism." In *The Southeastern Ceremonial Complex: Artifacts and Analysis,* ed. Patricia Galloway, 45–92. University of Nebraska Press, Lincoln.

1997   *Cahokia and the Archaeology of Power.* University of Alabama Press, Tuscaloosa.

Estioko-Griffin, Agnes, and P. Bion Griffin

1997   "Woman the Hunter: The Agta." In *Gender in Cross-Cultural Perspective, Second Edition,* ed. Carolina B. Brettell and Carolyn F. Sargent, 219–28. Prentice Hall, Upper Saddle River, New Jersey.

Faulkner, Charles H.

1978   "Origin and Evolution of the Cherokee Winter House." *Journal of Cherokee Studies* 3:87–93.

Feinman, Gary M., and Jill E. Neitzel
1984 "Too Many Types: An Overview of Sedentary Prestate Societies in the Americas." *Advances in Archaeological Method and Theory* 7:39–102.

Fenton, William N.
1978 "Northern Iroquoian Culture Patterns." In *Handbook of North American Indians, Volume 15: Northeast,* ed. Bruce G. Trigger, 296–321. Smithsonian Institution Press, Washington, D.C.

Ferguson, Leland G.
1971 "South Appalachian Mississippian." Doctoral dissertation for the Department of Anthropology, University of North Carolina, Chapel Hill.

Firestone, Shulamith
1972 *The Dialectic of Sex.* Bantam, New York.

Flannery, Kent V.
1972 "The Cultural Evolution of Civilizations." *Annual Review of Ecology and Systematics* 3:399–426.

Foreman, Grant
1936 *Indians and Pioneers: The Story of the American Southwest Before 1830.* University of Oklahoma Press, Norman.

Fowler, E., Jr., and P. Osmon
1942 "New Bone Growth Due to Cold Water in the Ears." *Archives of Otolaryngology* 36:455–66.

Fratt, Lee
1991 "A Preliminary Analysis of Gender Bias in the Sixteenth and Seventeenth Century Spanish Colonial Documents of the American Southwest." In *The Archaeology of Gender,* ed. Dale Walde and Noreen D. Willows, 245–51. Archaeological Association of the University of Calgary, Proceedings of the Chacmool Conference 22, Calgary, Alberta, Canada.

Frayer, David W.
1988 "Auditory Exostoses and Evidence for Fishing at Vlasic." *Current Anthropology* 29:346–49.

Friedl, Ernestine
1967 "The Position of Women: Appearance and Reality." *Anthropological Quarterly* 40(3):97–108.

Galloway, Patricia K.
1989 "'The Chief Who Is Your Father': Choctaw and French Views of the Diplomatic Relation." In *Powhatan's Mantle: Indians in the Colonial Southeast,* ed. Peter H. Wood, Gregory A. Waselkov, and M. Thomas Hatley, 254–78. University of Nebraska Press, Lincoln.
1993 "Ethnohistory." In *The Development of Southeastern Archaeology,* ed. Jay K. Johnson, 78–108. University of Alabama Press, Tuscaloosa.
1995 *The Choctaw Genesis, 1500–1700.* University of Nebraska Press, Lincoln.
1997 "Where Have All the Menstrual Huts Gone? The Invisibility of Menstrual

Seclusion in the Late Prehistoric Southeast." In *Women in Prehistory: North America and Mesoamerica*, ed. Cheryl Claassen and Rosemary A. Joyce, 47–62. University of Pennsylvania Press, Philadelphia.

Gearing, Frederick O.

1958 "The Structural Poses of Eighteenth-Century Cherokee Villages." *American Anthropologist* 60:1148–57.

1962 *Priests and Warriors: Social Structures for Cherokee Politics in the Eighteenth Century.* Memoirs of the American Anthropological Association 93, Washington, D.C.

Gero, Joan M.

1991 "Genderlithics: Women's Roles in Stone Tool Production." In *Engendering Archaeology: Women and Prehistory*, ed. Joan M. Gero and Margaret W. Conkey, 163–93. Blackwell, Oxford.

1996 "Archaeological Practice and Gendered Encounters with Field Data." In *Gender and Archaeology*, ed. Rita P. Wright, 251–80. University of Pennsylvania Press, Philadelphia.

Gilchrist, Roberta

1994 *Gender and Material Culture: The Archaeology of Religious Women.* Routledge, London.

1997 "Ambivalent Bodies: Gender and Medieval Archaeology." In *Invisible People and Processes: Writing Gender and Childhood into European Archaeology*, ed. Jenny Moore and Eleanor Scott, 42–58. Leicester University Press, London.

Ginn, Jay, and Sara Arber

1995 "'Only Connect': Gender Relations and Ageing." In *Connecting Gender and Ageing: A Sociological Approach*, ed. Sara Arber and Jay Ginn, 1–14. Open University Press, Philadelphia, Pennsylvania.

Goldstein, Lynne G.

1980 *Mississippian Mortuary Practices: A Case Study of Two Cemeteries in the Lower Illinois Valley.* Northwestern University Archaeological Program, Scientific Papers 4, Evanston, Illinois.

1995 "Landscapes and Mortuary Practices: A Case for Regional Perspectives." In *Regional Approaches to Mortuary Analysis*, ed. Lane Anderson Beck, 101–21. Plenum Press, New York.

Goodenough, Ward H.

1965 "Rethinking 'Status' and 'Role': Toward a General Model of the Cultural Organization of Social Relationships." In *The Relevance of Models for Social Relationships*, ed. Michael P. Banton, 1–24. Tavistock Publications, Association of Social Anthropologists of the Commonwealth Monographs 1, London.

Goodwin, Gary C.

1977 *Cherokees in Transition: A Study of Changing Culture and Environment Prior to 1775.* University of Chicago, Department of Geography Research Paper 181, Chicago.

Gregg, J. B., J. P. Steele, L. Zimmerman, H. Ferwerda, and P. S. Gregg
1981 "Otolaryngic Osteopathology in Fourteenth-Century Mid-America. The Crow Creek Massacre." *Ann. Otol. Rhinol. Laryngol.* 90(3 pt. 1):288–93.

Guthe, Alfred K.
1977 "The Eighteenth-Century Overhill Cherokee." In *For the Director: Essays in Honor of James B. Griffin*, ed. Charles E. Cleland, 212–29. University of Michigan, Museum of Anthropology Anthropological Papers 61, Ann Arbor.

Hale, Stephen, Domingo Diaz, and Marucio Mendez
1996 "Mammals to Land, Fish to the Sea and Garbage to the New Land: The Taphonomy of Midden Formation among the Maritime Kuna of Panama and Implications for Midden Interpretation." Paper presented at the 53rd Annual Meeting of the Southeastern Archaeological Conference, Birmingham, Alabama.

Hall, Robert L.
1997 *Archaeology of the Soul*. University of Illinois Press, Urbana-Champaign.

Hall, Simon
1998 "A Consideration of Gender Relations in the Late Iron Age 'Sotho' Sequence of the Western Highveld, Southern Africa." In *Gender in African Prehistory*, ed. Susan Kent, 235–58. Alta Mira Press, Walnut Creek, California.

Hally, David J.
1986 "The Cherokee Archaeology of Georgia." In *The Conference on Cherokee Prehistory*, comp. David G. Moore, 95–121. Warren Wilson College, Swannanoa, North Carolina.

1994a "An Overview of Lamar Culture." In *Ocmulgee Archaeology, 1936–1986*, ed. David J. Hally, 144–74. University of Georgia Press, Athens.

1994b "The Chiefdom of Coosa." In *The Forgotten Centuries: Indians and Europeans in the American South, 1521–1704*, ed. Charles Hudson and Carmen Chaves Tesser, 227–53. University of Georgia Press, Athens.

1996 "Platform Mound Construction and the Instability of Mississippian Chiefdoms." In *Political Structure and Change in the Prehistoric Southeastern United States*, ed. John F. Scarry, 92–127. University Press of Florida, Gainesville.

Hally, David J., and Hypatia Kelly
1998 "The Nature of Mississippian Towns in Georgia: The King Site Example." In *Mississippian Towns and Sacred Spaces*, ed. R. Barry Lewis and Charles Stout, 49–63. University of Alabama Press, Tuscaloosa.

Hally, David J., and James B. Langford, Jr.
1988 *Mississippi Period Archaeology of the Georgia Valley and Ridge Province*. University of Georgia, Laboratory of Archaeology Report 25, Athens.

Hally, David J., and James L. Rudolph
1986 *Mississippi Period Archaeology of the Georgia Piedmont*. University of Georgia, Laboratory of Archaeology Report 24, Athens.

Hally, David J., Marvin T. Smith and James B. Langford, Jr.
1990 "The Archaeological Reality of De Soto's Coosa." In *Columbian Conse-*

quences, Volume II: Archaeological and Historical Perspectives on the Spanish Borderlands East, ed. David Hurst Thomas, 121–38. Smithsonian Institution Press, Washington, D.C.

Hamell, George

1983   "Trading in Metaphors: The Magic of Beads, Another Perspective upon Indian-European Contact in Northeastern North America." In Proceedings of the 1982 Glass Trade Bead Conference, ed. C. Hayes, 5–28. Rochester Museum and Science Center Research Records 16, Rochester, New York.

1987   "Strawberries, Floating Islands, and Rabbit Captains: Mythical Realities and European Contact in the Northeast during the Sixteenth and Seventeenth Centuries." Journal of Canadian Studies 21:72–94.

Handsman, Russell G.

1991   "Whose Art Was Found at Lepinski Vir? Gender Relations and Power in Archaeology." In Engendering Archaeology: Women in Prehistory, ed. Joan M. Gero and Margaret W. Conkey, 329–65. Blackwell, Oxford.

Harmon, Michael A.

1986   Eighteenth Century Lower Cherokee Adaptation and Use of Material Cultures. South Carolina, Institute of Archaeology and Anthropology Volumes in Historical Archaeology 2, Columbia.

Harris, Marvin

1993   "The Evolution of Human Gender Hierarchies: A Trial Formulation." In Sex and Gender Hierarchies, ed. Barbara D. Miller, 57–79. Cambridge University Press, Cambridge.

Hastorf, Christine A.

1991   "Gender, Space, and Food in Prehistory." In Engendering Archaeology: Women and Prehistory, ed. Joan M. Gero and Margaret W. Conkey, 132–59. Blackwell, Oxford.

Hatch, James W.

1974   "Social Dimensions of Dallas Mortuary Practices." Master's thesis for the Department of Anthropology, Pennsylvania State University, University.

1975   "Social Dimensions of Dallas Burials." Southeastern Archaeological Conference Bulletin 18:132–38.

1976   "Status in Death: Principles of Ranking in Dallas Culture Mortuary Remains." Doctoral dissertation for the Department of Anthropology, Pennsylvania State University, University.

1987   "Mortuary Indicators of Organizational Variability among Late Prehistoric Chiefdoms in the Southeastern U.S. Interior." In Chiefdoms in the Americas, ed. Robert D. Drennan and Cathryn A. Uribe, 9–19. University Press of America, Lanham, Maryland.

Hatley, M. Thomas

1989   "The Three Lives of Keowee: Loss and Recovery in Eighteenth-Century Cherokee Villages." In Powhatan's Mantle: Indians in the Colonial Southeast, ed. Peter H. Wood, Gregory A. Waselkov, and M. Thomas Hatley, 223–48. University of Nebraska Press, Lincoln.

1991 "Cherokee Women Farmers Hold Their Ground." In *Appalachian Frontiers: Settlement, Society, and Development in the Preindustrial Era,* ed. Robert D. Mitchell, 37–51. University Press of Kentucky, Lexington.

1995 *The Dividing Paths: Cherokees and South Carolinians through the Revolutionary Era.* Oxford University Press, Oxford.

Hendon, Julia A.

1996 "Archaeological Approaches to the Organization of Domestic Labor: Household Practice and Domestic Relations." *Annual Review of Anthropology* 25:45–61.

1997 "Women's Work, Women's Space, and Women's Status among the Classic Period Maya Elite of the Copan Valley, Honduras." In *Women in Prehistory: North America and Mesoamerica,* ed. Cheryl Claassen and Rosemary A. Joyce, 33–46. University of Pennsylvania Press, Philadelphia.

Hermann, Anne, and Abigail Stewart, editors

1994 *Theorizing Feminism: Parallel Trends in the Humanities and Social Sciences.* Westview Press, Boulder, Colorado.

Hill, Sarah H.

1997 *Weaving New Worlds: Southeastern Cherokee Women and Their Basketry.* University of North Carolina Press, Chapel Hill.

Hingley, Richard

1990 "Domestic Organisation and Gender Relations in Iron Age and Romano-British Households." In *The Social Archaeology of Houses,* ed. Ross Samson, 125–47. Edinburgh University Press, Edinburgh.

Hodder, Ian

1982 "Theoretical Archaeology: A Reactionary View." In *Symbolic and Structural Archaeology,* ed. Ian Hodder, 1–16. Cambridge University Press, Cambridge.

1984 "Burials, Houses, Women and Men in the European Neolithic." In *Ideology, Power, and Prehistory,* ed. Daniel Miller and Christopher Tilley, 51–68. Cambridge University Press, Cambridge.

Hogue, Susan Homes

1988 "A Bioarchaeological Study of Mortuary Practice and Change among the Piedmont Siouan Indians." Doctoral dissertation for the Department of Anthropology, University of North Carolina, Chapel Hill.

Holden, Patricia P.

1966 "An Archaeological Survey of Transylvania County, North Carolina." Master's thesis for the Department of Anthropology, University of North Carolina, Chapel Hill.

Hollimon, Sandra E.

1991 "Health Consequences of Divisions of Labor among the Chumash Indians of Southern California." In *The Archaeology of Gender,* ed. Dale Walde and Noreen D. Willows, 462–69. Archaeological Association of the University of Calgary, Proceedings of the Chacmool Conference 22, Calgary, Alberta, Canada.

1992   "Health Consequences of Sexual Division of Labor among Prehistoric Native Americans: The Chumash of California and the Arikara of the Northern Plains." In *Exploring Gender through Archaeology,* ed. Cheryl Claassen, 81–88. Prehistory Press, Monographs in World Archaeology 11, Madison, Wisconsin.

1997   "The Third Gender in Native California: Two-Spirit Undertakers among the Chumash and Their Neighbors." In *Women in Prehistory: North America and Mesoamerica,* ed. Cheryl Claassen and Rosemary A. Joyce, 173–88. University of Pennsylvania Press, Philadelphia.

Holmes, William H.

1903   *Aboriginal Pottery of the Eastern United States.* Smithsonian Institution, Bureau of American Ethnology Report 20:1–237, Washington, D.C.

Howell, Todd L.

1995   "Tracking Zuni Gender and Leadership Roles across the Contact Period." *Journal of Anthropological Research* 51:125–48.

Howell, Todd L., and Keith W. Kintigh

1996   "Archaeological Identification of Kin Groups Using Mortuary and Biological Data: An Example from the American Southwest." *American Antiquity* 61:537–54.

Hrdlička, Aleš

1935   *Ear Exostoses.* Smithsonian Institution, Smithsonian Miscellaneous Collections 93:6:47–98, Washington, D.C.

Hudson, Charles M.

1976   *The Southeastern Indians.* University of Tennessee Press, Knoxville.

1977   "James Adair as Anthropologist." *Ethnohistory* 24:311–28.

1986   "Some Thoughts on the Early Social History of the Cherokees." In *The Conference on Cherokee Prehistory,* comp. David G. Moore, 139–53. Warren Wilson College, Swannanoa, North Carolina.

1990   *The Juan Pardo Expeditions: Exploration of the Carolinas and Tennessee, 1566–1568.* Smithsonian Institution Press, Washington, D.C.

1997   *Knights of Spain, Warriors of the Sun: Hernando de Soto and the South's Ancient Cheifdoms.* University of Georgia Press, Athens.

Hudson, Charles M., Marvin T. Smith, and Chester B. DePratter

1984   "The Hernando DeSoto Expedition from Apalachee to Chiaha." *Southeastern Archaeology* 3:65–77.

Huntington, Richard, and Peter Metcalf

1979   *Celebrations of Death.* Cambridge University Press, Cambridge.

Hutchinson, Dale L., C. B. Denise, Hal J. Daniel, and G. W. Kalmus

1997   "A Reevaluation of the Cold Water Etiology of External Auditory Exostoses." *American Journal of Physical Anthropology* 103:417–22.

Ito, M., and M. Ikeda

1998   "Does Cold Water Truly Promote Diver's Ear?" *Undersea Hyperbolic Medicine* 25:59–62.

Jackson, Thomas L.

1991 "Pounding Acorn: Women's Production as Social and Economic Focus." In *Engendering Archaeology: Women and Prehistory*, ed. Joan M. Gero and Margaret W. Conkey, 301–25. Blackwell, Oxford.

Johnson, Jay K.

1994 "Prehistoric Exchange in the Southeast." In *Prehistoric Exchange Systems in North America*, ed. Timothy G. Baugh and Jonathon E. Ericson, 99–125. Plenum Press, New York.

Johnson, Jay K., editor

1993 *The Development of Southeastern Archaeology*. University of Alabama Press, Tuscaloosa.

Joyce, Rosemary A.

1994 "Dorothy Hughes Popenoe: Eve in an Archaeological Garden." In *Women in Archaeology*, ed. Cheryl Claassen, 51–66. University of Pennsylvania Press, Philadelphia.

Joyce, Rosemary A., and Cheryl Claassen

1997 "Women in the Ancient Americas: Archaeologists, Gender, and the Making of Prehistory." In *Women in Prehistory: North America and Mesoamerica*, ed. Cheryl Claassen and Rosemary A. Joyce, 1–14. University of Pennsylvania Press, Philadelphia.

Karegeannes, J. C.

1995 "Incidence of Bony Outgrowths of the External Ear Canal in U.S. Navy Divers." *Undersea Hyperbolic Medicine* 22:301–6.

Keel, Bennie C.

1976 *Cherokee Archaeology: A Study of the Appalachian Summit*. University of Tennessee Press, Knoxville.

Keel, Bennie C., and Brian J. Egloff

1999 "Archaeological Fieldwork at Coweeta Creek in Southwestern North Carolina." Paper presented at the 56th Annual Meeting of the Southeastern Archaeological Conference, Pensacola, Florida.

Kehoe, Alice

1996 "Mississippian Weavers." Paper presented at the 4th Biennial Gender and Archaeology Conference, East Lansing, Michigan.

1998 "Appropriate Terms." *Bulletin of the Society for American Archaeology* 16(2): 23.

Kelley, Marc

1980 "Disease and Environment: A Comparative Analysis of Three Early American Indian Skeletal Collections." Doctoral dissertation for the Department of Anthropology, Case Western Reserve University, Cleveland, Ohio.

Kennedy, Gail E.

1986 "The Relationship between Auditory Exostoses and Cold Water: A Latitudinal Analysis." *American Journal of Physical Anthropology* 71:401–15.

Kent, Susan
1992   "The Current Forager Controversy: Real versus Ideal Views of Hunt-er-Gatherers." *Man* 27:40–65.
1995   "Does Sedentarization Promote Gender Inequality? A Case Study from the Kalahari." *Journal of the Royal Anthropological Institute* 1:513–36.
1998a "Gender and Prehistory in Africa." In *Gender in African Prehistory*, ed. Susan Kent, 9–24. Alta Mira Press, Walnut Creek, California.
1998b "Invisible Gender—Invisible Foragers: Southern African Hunter-Gatherer Spatial Patterning and the Archaeological Record." In *Gender in African Prehistory*, ed. Susan Kent, 39–67. Alta Mira Press, Walnut Creek, California.
1999   "Egalitarianism, Equality, and Equitable Power." In *Gender and Power*, ed. Tracy L. Sweely, 30–48. Routledge, London.
King, Duane H.
1979   "Introduction." In *The Cherokee Indian Nation: A Troubled History*, ed. Duane H. King, ix–xix. University of Tennessee Press, Knoxville.
King, Duane H., and E. Raymond Evans, editors
1977   "Memoirs of the Grant Expedition against the Cherokees, 1761." *Journal of Cherokee Studies* 2:272–337.
King, Duane H., and Danny E. Olinger
1972   "Oconostota." *American Antiquity* 37:322–78.
Knight, Vernon J., Jr.
1986   "The Institutional Organization of Mississippian Religion." *American Antiquity* 51:675–87.
1990   "Social Organization and the Evolution of Hierarchy in Southeastern Chiefdoms." *Journal of Anthropological Research* 46:1–23.
1998   "Moundville as a Diagrammatic Ceremonial Center." In *Archaeology of the Moundville Chiefdom*, ed. Vernon J. Knight Jr. and Vincas P. Steponaitis, 44–62. Smithsonian Institution Press, Washington, D.C.
Knight, Vernon J., Jr., and Vincas P. Steponaitis, editors
1998   *Archaeology of the Moundville Chiefdom*. Smithsonian Institution Press, Washington, D.C.
Koehler, Lyle
1997   "Earth Mothers, Warriors, Horticulturalists, Artists, and Chiefs: Women among the Mississippian and Mississippian-Oneota Peoples, A.D. 1211–1750." In *Women in Prehistory: North America and Mesoamerica*, ed. Cheryl Claassen and Rosemary A. Joyce, 211–26. University of Pennsylvania Press, Philadelphia.
Kornfeld, Marcel, and Julie Francis
1991   "A Preliminary Historical Outline of Northwestern High Plains Gender Systems." In *The Archaeology of Gender*, ed. Dale Walde and Noreen D. Willows, 444–51. Archaeological Association of the University of Calgary, Proceedings of the Chacmool Conference 22, Calgary, Alberta, Canada.

Kozuch, Laura

1993 *Sharks and Shark Products in Prehistoric South Florida.* University of Florida, Institute of Archeology and Paleoenvironmental Studies Monograph 2, Gainesville.

Lambert, Patricia M.

1993 "Health in Prehistoric Populations of the Santa Barbara Channel Islands." *American Antiquity* 58:509–21.

Lambert, Patricia M., editor

1999 *Bioarchaeological Studies of Life in the Age of Agriculture.* University of Alabama Press, Tuscaloosa.

Lamphere, Louise

1974 "Strategies, Cooperation and Conflict among Women in Domestic Groups." In *Women, Culture, and Society,* ed. Michelle Zimbalist Rosaldo and Louise Lamphere, 97–112. Stanford University Press, Stanford, California.

Lane, Paul

1998 "Engendered Spaces and Bodily Practices in the Iron Age of Southern Africa." In *Gender in African Prehistory,* ed. Susan Kent, 179–203. Alta Mira Press, Walnut Creek, California.

Larsen, Clark Spencer

1994 "In the Wake of Columbus: Native Population Biology in the Postcontact Americas." *Yearbook of Physical Anthropology* 37:109–54.

1995a "Biological Changes in Human Populations with Agriculture." *Annual Review of Anthropology* 24:185–213.

1995b "Regional Perspectives on Mortuary Analysis." In *Regional Approaches to Mortuary Analysis,* ed. Lane Anderson Beck, 247–64. Plenum Press, New York.

1997 *Bioarchaeology: Interpreting Behavior from the Human Skeleton.* Cambridge University Press, Cambridge.

Larsen, Clark Spencer, Margaret Schoeninger, Nicholas van der Merwe, Katherine Moore, and Julia Lee Thorp

1992 "Carbon and Nitrogen Stable Isotopic Signatures of Human Dietary Change in the Georgia Bight." *American Journal of Physical Anthropology* 89:197–214.

Latta, Martha

1991 "The Captive Bride Syndrome: Iroquoian Behavior or Archaeological Myth?" In *The Archaeology of Gender,* ed. Dale Walde and Noreen D. Willows, 375–83. Archaeological Association of the University of Calgary, Proceedings of the Chacmool Conference 22, Calgary, Alberta, Canada.

Lawrence, Denise L., and Setha M. Low

1990 "The Built Environment and Spatial Form." *Annual Review of Anthropology* 19:453–505.

Leacock, Eleanor B., editor

1981 *Myths of Male Dominance: Collected Articles on Women Cross-Culturally: Change and Challenge.* Monthly Review Press, New York.

Lefler, Hugh T., editor
1967   *A New Voyage to Carolina*, by John Lawson. University of North Carolina Press, Chapel Hill.

Lengyel, Stacey N., Jeffrey L. Eighmy, and Lynne P. Sullivan
1999   "On the Potential of Archaeomagnetic Dating in the Midcontinent Region of North America: Toqua Site Results." *Southeastern Archaeology* 18(2): 156–71.

Lesick, Kurtis S.
1997   "Re-Engendering Gender: Some Theoretical and Methodological Concerns on a Burgeoning Archaeological Pursuit." In *Invisible People and Processes: Writing Gender and Childhood into European Archaeology*, ed. Jenny Moore and Eleanor Scott, 31–41. Leicester University Press, London.

Levy, Janet E.
1995   "Heterarchy in Bronze Age Denmark: Settlement Pattern, Gender, and Ritual." In *Heterarchy and the Analysis of Complex Societies*, ed. Robert M. Ehrenreich, Carole L. Crumley, and Janet E. Levy, 41–53. Archeological Papers of the American Anthropological Association 6, Washington, D.C.
1999   "Gender, Power, and Heterarchy in Middle-Level Societies." In *Manifesting Power: Gender and the Interpretation of Power in Archaeology*, ed. Tracy L. Sweely, 62–78. Routledge, London.

Lewis, R. Barry
1996   "Mississippian Farmers." In *Kentucky Archaeology*, ed. R. Barry Lewis, 127–59. University Press of Kentucky, Lexington.

Lewis, R. Barry, and Charles Stout
1998   "Preface." In *Mississippian Towns and Sacred Spaces: Searching for an Architectural Grammar*, ed. R. Barry Lewis and Charles Stout, xi–xii. University of Alabama Press, Tuscaloosa.

Lewis, R. Barry, Charles Stout, and Cameron B. Wesson
1998   "The Design of Mississippian Towns." In *Mississippian Towns and Sacred Spaces: Searching for an Architectural Grammar*, ed. R. Barry Lewis and Charles Stout, 1–21. University of Alabama Press, Tuscaloosa.

Lewis, Thomas M. N., and Madeline D. Kneberg
1946   *Hiwassee Island: An Archaeological Account of Four Tennessee Indian Peoples.* University of Tennessee Press, Knoxville.

Lewis, Thomas M. N., Madeline D. Kneberg Lewis, and Lynne P. Sullivan, editors and compilers
1995   *The Prehistory of the Chickamauga Basin.* University of Tennessee Press, Knoxville.

Lopinot, Neal H.
1984   "Seasonal Subsistence in the Shawnee Hills." In *Cultural Frontiers in the Upper Cache Valley, Illinois*, ed. Veletta Canouts, Ernest May, Neal H. Lopinot, and Jon Muller, 91–105. Southern Illinois University, Center for Archaeological Investigations Research Paper 16, Carbondale.
1990   "Appendix C: Plant Remains from the Great Salt Spring." In *The Great Salt*

Spring: Mississippian Production and Specialization, ed. Jon Muller, 388–400. Report submitted to the United States Forest Service, Shawnee National Forest, Harrisburg, Illinois.

MacCormack, C. P.

1980   "Nature, Culture and Gender: A Critique." In *Nature, Culture and Gender,* ed. C. P. MacCormack and M. Strathern, 1–24. Cambridge University Press, Cambridge.

Mainfort, Robert C., Jr.

1985   "Wealth, Space, and Status in a Historic Indian Cemetery." *American Antiquity* 50:555–79.

Manzi, Giorgio, Alessandra Sperduti, and Pietro Passarello

1991   "Behavior-Induced Auditory Exostoses in Imperial Roman Society: Evidence from Coeval Urban and Rural Communities Near Rome." *American Journal of Physical Anthropology* 85:253–60.

Mathews, H. F.

1985   "We Are Mayordomo: A Reinterpretation of Women's Roles in the Mexican Cargo System." *American Ethnologist* 14:210–25.

Merrell, James H.

1987   "'This Western World': The Evolution of the Piedmont, 1525–1725." In *The Siouan Project: Seasons I and II,* ed. Roy S. Dickens, Jr., H. Trawick Ward, and R. P. Stephen Davis Jr., 19–27. University of North Carolina, Research Laboratories of Anthropology Monograph 2, Chapel Hill.

1989   *The Indians' New World: Catawbas and Their Neighbors from European Contact through the Era of Removal.* University of North Carolina Press, Chapel Hill.

Miller, Barbara Diane

1993   "The Anthropology of Sex and Gender Hierarchies." In *Sex and Gender Hierarchies,* ed. Barbara Diane Miller, 3–31. Cambridge University Press, Cambridge.

Miller-Shaivitz, Patricia, and Mehmet Yasar Iscan

1991   "The Prehistoric People of Fort Center: Physical and Health Characteristics." In *What Mean These Bones: Studies in Southeastern Bioarchaeology,* ed. Mary Lucas Powell, Patricia S. Bridges, and Ann Marie Wagner Mires, 131–47. University of Alabama Press, Tuscaloosa.

Milner, George R.

1998   *The Cahokia Chiefdom: The Archaeology of a Mississippian Society.* Smithsonian Institution Press, Washington, D.C.

Mooney, James

1890   "Cherokee Theory and Practice of Medicine." *Journal of American Folklore* 3:44–50.

1894   *The Siouan Tribes of the East.* Smithsonian Institution, Bureau of American Ethnology Bulletin 22, Washington, D.C.

1900   *History, Myths, and Sacred Formulas of the Cherokees.* Smithsonian Institution, Bureau of American Ethnology Annual Report 19:3–548, Washington, D.C.

Mooney, Timothy Paul

1992   "Migration of the Chickasawhays into the Choctaw Homeland." *Mississippi Archaeology* 27:28–39.

1994   "Many Choctaw Standing: An Archaeological Study of Culture Change in the Early Historic Period." Master's thesis for the Department of Anthropology, University of North Carolina, Chapel Hill.

1995   "Choctaw Culture Compromise and Change between the Eighteenth and Early Nineteenth Centuries: An Analysis of the Collections from Seven Sites from the Choctaw Homeland in East-Central Mississippi." *Journal of Alabama Archaeology* 41:162–79.

1997   *Many Choctaw Standing: An Archaeological Study of Culture Change in the Early Historic Period.* Mississippi Department of Archives and History, Archaeological Report 38, Jackson.

Moore, Alexander, editor

1988   *Nairne's Muskogean Journals: The 1708 Expedition to the Mississippi River.* University Press of Mississippi, Jackson.

Moore, David G.

1990   "An Overview of Historic Aboriginal Public Architecture in Western North Carolina." Paper presented at the 47th Annual Meeting of the Southeastern Archaeological Conference, Mobile, Alabama.

Moore, Henrietta

1988   *Feminism and Anthropology.* University of Minnesota Press, Minneapolis.

Moore, Jenny

1997   "Conclusion: The Visibility of the Invisible." In *Invisible People and Processes: Writing Gender and Childhood into European Archaeology,* ed. Jenny Moore and Eleanor Scott, 251–57. Leicester University Press, London.

Morse, Dan

1967   "The Robinson Site and Shell Mound Archaic Culture in the Middle South." Doctoral dissertation for the Department of Anthropology, University of Michigan, Ann Arbor.

Moss, Madonna

1993   "Shellfish, Gender, and Status on the Northwest Coast: Reconciling Archaeological, Ethnographic, and Ethnohistorical Records of the Tlingit." *American Anthropologist* 95:631–52.

Mukhopadhyay, Carol C., and Patricia J. Higgins

1988   "Anthropological Studies of Women's Status Revisited: 1977–1987." *Annual Review of Anthropology* 17:461–95.

Muller, Jon

1984   "Mississippian Specialization and Salt." *American Antiquity* 49:489–507.

1986   *Archaeology of the Lower Ohio River Valley.* Academic Press, New York.

1987   "Salt, Chert, and Shell: Mississippian Exchange and Economy." In *Specialization, Exchange, and Social Complexity,* ed. Elizabeth M. Brumfiel and Timothy K. Earle, 10–21. Cambridge University Press, Cambridge.

1990   *The Great Salt Spring: Mississippian Production and Specialization*. Report submitted to the United States Forest Service, Shawnee National Forest, Harrisburg, Illinois.

1991   *Great Salt Spring Structure*. Report submitted to the United States Forest Service, Shawnee National Forest, Harrisburg, Illinois.

1997   *Mississippian Political Economy*. Plenum Press, New York.

Muller, Jon, and George Avery

1990   "Site-Location Survey." In *The Great Salt Spring: Mississippian Production and Specialization*, ed. Jon Muller, 67–82. Report submitted to the United States Forest Service, Shawnee National Forest, Harrisburg, Illinois.

Muller, Jon, and Lisa Renken

1989   "Radiocarbon Dates for the Great Salt Spring Site: Dating Saltpan Variation." *Illinois Archaeology* 1:150–60.

Murdock, George P.

1967   *Ethnographic Atlas*. University of Pittsburgh Press, Pittsburgh, Pennsylvania.

Nassaney, Michael S., and Kendra Pyle

1999   "The Adoption of the Bow and Arrow in Eastern North America: A View from Central Arkansas." *American Antiquity* 64:243–65.

Navey, Liane

1982   "An Introduction to the Mortuary Practices of the Historic Sara." Master's thesis for the Department of Anthropology, University of North Carolina, Chapel Hill.

Nelson, Sarah Milledge

1997   *Gender in Archaeology: Analyzing Power and Prestige*. Alta Mira Press, Walnut Creek, California.

1998   "Reflections on Gender Studies in African and Asian Archaeology." In *Gender in African Prehistory*, ed. Susan Kent, 285–94. Alta Mira Press, Walnut Creek, California.

O'Brien, Patricia J.

1995   "Taxonomic Determinism in Evolutionary Theory: Another Model of Multilinear Cultural Evolution with an Example from the Plains." In *Beyond Subsistence: Plains Archaeology and the Postprocessual Critique*, ed. Philip Duke and Michael C. Wilson, 66–89. University of Alabama Press, Tuscaloosa.

Ortner, Donald J., and W. G. J. Putschar

1981   *Identification of Pathological Conditions in Human Skeletal Remains*. Smithsonian Institution, Contributions to Anthropology 28, Washington, D.C.

O'Shea, John M.

1984   *Mortuary Variability: An Archaeological Investigation*. Academic Press, New York.

Parham, Kenneth

1987   "Toqua Skeletal Biology: A Biocultural Approach." In *The Toqua Site: A Late*

Mississippian Dallas Phase Town, ed. Richard R. Polhemus, 431–551. University of Tennessee, Department of Anthropology Report of Investigations 41, Knoxville.

Parker Pearson, Michael

1982 "Mortuary Practices, Society, and Ideology." In *Symbolic and Structural Archaeology,* ed. Ian Hodder, 99–113. Cambridge University Press, Cambridge.

Parkington, John

1998 "Resolving the Past: Gender in the Stone Age Archaeological Record of the Western Cape." In *Gender in African Prehistory,* ed. Susan Kent, 25–37. Alta Mira Press, Walnut Creek, California.

Parmalee, Paul W., Andreas A. Paloumpis, and Nancy Wilson

1972 *Animals Utilized by Woodland Peoples Occupying the Apple Creek Site, Illinois.* Illinois State Museum, Reports of Investigations 23, Springfield.

Parrelli, Douglas

1994 "Gender, Mobility, and Subsistence in Iroquois Prehistory: An Ethnohistorical Approach to Archaeological Interpretation." Master's thesis for the Department of Anthropology, State University of New York, Buffalo.

Pauketat, Timothy R.

1987 "Mississippian Domestic Economy and Formation Processes." *Midcontinental Journal of Archaeology* 12:77–88.

1989 "Monitoring Mississippian Homestead Occupation Span and Economy Using Ceramic Refuse." *American Antiquity* 54:288–310.

1994 *The Ascent of Chiefs: Cahokia and Mississippian Politics in Native North America.* University of Alabama Press, Tuscaloosa.

1997 "Specialization, Political Symbols, and the Crafty Elite of Cahokia." *Southeastern Archaeology* 16:1–15.

Peebles, Christopher S.

1974 "Moundville: The Organization of a Prehistoric Community and Culture." Doctoral dissertation for the Department of Anthropology, University of California, Santa Barbara.

Peebles, Christopher S., and Susan M. Kus

1977 "Some Archaeological Correlates of Ranked Societies." *American Antiquity* 42:421–48.

Perdue, Theda

1998 *Cherokee Women: Gender and Culture Change, 1700–1835.* University of Nebraska Press, Lincoln.

Persico, V. Richard, Jr.

1979 "Early Nineteenth-Century Cherokee Political Organization." In *The Cherokee Indian Nation: A Troubled History,* ed. Duane H. King, 92–109. University of Tennessee Press, Knoxville.

Phillips, William A.

1900 "Aboriginal Quarries and Shops at Mill Creek, Illinois." *American Anthropologist* 2:37–52.

Pietrusewsky, M.
1981   "Metric and Non-Metric Cranial Variation in Australian Aboriginal Populations Compared with Populations from the Pacific and Asia." *Australian Institute for Aboriginal Studies Occasional Papers in Human Biology* 3:1–113. Australian Institute for Aboriginal Studies, Canberra.

Polhemus, Richard R.
1990   "Dallas Phase Architecture and Sociopolitical Structure." In *Lamar Archaeology: Mississippian Chiefdoms of the Deep South*, ed. Mark Williams and Gary Shapiro, 125–38. University of Alabama Press, Tuscaloosa.

Polhemus, Richard R., editor
1987   *The Toqua Site: A Late Mississippian Dallas Phase Town.* University of Tennessee, Department of Anthropology Report of Investigations 41, Knoxville.

Powell, Mary Lucas
1986   "Late Prehistoric Community Health in the Central Deep South: Biological and Social Dimensions of the Mississippian Chiefdom at Moundville, Alabama." In *Skeletal Analysis in Southeastern Archaeology*, ed. Janet Levy, 127–50. North Carolina Archaeological Council Publication 24, Raleigh.
1988   *Status and Health in Prehistory: A Case Study of the Moundville Chiefdom.* Smithsonian Institution Press, Washington, D.C.
1991   "Ranked Status and Health in the Mississippian Chiefdom at Moundville." In *What Mean These Bones: Studies in Southeastern Bioarchaeology*, ed. Mary Lucas Powell, Patricia S. Bridges, and Ann Marie Wagner Mires, 22–51. University of Alabama Press, Tuscaloosa.

Prentice, Guy
1983   "Cottage Industries: Concepts and Implications." *Midcontinental Journal of Archaeology* 8:17–48.
1985   "Economic Differentiation among Mississippian Farmsteads." *Midcontinental Journal of Archaeology* 10:77–122.

Prezzano, Susan C.
1997   "Warfare, Women, and Households: The Development of Iroquois Culture." In *Women in Prehistory: North America and Mesoamerica*, ed. Cheryl Claassen and Rosemary A. Joyce, 88–99. University of Pennsylvania Press, Philadelphia.

Ramenofsky, Ann F.
1987   *Vectors of Death: The Archaeology of European Contact.* University of New Mexico Press, Albuquerque.

Randolph, J. Ralph
1973   *British Travelers among the Southern Indians, 1660–1763.* University of Oklahoma Press, Norman.

Rapoport, Amos
1994   "Spatial Organization and the Built Environment." In *Companion Encyclopedia of Anthropology*, ed. Tim Ingold, 460–502. Routledge, London.

Riggs, Brett H.
1989   "Ethnohistorical and Archaeological Dimensions of Early Nineteenth-Cen-

tury Cherokee Intrahousehold Variation." In *Households and Communities,* ed. Scott MacEachern, David Archer, and Richard Garvin, 328–38. Archaeological Association of the University of Calgary, Proceedings of the Chacmool Conference 21, Calgary, Alberta, Canada.

Rights, Douglas L.
1957   *The American Indian in North Carolina.* John F. Blair, Winston-Salem, North Carolina.

Rodning, Christopher B.
1996   "Towns and Clans: Social Institutions and Organization of Native Communities on the Appalachian Summit." Fourth-semester paper for the Department of Anthropology, University of North Carolina, Chapel Hill.
1999a   "Archaeological Perspectives on Gender and Women in Traditional Cherokee Society." *Journal of Cherokee Studies* 20:3–27.
1999b   "Landscaping Communal Space at the Confluence of Coweeta Creek and the Little Tennessee River." Paper presented at the 56th Annual Meeting of the Southeastern Archaeological Conference, Pensacola, Florida.

Rosaldo, Michelle Zimbalist
1980   "The Use and Misuse of Anthropology: Reflections on Feminism and Cross-Cultural Understanding." *Signs* 5:389–441.

Rose, Jerome C., Murray K. Marks, and Larry L. Tieszen
1991   "Bioarchaeology and Subsistence in the Central and Lower Portions of the Mississippi Valley." In *What Mean These Bones: Studies in Southeastern Bioarchaeology,* ed. Mary Lucas Powell, Patricia S. Bridges, and Ann Marie Wagner Mires, 7–21. University of Alabama Press, Tuscaloosa.

Rothschild, Nan
1979   "Mortuary Behavior and Social Organization at Indian Knoll and Dickson Mounds." *American Antiquity* 44:658–75.

Rothstein, F. A.
1982   *Three Different Worlds: Women, Men and Children in an Industrializing Community.* Greenwood Press, Westport, Connecticut.

Rubinstein, Robert L.
1990   "Nature, Culture, Gender, Age: A Critical Review." In *Anthropology and Aging: Comprehensive Reviews,* ed. Robert L. Rubinstein, with J. Keith, D. Shenk, and D. Wieland, 109–28. Kluwer Academic Publishers, Boston.

Russ, Kurt C., and Jefferson Chapman
1983   *Archaeological Investigations at the Eighteenth Century Overhill Cherokee Town of Mialoquo.* University of Tennessee, Department of Anthropology Report of Investigations 37, Knoxville.

Sahlins, Marshall D.
1972   *Stone Age Economics.* Aldine, Chicago.

Sanday, Peggy R.
1981   *Female Power and Male Dominance: On the Origins of Sexual Inequality.* Cambridge University Press, Cambridge.

Sassaman, Kenneth E.

1992 "Lithic Technology and the Hunter-Gatherer Sexual Division of Labor." *North American Archaeologist* 13:249–62.

1993 *Early Pottery in the Southeast: Tradition and Innovation in Cooking Technology.* University of Alabama Press, Tuscaloosa.

1996 "Left-Handed Potters, Unilineal Descent, and the Social Power of Gender." Paper presented at the 53rd Annual Meeting of the Southeastern Archaeological Conference, Birmingham, Alabama.

Sattler, Richard A.

1995 "Women's Status among the Muskogee and Cherokee." In *Women and Power in Native North America,* ed. Laura F. Klein and Lillian A. Ackerman, 214–29. University of Oklahoma Press, Norman.

Saxe, Arthur A.

1970 "Social Dimensions of Mortuary Practices." Doctoral dissertation for the Department of Anthropology, University of Michigan, Ann Arbor.

1971 "Social Dimensions of Mortuary Practices in Mesolithic Populations from Wadi Halfa, Sudan." In *Approaches to the Social Dimensions of Mortuary Practices,* ed. James A. Brown, 39–56. Memoirs of the Society for American Archaeology 25, Washington, D.C.

Scarry, John F.

1992 "Political Offices and Political Structure: Ethnohistoric and Archaeological Perspectives on the Native Lords of Apalachee." In *Lords of the Southeast: Social Inequality and the Native Elites of Southeastern North America,* ed. Alex W. Barker and Timothy R. Pauketat, 163–83. Archeological Papers of the American Anthropological Association 3, Washington, D.C.

Scarry, John F., editor

1996 *Political Structure and Change in the Prehistoric Southeastern United States.* University Press of Florida, Gainesville.

Schiffer, Michael B.

1976 *Behavioral Archaeology.* Academic Press, New York.

1995 *Behavioral Archaeology: First Principles.* University of Utah Press, Salt Lake City.

Schildkrout, E.

1978 "Roles of Children in Urban Kano." In *Sex and Age as Principles of Social Differentiation,* ed. Jean Sybil La Fontaine, 109–38. Academic Press, Association of Social Anthropologists of the Commonwealth Monograph 17, New York.

Schmidt, Peter

1998 Reading Gender in the Ancient Iron Age Technology of Africa." In *Gender in African Prehistory,* ed. Susan Kent, 139–62. Alta Mira Press, Walnut Creek, California.

Schoeninger, Margaret, and Christopher S. Peebles

1981 "Notes on the Relationship between Social Status and Diet at Moundville." *Southeastern Archaeological Conference Bulletin* 24:96–97.

Schroedl, Gerald F.
1978   "Louis-Phillipe's Journal and Archaeological Investigations at the Overhill Town of Toqua." *Journal of Cherokee Studies* 3:206–20.
1986a "Toward an Explanation of Cherokee Origins in East Tennessee." In *The Conference on Cherokee Prehistory*, comp. David G. Moore, 122–38. Warren Wilson College, Swannanoa, North Carolina.
1989   "Overhill Cherokee Household and Village Patterns in the Eighteenth Century." In *Households and Communities*, ed. Scott MacEachern, David Archer, and Richard Garvin, 350–60. Archaeological Association of the University of Calgary, Proceedings of the Chacmool Conference 21, Calgary, Alberta, Canada.
1998   "Mississippian Towns in the Eastern Tennessee Valley." In *Mississippian Towns and Sacred Spaces: Searching for an Architectural Grammar*, ed. R. Barry Lewis and Charles Stout, 64–92. University of Alabama Press, Tuscaloosa.
Schroedl, Gerald F., editor
1986b *Overhill Cherokee Archaeology at Chota-Tanasee*. University of Tennessee, Department of Anthropology Report of Investigations 38, Knoxville.
Schroedl, Gerald F., and Emanuel D. Breitburg
1986   "Burials." In *Overhill Cherokee Archaeology at Chota-Tanasee*, ed. Gerald F. Schroedl, 125–206. University of Tennessee, Department of Anthropology Report of Investigations 38, Knoxville.
Schroedl, Gerald F., and Brett H. Riggs
1990   "Investigations of Cherokee Village Patterning and Public Architecture at the Chattooga Site." Paper presented at the 47th Annual Meeting of the Southeastern Archaeological Conference, Mobile, Alabama.
Schroedl, Gerald F., C. Clifford Boyd, Jr., and R. P. Stephen Davis, Jr.
1990   "Explaining Mississippian Origins in East Tennessee." In *The Mississippian Emergence*, ed. Bruce D. Smith, 175–96. Smithsonian Institution Press, Washington, D.C.
Scott, Gary, and Richard R. Polhemus
1987   "Mortuary Patterns." In *The Toqua Site: A Late Mississippian Dallas Phase Town*, ed. Richard R. Polhemus, 378–431. University of Tennessee, Department of Anthropology Report of Investigations 41, Knoxville.
Seligman, E.
1864   *Uber Exostosen an Peruanerschadeln*. Wein. Kais. Akad. Wiss., Sitzungsber.
Setzler, Frank M., and Jesse D. Jennings
1941   *Peachtree Mound and Village Site, Cherokee County, North Carolina*. Smithsonian Institution, Bureau of American Ethnology Bulletin 131, Washington, D.C.
Shanks, Michael, and Christopher Tilley
1982   "Ideology, Symbolic Power and Ritual Communication: A Reinterpretation of Neolithic Mortuary Practices." In *Symbolic and Structural Archaeology*, ed. Ian Hodder, 129–54. Cambridge University Press, Cambridge.

Shennan, Susan

1975   "The Social Organization at Branc." *Antiquity* 49:279–88.

Sherratt, Andrew G.

1982   "Mobile Resources: Settlement and Exchange in Early Agricultural Europe." In *Ranking, Resource and Exchange: Aspects of the Archaeology of Early European Society,* ed. A. Colin Renfrew and Stephen J. Shennan, 13–26. Cambridge University Press, Cambridge.

Sillitoe, Paul

1985   "Divide and No One Rules: The Implications of Sexual Divisions of Labor in Papua New Guinea." *Man* 20:494–522.

Silverman, Sydel F.

1975   "The Life Crisis as a Clue to Social Function: The Case of Italy." In *Toward an Anthropology of Women,* ed. Rayna R. Reiter, 309–21. Monthly Review Press, New York.

Smith, Betty Anderson

1979   "Distribution of Eighteenth-Century Cherokee Settlements." In *The Cherokee Indian Nation: A Troubled History,* ed. Duane H. King, 46–60. University of Tennessee Press, Knoxville.

Smith, Bruce D.

1975   *Middle Mississippi Exploitation of Animal Populations.* University of Michigan, Museum of Anthropology Anthropological Papers 52, Ann Arbor.

1986   "Archaeology in the Southeastern United States: From Dalton to de Soto, 10,500–500 B.P." *Advances in World Archaeology* 5:1–92.

Smith, Kevin E.

1991   "The Mississippian Figurine Complex and Symbolic Systems of the Southeastern United States." In *The New World Figurine Project, Volume 1,* ed. Terry Stocker, 123–37. Research Press, Provo, Utah.

Smith, Maria O.

1996   "Bioarchaeological Inquiry into Archaic Period Populations of the Southeast: Trauma and Occupational Stress." In *Archaeology of the Mid-Holocene Southeast,* ed. Kenneth E. Sassaman and David G. Anderson, 134–54. University Press of Florida, Gainesville.

Smith, Marvin T.

1987   *The Archaeology of Aboriginal Culture Change: Depopulation during the Early Historic Period.* University Press of Florida, Gainesville.

1992   *Historic Period Indian Archaeology of Northern Georgia.* University of Georgia, Laboratory of Archaeology Report 30, Athens.

Smith, Marvin T., and David J. Hally

1992   "Chiefly Behavior: Evidence from Sixteenth Century Spanish Accounts." In *Lords of the Southeast: Social Inequality and the Native Elites of Southeastern North America,* ed. Alex W. Barker and Timothy R. Pauketat, 99–109. Archeological Papers of the American Anthropological Association 3, Washington, D.C.

Smith, Marvin T., and Julie Barnes Smith
1989   "Engraved Shell Masks in North America." *Southeastern Archaeology* 8:9–18.

Smith, Marvin T., and Mark Williams
1994   "Mississippian Mound Refuse Disposal Patterns and Implications for Archaeological Research." *Southeastern Archaeology* 13:27–35.

Smith, Philip W.
1979   *The Fishes of Illinois.* University of Illinois Press, Urbana-Champaign.

Sobolik, Kristin D.
1996   "Experiments on Determining Gender from Coprolites by DNA Analysis." *Journal of Archaeological Science* 23:263–67.

Sobolik, Kristin D., Kristen J. Gremillion, and Patty Jo Watson
1996   "Technology Note: Sex Determination of Prehistoric Human Paleofeces." *American Journal of Physical Anthropology* 101:283–90.

Spain, Daphne
1992   *Gendered Spaces.* University of North Carolina Press, Chapel Hill.

Speck, Frank G.
1935   "Siouan Tribes of the Carolinas as Known from Catawba, Tutelo, and Documentary Sources." *American Anthropologist* 37:201–25.

1946   *Catawba Hunting, Trapping and Fishing.* Museum of the University of Pennsylvania and the Philadelphia Anthropological Society, Joint Publications 2, Philadelphia.

Spector, Janet D.
1983   "Male/Female Task Differentiation among the Hidasta: Toward the Development of an Archaeological Approach to the Study of Gender." In *The Hidden Half: Studies of Plains Indian Women,* ed. Patricia Albers and Beatrice Medicine, 77–99. University Press of America, Lanham, Maryland.

1991   "What This Awl Means: Toward a Feminist Archaeology." In *Engendering Archaeology: Women and Prehistory,* ed. Joan M. Gero and Margaret W. Conkey, 388–406. Blackwell, Oxford.

1993   *"What This Awl Means: Feminist Archaeology at a Wahpeton Dakota Village.* Minnesota Historical Society, Saint Paul.

Spector, Janet D., and Mary K. Whelan
1989   "Incorporating Gender into Archaeology Courses." In *Gender and Anthropology: Critical Reviews for Research and Teaching,* ed. Sandra Morgen, 65–94. American Anthropological Association, Washington, D.C.

Spielmann, Katherine A.
1995   "Glimpses of Gender in the Prehistoric Southwest." *Journal of Anthropological Research* 51:91–102.

Standen, V. G., B. T. Arriaza, and C. M. Santoro
1997   "External Auditory Exostosis in Prehistoric Chilean Populations: A Test of the Cold Water Hypothesis." *American Journal of Physical Anthropology* 103:119–29.

Starachowicz, J., and E. Koterba
1977 "Changes in the External Auditory Meatus in Swimmers." *Otolaryn. Pol.* 28:79–82.

Steponaitis, Vincas P.
1986 "Prehistoric Archaeology in the Southeastern United States, 1970–1985." *Annual Review of Anthropology* 15:363–404.

Stone, Andrea
1997 "Ethnographic Spatial Models and Artifact Distribution in Maya Caves." Paper presented at the 63rd Annual Meeting of the Society of American Archaeology, Nashville, Tennessee.

Sudarkasa, N.
1981 "Female Employment and Family Organization in West Africa." In *The Black Woman Cross-Culturally,* ed. Filomina Chioma Steady, 49–63. Schenkman, Cambridge, Massachusetts.

Sullivan, Lynne P.
1986 "The Late Mississippian Village: Community and Society of the Mouse Creek Phase in Southeastern Tennessee." Doctoral dissertation for the Department of Anthropology, University of Wisconsin, Milwaukee.
1987 "The Mouse Creek Phase Household." *Southeastern Archaeology* 6:16–29.
1989 "Household, Community, and Society: An Analysis of Mouse Creek Settlements." In *Households and Communities,* ed. Scott MacEachern, David Archer, and Richard Garvin, 317–27. Archaeological Association of the University of Calgary, Proceedings of the Chacmool Conference 21, Calgary, Alberta, Canada.
1995 "Mississippian Household and Community Organization in Eastern Tennessee." In *Mississippian Communities and Households,* ed. J. Daniel Rogers and Bruce D. Smith, 99–123. University of Alabama Press, Tuscaloosa.

Swanton, John R.
1928 *Aboriginal Culture of the Southeast.* Smithsonian Institution, Bureau of American Ethnology Annual Report 42:673–726. Washington, D.C.
1946 *The Indians of the Southeastern United States.* Smithsonian Institution, Bureau of American Ethnology Bulletin 137, Washington, D.C.

Tainter, Joseph A.
1978 "Mortuary Practices and the Study of Prehistoric Social Systems." *Advances in Archaeological Method and Theory* 1:105–41.

Thomas, Larissa A.
1996 "A Study of Shell Beads and Their Social Context in the Mississippian Period: A Case from the Carolina Piedmont and Mountains." *Southeastern Archaeology* 15:29–46.
1997 "Hoe Production and Household Production at Dillow's Ridge: Gender Division of Labor and the Place of Production for Exchange in Mississippian Economy." Doctoral dissertation for the Department of Anthropology, State University of New York, Binghamton.

Tilley, Christopher

1984   "Ideology and Legitimation of Power in the Middle Neolithic of Southern Sweden." In *Ideology, Power, and Prehistory,* ed. Daniel Miller and Christopher Tilley, 111–46. Cambridge University Press, Cambridge.

1994   *A Phenomenology of Landscape: Places, Paths, and Monuments.* Berg, London.

Tosi, Maurizio

1984   "The Notion of Craft Specialization and Its Representation in the Archaeological Record of Early States in the Turanian Basin." In *Marxist Perspectives in Archaeology,* ed. Matthew Spriggs, 22–52. Cambridge University Press, Cambridge.

Tregle, Joseph G., Jr., editor

1975   *The History of Louisiana or of the Western Parts of Virginia and Carolina,* by Antoine S. Le Page du Pratz. Louisiana State University Press, Baton Rouge.

Trigger, Bruce G.

1978   "Cultural Unity and Diversity." In *Handbook of North American Indians, Volume 15: Northeast,* ed. Bruce G. Trigger, 798–804. Smithsonian Institution Press, Washington, D.C.

1989   *History of Archaeological Thought.* Cambridge University Press, Cambridge.

Tringham, Ruth E.

1991   "Households with Faces: The Challenge of Gender in Prehistoric Architectural Remains." In *Engendering Archaeology: Women and Prehistory,* ed. Joan M. Gero and Margaret W. Conkey, 93–131. Blackwell, Oxford.

Trinkaus, Kathryn M.

1995   "Mortuary Behavior, Labor Organization and Social Rank." In *Regional Approaches to Mortuary Analysis,* ed. Lane Anderson Beck, 53–76. Plenum Press, New York.

Trocolli, Ruth

1992   "Colonization and Women's Production: The Timucua of Florida." In *Exploring Gender through Archaeology,* ed. Cheryl Claassen, 95–102. Prehistory Press, Monographs in World Archaeology 11, Madison, Wisconsin.

1999   "Women Leaders in Native North American Societies: Invisible Women of Power." In *Manifesting Power: Gender and the Interpretation of Power in Archaeology,* ed. Tracy L. Sweely, 49–61. Routledge, London.

Tuross, Noreen, and Marilyn Fogel

1994   "Stable Isotope Analysis and Subsistence Patterns at the Sully Site." In *Skeletal Biology in the Great Plains: Migration, Warfare, Health, and Subsistence,* ed. Douglas W. Owsley and Richard L. Jantz, 283–89. Smithsonian Institution Press, Washington, D.C.

Umeda, Y., M. Nakajima, and H. Hoshioka

1989   "Surfer's Ear in Japan." *Laryngoscope* 99(6 pt. 1):639–41.

van der Merwe, Nicholas, and Joseph Vogel

1978   "^{13}C Content of Human Collagen as a Measure of Prehistoric Diet in Woodland North America." *Nature* 276:815–16.

Victor, Katherine L., and Mary C. Beaudry
1992 "Women's Participation in American Prehistoric and Historic Archaeology: A Comparative Look at the Journals *American Antiquity* and *Historical
Archaeology*." In *Exploring Gender through Archaeology*, ed. Cheryl Claassen,
11–21. Prehistory Press, Monographs in World Prehistory 11, Madison,
Wisconsin.
Ward, H. Trawick
1987 "Mortuary Patterns at the Fredricks, Wall, and Mitchum Sites." In *The
Siouan Project, Seasons I and II*, ed. Roy S. Dickens Jr., H. Trawick Ward,
and R. P. Stephen Davis Jr., 81–110. University of North Carolina, Research
Laboratories of Anthropology Monograph 1, Chapel Hill.
Ward, H. Trawick, and R. P. Stephen Davis Jr.
1991 "The Impact of Old World Diseases on the Native Inhabitants of the North
Carolina Piedmont." *Archaeology of Eastern North America* 19:171–81.
1993 *Indian Communities on the North Carolina Piedmont, A.D. 1000 to 1700*. University of North Carolina, Research Laboratories of Anthropology Monograph 2, Chapel Hill.
1999 *Time before History: The Archaeology of North Carolina*. University of North
Carolina Press, Chapel Hill.
Ward, H. Trawick, and R. P. Stephen Davis Jr., editors
1988 "Archaeology of the Historic Occaneechi Indians." *Southern Indian Studies*
36–37.
Waselkov, Gregory A.
1987 "Shellfish Gathering and Shell Midden Archaeology." *Advances in Archaeological Method and Theory* 10:93–210.
Waselkov, Gregory A., and Kathryn E. H. Braund, editors
1995 *William Bartram on the Southeastern Indians*. University of Nebraska Press,
Lincoln.
Watson, Patty Jo, and Mary C. Kennedy
1991 "The Development of Horticulture in the Eastern Woodlands of North
America: Women's Role." In *Engendering Archaeology: Women and Prehisto-
ry*, ed. Joan M. Gero and Margaret W. Conkey, 255–75. Blackwell, Oxford.
Webb, William S.
1974 *Indian Knoll*. University of Tennessee Press, Knoxville.
Weiss, Kenneth M.
1972 "On the Systematic Bias in Skeletal Sexing." *American Journal of Physical
Anthropology* 37:239–49.
1973 *Demographic Models for Anthropology*. Memoirs of the Society for American
Archaeology 27, Washington, D.C.
1974 "On the Systematic Bias in Skeletal Sexing." *American Journal of Physical
Anthropology* 37:239–49.
Welch, Paul D.
1991 *Moundville's Economy*. University of Alabama Press, Tuscaloosa.

1996   "Control over Goods and the Political Stability of the Moundville Chiefdom." In *Political Structure and Change in the Prehistoric Southeastern United States,* ed. John F. Scarry, 69–91. University Press of Florida, Gainesville.

Wessen, Gary
1982   "Shell Middens as Cultural Deposits: A Case Study from Ozette." Doctoral dissertation for the Department of Anthropology, Washington State University, Pullman.

Wetmore, Ruth Y.
1983   "The Green Corn Ceremony of the Eastern Cherokees." *Journal of Cherokee Studies* 8:46–56.

Whelan, Mary K.
1991a   "Gender and Historical Archaeology: Eastern Dakota Patterns in the Nineteenth Century." *Historical Archaeology* 25:17–32.
1991b   "Gender and Archaeology: Mortuary Studies and the Search for the Origins of Gender Differentiation." In *The Archaeology of Gender,* ed. Dale Walde and Noreen D. Willows, 358–65. Archaeological Association of Calgary, Proceedings of the Chacmool Conference 22, Calgary, Alberta, Canada.
1995   "Beyond Hearth and Home on the Range: Feminist Approaches to Plains Archaeology." In *Plains Archaeology and the Postprocessual Critique,* ed. Philip Duke and Michael C. Wilson, 46–65. University of Alabama Press, Tuscaloosa.

White, Nancy M.
1999   "Women in Southeastern U.S. Archaeology." In *Grit-Tempered: Early Women Archaeologists in the Southeastern United States,* ed. Nancy M. White, Lynne P. Sullivan, and Rochelle A. Marrinan, 1–24. University Press of Florida, Gainesville.

White, Nancy M., Lynne P. Sullivan, and Rochelle A. Marrinan, editors
1999   *Grit-Tempered: Early Women Archaeologists in the Southeastern United States.* University Press of Florida, Gainesville.

White, Tim D.
1991   *Human Osteology.* Academic Press, New York.

Whitehead, Harriet
1981   "The Bow and the Burden Strap: A New Look at Institutionalized Homosexuality in Native North America." In *Sexual Meanings: The Cultural Construction of Gender,* ed. Sherry B. Ortner and Harriet Whitehead, 80–115. Cambridge University Press, Cambridge.

Wilk, Richard R.
1989   "Decision Making and Resource Flows within the Household: Beyond the Black Box." In *The Household Economy: Reconsidering the Domestic Mode of Production,* ed. Richard R. Wilk, 23–52. Westview Press, Boulder, Colorado.

Wilkinson, Leland, MaryAnn Hill, Jeffrey P. Welna, and Gregory K. Birkenbeuel
1992   *SYSTAT for Windows: Statistics, Version 5 Edition.* SYSTAT, Inc., Evanston, Illinois.

Williams, Mark, and Gary Shapiro, editors
1990 *Lamar Archaeology: Mississippian Chiefdoms in the Deep South.* University of Alabama Press, Tuscaloosa.

Wilson, Diane
1994 "Division of Labor and Stress Loads at the Sanders Site (41Lr2), Lamar County, Texas." *Bulletin of the Texas Archaeological Society* 65:129–60.
1997 "Gender, Diet, Health, and Social Status in Mississippian Powers Phase Turner Cemetery Population." In *Women in Prehistory: North America and Mesoamerica,* ed. Cheryl Claassen and Rosemary A. Joyce, 119–35. University of Pennsylvania Press, Philadelphia.

Wilson, Homes Hogue
1986 "Burials from the Warren Wilson Site: Some Biological and Behavioral Considerations." In *The Conference on Cherokee Prehistory,* comp. David G. Moore, 42–72. Warren Wilson College, Swannanoa, North Carolina.
1987 "Human Skeletal Remains from the Wall and Fredricks Sites." In *The Siouan Project, Seasons I and II,* ed. Roy S. Dickens Jr., H. Trawick Ward, and R. P. Stephen Davis Jr., 111–39. University of North Carolina, Research Laboratories of Anthropology Monograph 1, Chapel Hill.

Winters, Howard D.
1968 "Value Systems and Trade Cycles of the Late Archaic in the Midwest." In *New Perspectives in Archaeology,* ed. Sally R. Binford and Lewis R. Binford, 175–221. Aldine, Chicago.
1981 "Excavating in Museums: Notes on Mississippian Hoes and Middle Woodland Copper Gouges and Celts." In *The Research Potential of Anthropological Museum Collections,* ed. A. E. Cantwell, James B. Griffin, and Nan A. Rothschild, 17–34. Annals of the New York Academy of Sciences 376, New York.

Wong, B. J., W. Cervantes, K. J. Doyle, A. M. Karamzadeh, P. Boys, G. Brauel, and E. Mushtaq
1999 "Prevalence of External Auditory Canal Exostoses in Surfers." *Archives of Otolaryngology-Head and Neck Surgery* 125:969–72.

Wood, Alice S.
1974 "A Catalogue of Jesuit and Ornamental Rings from Western New York State: Collections of Charles Wray and the Rochester Museum and Science Center." *Historical Archaeology* 8:83–104.

Wright, Louis B., editor
1966 *The Prose Works of William Byrd of Westover: Narratives of a Colonial Virginian.* Harvard University Press, Cambridge.

Wright, Rita P.
1991 "Women's Pottery Production in Prehistory." In *Engendering Archaeology: Women and Prehistory,* ed. Joan M. Gero and Margaret W. Conkey, 194–223. Blackwell, Oxford.
1996a "Introduction: Gendered Ways of Knowing in Archaeology." In *Gender and*

Archaeology, ed. Rita P. Wright, 1–19. University of Pennsylvania Press, Philadelphia.

1996b "Technology, Gender, and Class: Worlds of Difference in Ur III Mesopotamia." In *Gender and Archaeology,* ed. Rita P. Wright, 79–110. University of Pennsylvania Press, Philadelphia.

Wylie, Alison

1991a "Gender Theory and the Archaeological Record: Why Is There No Archaeology of Gender?" In *Engendering Archaeology: Women and Prehistory,* ed. Joan M. Gero and Margaret W. Conkey, 31–54. Blackwell, Oxford.

1991b "Feminist Critiques and Archaeological Challenges." In *The Archaeology of Gender,* ed. Dale Walde and Noreen D. Willows, 17–23. Archaeological Association of the University of Calgary, Proceedings of the Chacmool Conference 22, Calgary, Alberta, Canada.

1992   "The Interplay of Evidential Constraints and Political Interests: Recent Archaeological Research on Gender." *American Antiquity* 57:15–35.

Wynn, Jack T.

1990   *The Mississippi Period Archaeology of the Georgia Blue Ridge.* University of Georgia, Laboratory of Archaeology Report 27, Athens.

Yanagisako, Sylvia J., and Jane F. Collier

1987   "Toward a Unified Analysis of Gender and Kinship." In *Gender and Kinship: Essays toward a Unified Analysis,* ed. Sylvia J. Yanagisako and Jane F. Collier, 14–50. Stanford University Press, Stanford, California.

Yarnell, Richard A.

1976   "Early Plant Husbandry in Eastern North America." In *Cultural Change and Continuity: Essays in Honor of James Bennett Griffin,* ed. Charles E. Cleland, 265–73. Academic Press, New York.

Yerkes, Richard W.

1983   "Microwear, Microdrills, and Mississippian Craft Specialization." *American Antiquity* 48:499–518.

1986   "Licks, Pans, and Chiefs: A Comment on Mississippian Specialization and Salt." *American Antiquity* 51:402–4.

1989   "Mississippian Craft Specialization on the American Bottom." *Southeastern Archaeology* 8:93–106.

1991   "Specialization in Shell Artifact Production at Cahokia." In *New Perspectives on Cahokia: Views from the Periphery,* ed. James B. Stoltman, 49–64. Prehistory Press, Monographs in World Prehistory 2, Madison, Wisconsin.

Contributors

Cheryl Claassen is professor of anthropology at Appalachian State University in Boone, N.C. She received her doctorate from Harvard University. Her archaeological interests include gender studies, Archaic shell middens in the Southeast, and the sociology of archaeology. She is co-editor with Rosemary Joyce of *Women in Prehistory: North America and Mesoamerica*, published by the University of Pennsylvania Press, 1997.

R. P. Stephen Davis, Jr., is research associate at the Research Laboratories of Archaeology, University of North Carolina, Chapel Hill. His dissertation at the University of Tennessee was a study of settlement patterns in the lower Little Tennessee Valley region. His recent interests have been culture continuity and change in Piedmont Siouan communities of North Carolina at European contact. He is coauthor with H. Trawick Ward of *Time before History: The Archaeology of North Carolina*, published by the University of North Carolina Press, 1999.

Jane M. Eastman earned her doctorate from the University of North Carolina at Chapel Hill and is currently visiting assistant professor of anthropology at East Carolina University. Her archaeological interests are late prehistory and protohistory in the North Carolina and Virginia Piedmont.

Patricia M. Lambert is assistant professor of anthropology at Utah State University. She received her doctorate from the University of California at Santa Barbara. Recently she has been a postdoctoral fellow in anthropology at the University of North Carolina at Chapel Hill. She is editor of *Bioarchaeological Studies of Life in the Age of Agriculture*, published by the University of Alabama Press, 1999.

Janet E. Levy is associate professor of anthropology at the University of North Carolina at Charlotte. She studied anthropology at Brown University and earned her doctorate at Washington University in St. Louis. Her archaeological interests include gender and power in Mississippian chiefdoms and Danish Bronze Age societies.

Elizabeth Monahan Driscoll is a doctoral candidate in anthropology at the University of North Carolina at Chapel Hill. Her dissertation is a study of mortuary patterns at Town Creek in southern North Carolina.

Christopher B. Rodning is a doctoral candidate in anthropology at the University of North Carolina at Chapel Hill. His dissertation is a study of the protohistoric cultural landscape of the Appalachian Summit region in western North Carolina.

Lynne P. Sullivan is curator of archaeology at the Frank H. McClung Museum at the University of Tennessee in Knoxville. She earned her doctorate at the University of Wisconsin at Milwaukee for her dissertation about households and communities in late prehistoric eastern Tennessee. Her interests include late prehistory and protohistory in the southern Appalachian region and the social structure of Mississippian chiefdoms. She is compiler and coeditor with the late Thomas M. N. Lewis and the late Madeline D. Kneberg Lewis of *The Prehistory of the Chickamauga Basin*, published by the University of Tennessee Press, 1995.

Larissa Thomas is senior archaeologist at TRC Garrow Associates, Inc., in Atlanta. She received her doctorate in anthropology from the State University of New York at Binghamton. Her archaeological interests include household economy and the production and exchange of goods in native southeastern societies.

H. Trawick Ward is research associate at the Research Laboratories of Archaeology, University of North Carolina, Chapel Hill. He has conducted considerable archaeological fieldwork in many different parts of North Carolina and has published significant studies of storage and mortuary patterns in North Carolina. He is coauthor with R. P. Stephen Davis, Jr., of *Time before History: The Archaeology of North Carolina*, published by the University of North Carolina Press, 1999.

Index

Ripley P. Bullen Series
Florida Museum of Natural History
Edited by Jerald T. Milanich

www.ingramcontent.com/pod-product-compliance
Lightning Source LLC
Chambersburg PA
CBHW020857270326
41928CB00006B/752